Dark Attractions

The Theatre of Peter Barnes

BRIAN WOOLLAND

Methuen

Published by Methuen 2004

1 3 5 7 9 10 8 6 4 2

Published in 2004 by
Methuen Publishing Ltd
215 Vauxhall Bridge Road
London SW1V 1EJ
www.methuen.co.uk

Methuen Publishing Limited Reg. No. 3543167

ISBN 0 413 77442 2

A CIP catalogue for this title is available from the British Library.

Designed by Bryony Newhouse

Typeset by SX Composing DTP, Rayleigh, Essex

Printed and bound in Great Britain
by Mackays of Chatham plc, Chatham, Kent

CONTENTS

ACKNOWLEDGEMENTS

Although writing a supposedly 'single-authored' book such as this is often a lonely business, it is, like theatre itself, the product of a great many collaborations. Sometimes these collaborations are easy to recognise and acknowledge; sometimes a conversation about something apparently totally unrelated can spark new thoughts and challenge 'certainties'. The following acknowledgements represent but the tip of an iceberg.

My colleagues in the Department of Film, Theatre & Television at the University of Reading have been unfailingly supportive throughout the development of this project. I would particularly like to thank Teresa Murjas, who helped with translating correspondence with theatres in Poland, and Lib Taylor, who took on much of my administrative load whilst I enjoyed AHRB-funded research leave to complete my work on this book. My thanks also to all those students with whom I have worked on various theatre projects over many years, all of whom have given so much of their time and energy, and have contributed enormously to my understanding of theatre

Looking at the cast and company lists of Barnes' plays, one sees the same names recurring. In spite of the relative absence of his plays from the main stages of our major theatre companies in recent years, there are many producers, directors, designers, musicians and actors working in the theatre, in radio and in television who have shown great faith in Peter Barnes' writing. May their wisdom prevail.

My thanks to Stephen Lacey, who introduced me to the work of Meyerhold; to David Davis, for his friendship and support; to Elaine Turner, for her insights and her enthusiasm for the work of Peter Barnes; to Richard Cave and Michael Walling for their encouragement and for their invaluable feedback on draft chapters; and to Peter Tummons and Joanna Taylor at Methuen.

I am particularly grateful to Peter Barnes, who has been very generous with his time and has shared confidences and resources so openly, who never once tried to intervene in any way while I was writing this book, and yet has allowed me access to scripts, videos, photographs and correspondence; and to his lovely family, who always welcome me, however intrusive my visits might have been.

Finally, I owe the greatest debt of gratitude to my partner, Hilary Garrett, for her love and support through the process of developing and realising this project.

LIST OF PHOTOGRAPHS

The author and Methuen Publishing Limited gratefully acknowledge the permission granted to reproduce the photographs within this work.

1. David Neall as Dr Herder, Derek Godfrey as Jack in *The Ruling Class*, Nottingham, 1968. Photographer: Chris J. Arthur, Eye International.

2. Rosemary McHale as Queen Ana and Alan Howerd as Carlos in *The Bewitched*, an RSC production, London, 1974. Photographer: Nobby Clark.

3. Timothy West as Ivan in the Royal Court production of *Laughter!*, London, 1978. By kind permission of the photographer, Peter Moyse.

4./4a. From a 1994 production of *Red Noses* (*Czerwone Nosy*) at the Teatr Ludowy, Kraków, Poland. Photographer: Zbigniew Lagocki.

5. From a production of *Dreaming* at the Queen's Theatre, London, 1999. Christ (Luke Williams) comes down from the cross to talk to Sarah (Kate Isitt). Copyright © Sheila Burnett, 1999. Reproduced by kind permission of Peter Barnes and Sheila Burnett. This image is taken from a colour photograph.

6. A break from the recording of *After the Funeral,* from the series of radio plays *Barnes People III*, 1986. Front row (left to right): John Hurt, Sean Connery, Donald Pleasance. Back row: members of the production team and Peter Barnes (right). Copyright © BBC Photo Library.

7. Jown Plowright (Mary) and Paul Scofield (the Priest) preparing for the recording of *Worms* from the series of radio plays *Barnes People II*, 1984. Copyright © BBC Photo Library.

8. Harriet Walter as Queen Isabella in *Bye Bye Columbus*, a Greenpoint Production for BBC Television, 1992. Photographer: Ivan Kyncl.

9. (left to right) Nicholas Farrell as Hills, David Suchet as Carver, Michael Maloney as Powell in *More Than A Touch of Zen*, Channel 4, London, September 1989. Photographer: Ivan Kyncl.

10. The many faces of Peter Barnes. Contact strips. By kind permission of the photographer, Mark Gerson.

Front cover: Jim Hooper as Sonnerie and Antony Sher as Father Flote in *Red Noses*, an RSC production at the Barbican Theatre, London, 1985. Photographer: Ivan Kyncl.

Back cover: Peter Barnes on the set for *Nobody Here But Us Chickens*, Channel 4, London, 1989. Photographer: Ivan Kyncl.

Every effort has been made to trace the current copyright holders of the photographs included in this work. The publishers apologise for any unintended omissions and would be pleased to receive any information that would enable them to amend any inaccuracies or omissions in future editions.

FOREWORD

An actor recently described being in the audience at a Peter Barnes play. There was a sequence involving multiple bedpans and he was in such pain from laughing that he had to look away from the stage for fear of serious injury.

What was so funny? What was the joke Peter was always trying to tell? Always the same one: it has been described as the abyss yawning its head off at your feet, as you struggle with the monster that is trying to push you in.

It was this ever-present tension in Peter's work between the ridiculous and the sublime which made actors fall on it so hungrily, and it came from what a journalist called Peter's 'promiscuous' imagination. Nothing smaller than the world and its history was his reference book, and Peter was the magpie, bright-eyed and ruthless. If the right word didn't come to mind he would invent one. He created a lexicon of epic invention, energy and the most profound compassion. Now it is a legacy to be cherished and a challenge to be honoured.

Alan Rickman
July 2004

AUTHOR'S NOTE

Peter Barnes' death on 1 July 2004 came as a terrible shock and a great loss to all who knew him. His warmth, integrity and generosity of spirit are rare qualities. This book was, however, completed long before his death and was not conceived as a memorial to him, but as an urgently needed critical reappraisal of his work. I hope it might also now be read as a tribute to a fine writer and remarkable man.

Brian Woolland
July 2004

PROLOGUE

Peter Barnes is a prolific and versatile writer: a dramatist who has written for the theatre, radio and television, a screenwriter and an occasional essayist. At various moments in his career his work has been highly acclaimed. For *The Ruling Class* he won the John Whiting Award (shared in 1969 with Edward Bond); in 1969 he received the Evening Standard Award for Most Promising Playwright of the Year; and for *Red Noses* in 1985, the Laurence Olivier Award for the Best Drama of the Year. In 1981, for *Barnes' People*, he received the Giles Cooper Award for Radio Drama; the Royal Television Society Award for the Best Drama of 1989, *Nobody Here But Us Chickens*, and in 1991 his screenplay for *Enchanted April* was nominated for an Academy Award. In his introduction to the published edition of *The Ruling Class* Harold Hobson wrote: 'The most exciting thing that can happen to a dramatic critic is when he is suddenly and unexpectedly faced with the explosive blaze of an entirely new talent of a very high order. This happens very rarely. In twenty years of reviewing plays it has happened to me, for example, only four times.'[1] The first three of these occasions had been Samuel Beckett's *Waiting for Godot*, John Osborne's *Look Back in Anger* and Harold Pinter's *The Birthday Party*. The fourth was Peter Barnes's *The Ruling Class*. He concludes his introduction to the play by insisting that *The Ruling Class* 'is likely to prove a turning point in the drama of the second half of the twentieth century.' In his introduction to *The Bewitched* Ronald Bryden was similarly effusive, claiming the play is 'a work of genius . . . a major work of art'.[2]

In spite of these public accolades, there have been long periods when Barnes has struggled to find theatres willing to stage his plays. Even *The Bewitched*,[3] considered by many to be Barnes' finest play, had a run of only seventeen performances; and it has not enjoyed a professional revival in Britain since that first production.[4] *Red Noses*, written in 1978, was not staged until 1985, when it was produced by the RSC at the Barbican. In 1990 *Sunsets and Glories* opened at the West Yorkshire Playhouse in Leeds. In spite of largely positive reviews in the national press, its anticipated transfer to London's West End never materialised. *Dreaming*, which opened at the Royal Exchange Theatre in Manchester in March 1999, was, however, subsequently revived (in June 1999) for a five-week run at the Queen's Theatre, London, thus becoming Barnes' first major play to get a theatrical run in London since *Red Noses*. *Dreaming* had been warmly received when it opened in Manchester. Lyn Gardner, for the *Guardian*, wrote: 'Barnes . . . is a sly old devil and a brilliant craftsman . . . This is a major play.' In London the reviews were far more mixed. All Barnes' writing for radio and television has been commissioned, but to date the RSC is the only company to have commissioned a stage play from Barnes and that, surprisingly, was not *Red Noses* or *The Bewitched*, but *Jubilee*, which premiered at the Swan Theatre, Stratford-upon-Avon, in July 2001.

Much of Barnes' writing for theatre has provoked enormous controversy, but nothing he has written has outraged audiences to the extent that *Laughter!* did when it was produced at the Royal Court.[5] Although there are numerous accounts of audience hostility to *Laughter!*,[6] Irving Wardle (writing in *The Times* in January 1978) asserted: 'Nothing is more exciting in the theatre than a moment of genuine stylistic change: when . . . one sees a playwright not merely writing a play but reinventing what a play ought to be.'[7] It remains the most controversial of all Barnes' work. I have devoted an entire chapter to the play in Part Two of this book; I return to it in my discussion of comedy in Chapter 9, 'Laugh, I Could Have Died'.

Elsewhere in the review of *Dreaming* quoted above, Lyn Gardner wrote: 'It's the kind of play that demonstrates the difficulty of distinguishing between a giggle and a scream in your own throat.' What Gardner identifies here – a deliberate awkwardness, a crafted uncertainty of tone – is something that Hobson, Bryden and Wardle have all remarked upon in their own essays. At its best, Barnes' drama is disturbing and profoundly unsettling. It may not be easy to categorise, but it does have a very characteristic feel to it. His plays are steeped in an extensive knowledge of popular cinema, music hall, stand-up comic routines, dance, ventriloquism, vaudeville, popular song and grand theatrical spectacle. The wide-ranging references to and borrowings from popular culture, the use of anecdote, the constant coining of new jokes and the recycling of old ones are, however, all essential building blocks in formal structures that owe as much to the montage theories of the innovative Russian film-makers Sergei Eisenstein and Vsevolod Pudovkin as they do to the work of the Jacobean playwrights whom Barnes admires so much: Ben Jonson, Thomas Middleton and John Marston. This is not, however, the eclecticism of postmodernism. For all the extensive quotation (and often mischievously parodic misquotation) in the plays, Barnes' sensibilities are essentially modernist. His determined refusal of naturalism[8] is indicative of a desire to make audiences conscious of their own responses to

the theatrical events taking place before them. This desire to acti-
vate audiences is something he shares not only with his beloved
Jacobeans, but also with a wide range of practitioners in film and
theatre whose work he greatly admires: playwrights such as Frank
Wedekind and Georges Feydeau; theatre directors such as Bertolt
Brecht and Vsevolod Meyerhold; and film-makers as diverse as
Eisenstein, Jean Renoir, Preston Sturges and Ernst Lubitsch.

This book offers a critical reappraisal of Barnes' work, arguing
that the formal structures, the use of comedy, the appropriation
of history, the cultural eclecticism, the unstable tone, are all inte-
grally related to those central concerns which animate the plays.
Throughout his drama, Barnes returns to familiar themes: interrogating the social functions of humour and laughter; examining
the workings of authority and hierarchy; investigating the various
ways in which people become complicit with and acquiescent to
those who wield power.

The book is divided into four parts. Part One, 'An Introduction', places Barnes' career in a biographical context,
considers his early work for the theatre, and examines some of
the central concerns that run through his drama. Part Two, 'All
the Best Lies', offers detailed analyses of five of Barnes' major
plays for the theatre. These have been chosen because they can
be seen as landmarks in the development of his theatre. *Luna Park
Eclipses*, a short experimental play, written for and produced by
the National Theatre Studio, can also be seen as a landmark, but
I have not devoted a separate chapter to it because it has not yet
been published in full and it was performed only to an invited
audience.[9] It is discussed in the final chapter of Part Four. Several
other plays, not discussed elsewhere in the book, are considered
briefly in my Introduction; but it should be noted that although
the book does look closely at a large number and a wide range of
plays, it is not intended as a comprehensive overview. Part Three,

'Confessing Our Selves', considers a selection of those plays for radio and television which are not only significant in their own right but which also illuminate the thematic concerns and formal strategies which characterise his major work for the theatre.

The fourth part of the book, 'Reflections', places Barnes' work in relevant theatrical, critical, cultural and socio-political contexts. Chapter 7, 'Traditions and Contexts', focuses on the theatrical traditions that he uses, develops and subverts. Chapter 8 examines the relationships between Barnes' theatre and film, considering the value and the implications of reading the plays as a montage of attractions (which is also the title of this chapter). The final chapter, 'Laugh, I Could Have Died', proposes that Barnes has developed a kind of metacomedy, a comedy that interrogates the social functions of comedy; and that this use of comedy is one of many strategies that he has adopted to create texts which are far more 'open' than critics have usually acknowledged.

This final section of the book focuses unashamedly on the five stage plays discussed in Part Two. These are probably the best known of Peter Barnes' plays, although their relative absence from the stage means that they can hardly be referred to as canonical. Throughout the book I have assumed that the reader has an interest in Barnes' work, although I recognise that it is unlikely that most will know more than a few of his plays. For this reason, in my examination of the plays in Parts Two and Three I have included accounts of their content, integrating description and close analysis. My hope is that this approach will make the book useful to academics and to students of modern theatre, and accessible to the well-informed general reader with interests in contemporary theatre. If the book generates new interest in the work of one of the English theatre's most prolific, most exciting and most underrated playwrights, I will be delighted.

PART ONE
An Introduction

Peter Barnes was born on 10 January 1931 in Bow Road, East London. As he noted wryly, however, in a semi-autobiographical essay that he wrote in 1990, this made him only technically a Cockney: 'I *was* born in Bow, within the sound of Bow Bells, which makes me an authentic Cockney. But I never heard them ring.'[1] The essay is interesting for the contradictions it reveals, and for Barnes' insistence that autobiography is essentially an unreliable form. Some have, for example, attributed his fascination with popular culture and the carnivalesque to the influences of his childhood and adolescence. Although born in the East End of London, his family left London when he was a baby, moving to Clacton-on-Sea on the North Sea coast, some sixty miles north-east of London, and at that time (in the summer months at least) still a lively working-class seaside resort. His parents worked amusement stalls on the pier. But 'the problem with my carnival background is that it is both true and untrue. Those sights and sounds of the sea and amusement arcades, donkey rides, Punch and Judy shows, ice-cream salesmen, dodgem rides, speed-boats and sailing boats were all there, around and about me. That is me capturing a world in words as if they were enough, as if that was all there was to it. But I saw and heard very little of it. I was always reading. I tried to ignore what was going on around me and I usually succeeded.'[2] Fortunately, he did not succeed as well as he might have imagined, for one of the most distinctive characteristics of his mature work is its eclectic appropriation of a variety of popular forms, presenting them in a heady montage of juxtaposed 'attractions'.

When the Second World War broke out, the family went to Gloucestershire, where his father worked in a munitions factory and Peter attended Stroud Grammar School. During school holidays, however, in a characteristically eccentric 'reverse evacuation', he used regularly to visit an aunt who lived in London, where he developed a passionate love of cinema – a passion which is evident in even his earliest stage plays.

In 1948 he got work with London County Council (LCC), leaving for a spell of national service between 1949 and 1950. While with the LCC he wrote film reviews for the Council's in-house magazine. What had started as a ruse to get complimentary tickets to the movies soon became an important career move. In the early 1950s he became a freelance film critic, and his reviews appeared regularly in magazines such as *Films and Filming*. During this period he also organised programming for the National Film Theatre (on the South Bank, but not in the present building). One of the seasons for which he was responsible, and of which he is particularly proud, was entitled '100 Clowns'. The series brought together from all over the world films featuring great comic performers. The season covered work from very early silents to contemporary films, and included the familiar – Chaplin, Keaton, Harold Lloyd, W. C. Fields, George Formby, Laurel and Hardy – as well as the obscure and unexpected. Barnes still talks[3] with glowing pride of his discovery of a very early silent featuring a routine by Beatrice Lillie, a music hall performer.[4]

In 1956 Barnes joined Warwick Films as a story editor, and in

1958 began writing screenplays of his own. As a screenwriter he has been astonishingly prolific and successful. His numerous credits include *Ring of Spies* (1963), *Not With My Wife You Don't* (1966), *Enchanted April* (1991) for which he received an Academy Award nomination in 1992, *Merlin* (1998) and *Arabian Nights* (2000). Although *Arabian Nights* is discussed briefly on p. 217, it is beyond the scope of this book to consider Barnes' work as a screenwriter. It is, however, worth noting that in terms of audience figures, *Merlin* was the most successful miniseries ever to be broadcast on US TV. Barnes regards these screenplays as 'assignment work, craft work',[5] but he takes pride in the craft. The writing of these screenplays may be financially expedient, but is also crucial to the development of his theatrical style. Although he has a very strong sense of the different demands of each medium, there is a strong formal interplay between his stage plays and his film, TV and radio scripts. His writing for the theatre is not simply influenced by cinema, but is also informed by his own extensive knowledge of it. This interaction of influences is discussed at length in Chapter 8.

Early Work

It is, perhaps, a measure of Barnes' success as a screenwriter that his first, hitherto unpublished, stage play, *The Time of the Barracudas*, attracted Laurence Harvey and Elaine Stritch to play the leading roles. It opened in San Francisco in 1963 and moved on for a short run in Los Angeles. It closed, however, before the hoped-for transfer to Broadway. The title of the play is an allusion to the ruthless rapaciousness of business. Philip Weire's 'business' is to kill his wives for life insurance money. In the first scenes of the play Weire eliminates his third wife Jean, boasting to the theatre audience that she is his third 'success'. The main body of the play begins at Jean's funeral when he meets Stella. They marry and take out a joint life-insurance policy, soon realising that they are both in the same line of 'business'. She is 'a competitor!' (I.ix). As each tries to trick the other into death traps, Barnes establishes some of the techniques which he would subsequently explore in his major plays. *The Time of the Barracudas* is a social satire, playing with and subverting a popular theatrical form: the comic murder thriller. Its politics may be rather naive, but it is a political farce or, rather, a satirical farce with political aspirations.

Barnes' next play, *Sclerosis* (also as yet unpublished) is more overtly political. The play opened in June 1965 for a short run at the Traverse Theatre Club, Edinburgh. Under English law at that time theatrical performance to a general public was subject to censorship, but 'theatre clubs' could avoid this by playing to an audience of members only. Its subject matter (British involvement in Cyprus) was considered so inflammatory that when the RSC brought the play to London they could find only one Sunday night 'club' performance for it at the Aldwych Theatre. In 1966, after the production of *Sclerosis*, Barnes wrote *Clap Hands Here Comes Charlie*. The play has not received a professional production, although Barnes did revise it for publication in 1996.[6] In recent years several professional productions have been mooted, but none have come to fruition. Charlie Ketchum, the central character, is a dissolute tramp, an anarchist and an individualist with a facility for dismissive one-liners that does little to soften his outrageous self-importance. In both versions of the play a character named Peter Barnes appears and discusses the meanings and social functions of theatre. There are a number of ways in which the play is reminiscent of early Brecht, and in particular of *Baal*, which also boasts an eponymous central character whose rampant egotism disrupts the veneer of stability in bourgeois society. *Charlie* might also be considered Brechtian in the ways it attempts to create a reflective audience, an audience that is aware of its own active role in making meaning. The play eschews psychological characterisation, preferring to construct the excesses of Charlie's behaviour as the product of specific social structures. These concerns with activating an audience and with identity as a social negotiation become increasingly important in Barnes' plays, for although his politics are less explicit than Brecht's, he is a social analyst who is as fascinated by theatre as a social and cultural phenomenon as he is by its status as an art form.

The other key influences on Barnes' work are Frank Wedekind (1864–1918), whose hatred of hypocrisy informs his extravagant and grotesque appropriation of popular forms such as cabaret and circus; Georges Feydeau (1862–1921), who Barnes considers to be lamentably underrated as an incisive social critic illuminating the darker areas of human experience, and whom he praises as one of the theatre's greatest craftsmen; and Ben Jonson (1572–1637). In this context, what is significant is the way that Barnes perceives Jonson, for the greatest accolade he can imagine is to be considered a latter day Jonsonian. What he admires is the vitality and vulgarity of Jonson's comedy, its muscularity of language and its incisive social satire. Thus *Clap Hands Here Comes Charlie* can be seen as a deliberate move by Barnes towards inventing himself as a latter day Jonsonian comic writer. As in Jonson's *The Alchemist*, *The Devil is an Ass* and *Bartholomew Fair*, where the tricksters who gull their social superiors become the driving force behind the plays, Ketchum is from the under-class.

While all the influences noted above are evident in *The Ruling Class*,[7] Barnes' next major play, it was the first in which he clearly established his own theatrical voice and is, even now, probably the play for which he is best known. This is perhaps because it was made into a film which became something of a vehicle for Peter O'Toole (who was not cast for the stage production) to give one of his characteristically flamboyant performances. In the theatrical production, which opened at Nottingham Playhouse in 1968, transferring to the Piccadilly Theatre, London, in 1969, Jack Gurney, the central character, was played by Derek Godfrey. Although *The Ruling Class* is the play which undoubtedly established Barnes as a major writer for the theatre, with a recognisable voice and theatrical style of his own, there are two important ways in which it is uncharacteristic of the main body of his work. Firstly, it is less concerned with the functioning of a social group than almost all his other large-cast plays. Father Flote in *Red Noses*, Mallory in *Dreaming*, and even Carlos in *The Bewitched* can each be seen as a protagonist; but these plays are far more concerned with the social dynamics that surround them than with the individual's goals. Flote and Mallory are leaders, but the plays are concerned with the interaction of the group, and the group's responses to leadership. And although Carlos's inadequacies act as a catalyst for all the subsequent events of the play, *The Bewitched* is more concerned with the collective madness that grips the Spanish court than with the pitiable king's impotence and incompetence. In *The Ruling Class*, however, Jack Gurney's actions drive the plot of the play. What marks *The Ruling Class* as transitional in Barnes' development as a playwright is that although the play certainly focuses on Jack's madness(es), the target of the play's satire is the collective, social madness that allows such power to be invested in so few. But if the Earl of Gurney is an unlikely (because more theatrically familiar) protagonist for a Barnes play, the character of Tucker embodies concerns and dramatic methods that run throughout the plays. Tucker,[8] the family manservant, passed on like a Russian serf from one generation to the next, meets his demise when he stumbles upon the corpse of one of Gurney's murder victims, only to find himself used as a scapegoat and wrongly accused of murder. From early in the play, he has boasted to the audience that he is a closet revolutionary, yet he never actually takes action against his masters; his acts of minor disobedience are indicative of the security he finds in keeping to his station. This fascination with obedience is central to Barnes' work, which constantly returns to an examination of the mechanisms by which political power is exerted and maintained, and by which people collude with authority to participate in their own oppression.

History Plays

The second way in which *The Ruling Class* differs from the main body of Barnes' work for the theatre is that it is set firmly in the present day. With very few exceptions, his large-scale plays are history plays. When asked about this, he claims that it takes theatre managements so long to pluck up the courage to mount a production of a Barnes play, that even if he did set them in the present, the productions would still be history plays by the time they reached the stage. As always when Barnes talks about his own work, there is a certain wry self-deprecation mixed with a cynical and jaded view of theatre managements, but the comment is unexpectedly revealing in that it indicates a genuine concern to write plays which are relevant to the lives of their audiences, and which – even if they are set in fictionalised historical periods – explore contemporary concerns. Although the theatrical strategy is not new (Brecht followed the model of many Renaissance –

and even classical Greek – dramatists, whose plays are rooted in the contemporary experience of their audience but are often set in other times and places), Barnes is unusual amongst his own contemporaries in adopting it so wholeheartedly. Although, as I argue in the chapter devoted to the play, *The Ruling Class* can be read a scathing satire about power and privilege that is as relevant now as when it was written, there is also a sense in which it is very much of its time. Whether or not it was intended to be, it can be seen as a significant intervention in the debate about the abolition of the death penalty. Capital punishment had been suspended by an act of parliament in 1965 for a period of five years, but was not permanently abolished until December 1969,[9] more than a year after *The Ruling Class* opened.

It is worth noting that the history plays – *The Bewitched*, *Red Noses*, *Dreaming*, *Sunsets and Glories*, *Revolutionary Witness*, *The Spirit of Man* and *Bye Bye Columbus* – are all set in periods of massive social and political change – periods when the world has been, or is about to be, 'turned upside down'. The same can also be claimed for *Heaven's Blessings*[10] (published, but not yet produced, the play is set in Babylonian times, and is based on the story of Tobias and the Angel from the *Book of Tobit* in the *Apocrypha*) and *Eggs in Gravy*,[11] set in Italy in 1465. To date, *Jubilee*[12] enjoys the distinction of being the only full-length stage play that Barnes has written to commission – to commemorate David Garrick's 1769 Shakespeare festival. The immediate environment is not one of social upheaval, although it could be argued that the play's subject matter (which it dramatises with mischievous irreverence) – the events that unwittingly founded the 'Shakespeare industry' and began the elevation of Shakespeare from dead poet to global icon – marks a significant cultural upheaval. *The Butterfly Effect*[13] (the most recent of Barnes' plays that I have read, though also hitherto unpublished) begins in

1471, in the middle of the Wars of the Roses, with Act Two set in 1485, as Henry VII defeats Richard III at the Battle of Bosworth Field, and Act Three covering the period from Henry VIII's accession (1509) to his decision to divorce Katherine of Aragon and marry Anne Boleyn. Structurally the play echoes Schnitzler's *La Ronde*, substituting casual medieval killing for twentieth-century sexual liaisons. It opens in a woodland clearing as a butterfly wakes a sleeping peasant, and weaves its way through a series of short scenes, each new scene connected to the last by at least one character (who then drops out of the narrative or is killed). In the final scene Anne persuades Henry VIII to make himself head of the Church of England so that he can divorce Katherine. As they kiss, a white butterfly flutters overhead. Barnes has stipulated a cast of five for the play, which may make a production of it more affordable for theatre managements, but it also ensures that each actor plays characters from every rung on the social ladder.

In spite of Barnes' characteristic dark humour and unstable tone, which ranges from freewheeling knockabout to the sharpest of satire, there are very serious intentions behind the decision to set so many of his plays in times of such social turbulence. History is presented not as a given, but as a product of specific decisions. This is a significant factor behind Barnes' distaste for naturalism[14]: the fictional worlds of naturalism tend to create a sense of inevitability, a sense that this is the way the world is, whereas Barnes belongs alongside those playwrights, such as Bertolt Brecht, who deliberately seek to disturb this sense that there is anything determined about history, to remind us that the versions of history that we receive are highly selective and ideologically loaded, and to make interventions in the top-down model of history that is so often presented to us. In this sense, *Laughter!* is a pivotal play, as it contains within it a significant shift of focus from satirising the inadequacies of those who exercise power to dramatising the responses to power of those much lower down the social scale. Ivan the Terrible is the protagonist of Part One of *Laughter!*; Part Two focuses on Cranach, a minor bureaucrat in an office in Berlin. One of the great achievements of *Laughter!* (and it is by far the most controversial of all Barnes' plays) is to draw parallels between the actions of a tyrant who seeks personal responsibility for all his actions and those of a bureaucrat who hides behind a cloak of obedience, denying personal accountability.

Although there is a strong sense in which Barnes inherently mocks the authority of the histories that are handed down to us, his plays that are set in historical periods are always very thoroughly researched. Indeed, it comes as something of a surprise to find that some of the most unlikely characters and events in Barnes' plays have their origins in 'true stories': Velasquez, for example, painted Carlos's jester, Sebastien de Morra (who appears in *The Bewitched*); the Flagellants and the Ravens, in *Red Noses*, not only existed, but promoted much the same ideologies that they do in the play; all the characters in *Revolutionary Witness* are based on real people who have left behind their stories. Even some of the most extraordinary of his monologues for radio, such as *End of the World and After* and *Glory*, are based on historical records. Barnes' achievement is not to use these real-life stories to give his plays some spurious authenticity, but to mine them for the relevance they have for us today.

With the benefit of hindsight, evidence of these trends can be found in Barnes' first experiments with history plays, the double bill of one-act plays, *Leonardo's Last Supper* and *Noonday Demons*, which opened at the Open Space Theatre (a small, fairly short-lived studio space with a reputation for experimental theatre) in November 1969 under the direction of Charles Marowitz.

Leonardo's Last Supper is set in Ambois Charnel House in May 1519; *Noonday Demons* in a cave in Egypt, 392 AD. In the former, a family of down-at-heel undertakers at last get the job which they believe will make their name and fortune: they are about to prepare the corpse of Leonardo da Vinci for burial when the 'corpse' rises up and speaks. After the initial shock, they realise that letting Leonardo leave the charnel house will deprive them of their golden opportunity. In spite of his protestations that the family can conduct his 'final burial', they kill him and the play concludes with Maria, and then all, breaking into song: 'Mona Lisa, Mona Lisa, men have named you . . . Are you warm, are you real, Mona Lisa. Or just a cold and lonely, lovely work of art' (1989, pp. 151–2).[15] Richly comic, delightfully inventive, and wittily anachronistic, the play is reminiscent of Wedekind in its use of the grotesque and of Brecht in its dramatisation of the relationship between poverty, ethics and materialist priorities. As Lasca says to da Vinci, 'Thanks won't feed us, clothe us, give us back our villa . . . Thanks isn't good coin o' the realm . . . You can't keep a family together on thanks' (p. 147). And, like many plays by Brecht and Wedekind, both *Leonardo's Last Supper* and its companion piece *Noonday Demons* mock religious certainties as superstitious and repressive nonsense, thus developing the criticism of religious authority that is so evident in *The Ruling Class* and *The Bewitched*. There is a delicious irony that when Leonardo first revives from his catatonic state, he tries to convince the family that he is not a devil; it is only once he has established his humanity that he is forced to plead for his life.

Each of the ascetic saints in *Noonday Demons*, Saint Pior and Saint Eusebius, is convinced that the other is a devil: each tries to establish his own sanctity while convinced that the other is a demon in disguise come to tempt him. The violent, almost comic-book confrontation between them concludes with Eusebius brutally strangling Pior. This conflict between them is, however, an external manifestation of an internal struggle. Before Pior wanders in to his cave dwelling, Eusebius has been tempted by his own inner demons. The actor playing Eusebius is required to adopt a different voice for his inner demon, so that the character enters a tormenting dialogue with himself and a possible future: 'Now 'tis meet I shouldst endure mine own stench daily, that on Judgment Day God mayst deliver Christ's children from the unimaginable stench o' Hell,' says the saint – to which the tormenting alter ego replies: 'Believe me, compared to this hellhole, Hell is a blast' (p. 158). The comment echoes Pug's line in Jonson's *The Devil is an Ass* when the minor devil realises that Satan was right after all in advising him that he'll not be able to cope in London. 'Hell is a grammar school to this,' he admits. Barnes acknowledges Jonson as the most important single influence on his work, but has also been a great advocate for Jonson's theatre, editing and adapting several of his plays.[16] In Chapter 7 I explore these influences and relationships in depth, but I want to note that Jonson's theatre (like Barnes's after him) is crucially concerned with the social negotiation of identity.

Theatre Managements and Actors

Barnes' next play, *The Bewitched*, was produced by the RSC, directed by Terry Hands, opening at the Aldwych Theatre in May 1974, four and a half years after *Leonardo's Last Supper* and *Noonday Demons*. Another three and a half years elapsed before *Laughter!* opened at the Royal Court in January 1978. *Red Noses*, which opened in July 1985 (in an RSC production at the Barbican Theatre, London) had been written seven years before it was staged. Since *Red Noses*, no full-length Barnes play has premiered in London, although *Dreaming* did enjoy a West End run at the Queen's Theatre in June–July 1999. In the meantime, *Sunsets and Glories*, which opened at the West Yorkshire Playhouse, Leeds, in June 1990, did not transfer to London. I have devoted entire chapters to discussions and analyses of *The Bewitched, Red Noses, Laughter!* and *Dreaming*, and they are also referred to in the final part of the book. *Sunsets and Glories*, set in the papal courts of late thirteenth-century and early four-teenth-century Rome, is a fine play, but is in many ways a reca-pitulation of themes and methods refined in *The Bewitched* and *Red Noses* (though considerably darker in tone than the latter). For this reason I have not discussed it in this volume.

Barnes' plays evidently cause theatre managements a certain amount of consternation, but he inspires remarkable loyalty from many of those actors who work with him. A quick look at the cast lists of the collected editions of his plays reveals the same names frequently recurring. This might be expected in produc-tions at the same theatre, but the net goes far wider; there are times when it seems that there is almost an informally constituted Barnesonian[17] Repertory Company on which he can always draw. Those actors who are keen to perform in a Peter Barnes play are also keen to take part in his seventeenth-century adaptations. It is fair to assume, given BBC Radio 3's limited financial resources, that at least part of the attraction for actors on these projects was working with Barnes. The casts of his own radio plays (the *Barnes People* monologues, duologues and three-handers) are even more starry: they have included Sir Alec Guinness, Dame Peggy Ashcroft, Sir John Gielgud, Robert Stephens, Sean Connery, John Hurt and Simon Callow. This is not simply to eulogise Barnes' work by association, but to give an indication of its diversity and consistency throughout different media, and to raise the question: what is it about Barnes' writing that makes it so popular with actors? English actors, in particular, are said to relish psychologised characterisation. But whatever else he does with such panache, his characterisations are neither psychologised nor naturalistic. What attracts actors to Barnes is that his plays are so full-blooded, so rich linguistically, so surprising in their creation and evocation of imagery. Even the radio monologues create an extraordinary sense of theatrical spectacle in the minds of the audience. But I think what most appeals to actors about Barnes' work is that it makes them highly visible. As Dukore recounts (1995, p. 114), Timothy West, who played Ivan and Gottleb in the original production of *Laughter!*, remarked that Barnes' 'cheek, daring, energy . . . [makes for an] enormous stretching of the actor's resources.' Barnes assertion that these demands make theatre 'more fun for the actors'[18] is both accurate and revealing. It is evident that he gains enormous personal enjoyment from the performances of actors in his plays, and that they show great loyalty towards him and enormous enthusiasm for his work. The relationship is symbiotic, and it is highly significant in reading the plays. His theatre draws attention both to performance and to audience response, and makes the interrelationship between performer and spectator highly visible and crucially significant to the meanings of the theatrical event. Chapter 9 considers this relationship in depth, relating it to the self-reflexive qualities in Barnes' theatre, and examines the way that his plays interrogate the social functions of comedy itself. The chapter also considers various theories of comedy, drawing extensively on the work of Arthur Koestler.

Throughout his career Barnes has written comedies – dark, and sometimes cruel comedies, certainly – but comedies which deserve to be taken seriously. I hope that, while I have taken them seriously, I have not lost sight of their comic potential. In his book on the nature of humour, *Seriously Funny*, Howard

Jacobson (1997) argues that 'the primary comic disparity [is] between what we would like to be and what we are', that comedy reminds us that we are closer to animals than we are to gods. Barnes' humour, which may not always make us laugh, frequently places gods on stage or, rather, those who see themselves as gods and those who claim to have a direct line to God. In *The Ruling Class*, for example, the Earl of Gurney claims first to be Jesus Christ Mark II, and then an incarnation of the Old Testament Jehovah, God of fear and vengeance; and in *The Bewitched*, almost everybody seems to claim the authority of God for their obsessive brutality. This difference between what we are and what we aspire to be is not only a significant comic device in Barnes' theatre, but it is also a central concern – another correspondence between Barnes' theatre and that of Ben Jonson, whose great comedies brutally satirise greed and aspiration.

Chekhov and the Chinese Boxes

Much critical work on Barnes draws attention to the links between his work and Jonson's. Here I would like to note some rather more unlikely affinities – with Anton Chekhov. Barnes' distaste for naturalism would seem to make this a ridiculous comparison, but Chekhov was an uneasy naturalist: he was writing at a time when naturalism was a radical theatre form, and his own plays were as experimental in their use of naturalism as they were in their developments of vaudeville. Chekhov draws on popular forms far more than the notion of his work as 'high naturalism' allows; his full-length plays, vaudeville burlesques (such as *The Bear*, *The Proposal* and *Swan Song*) and short stories are all populated by characters whose aspirations bear little relation to the reality of their situations. Although *The Cherry Orchard* is a deeply serious play, it contains a wide range of comic devices: caricature, repeated catchphrases, misunderstandings between characters, running gags, farcical entrances and exits, bathos and even slapstick. That 'although' at the beginning of the last sentence, then, is perhaps misplaced: it is a mistake to question whether any given moment in *The Cherry Orchard* is tragic or comic. The sense of moments, of scenes, and indeed the entire action of the play, as being simultaneously tragic and comic, is important in understanding how Chekhov works as a dramatist. *The Cherry Orchard*, in particular, succeeds because it keeps tragedy and comedy in constant tension. Indeed it is this tension which becomes the driving force of the play. If as an audience we laugh at a scene, it's not because we're laughing at a character's tears – in real life these situations would be extraordinarily painful – but rather because we are encouraged simultaneously to feel the pain of the character and to see, more objectively, the social context that gives rise to the pain. Chekhov is as much a social dramatist as he is an astute observer of psychology. Chekhov coined the phrase 'laughter through tears' to describe the effect that he sought with comedy. The phrase is also particularly apposite for Peter Barnes' comedy of terrors, though whether it is more appropriate to think of his theatre as inciting laughter through tears, or tears through laughter is a moot point. Either way, although he is far less interested in individual psychology than Chekhov, he does use comedy for similar purposes.

When the Italian director Giorgio Strehler worked on Chekhov's *The Cherry Orchard*, he proposed a now celebrated theory of 'three Chinese boxes', a theory which is also surprisingly relevant to the work of Peter Barnes. While acknowledging that these comments refer specifically to *The Cherry Orchard*, it is worth quoting directly from Strehler:

In the first box we approach the play on the level of reality: that is to say through the story of a family, its life at a particular moment; in the second we shift to a historical level and in the conflict and struggles of the individual characters we see reflected the social and political conflicts of the period; in the third we are operating in the context of universal – let us call them abstract – values.[19]

In the case of *The Cherry Orchard*, the first box deals with ordinary human affairs: the buying and selling of an orchard, people returning to Russia from Paris. In the second box we get a glimpse of a wider socio-political perspective, of rural Russia in the late nineteenth century – a metonymic portrait of social upheaval, with Firs, the ageing family manservant, bemoaning the unexpected uncertainties that have resulted from the 'Freedom',[20] Lopakhin, a self-made businessman, riding high on the new financial opportunities, and Trofimov, the student, prevented from studying because of his political beliefs. In the third of Strehler's boxes we are aware of the wider context within which these events take place, of an 'eternal story of human existence, of suffering, resignation, the passage from birth to death'. Strehler employs the image of Chinese boxes because each progressive interpretation is a broadening of the perspective, yet the three are interdependent, existing inside 'a fourth box which must contain all three' (Hirst, 1993, p. 28). The challenge is to realise all these different levels of significance in equal depth. I refer to Strehler's theory in some detail because it can so usefully be applied to the plays of Peter Barnes. The boxes inevitably work in a different way because we are discussing satire, but the image of the Chinese boxes, containing meaning within meaning, is still resonant. In the case of *The Ruling Class*, for example, the play is a coruscating satire on the English aristocracy and the inextricable links between the English Establishment and the Church. But to see the play only in those terms is to confine it within Strehler's first Chinese box. It is set in a very particular historical moment, and the Earl of Gurney's 'madness' (his embracing of the values of the 'Love generation' in the first act, his psychotic violence in the second act) makes specific reference to the behaviour of peers of the realm in the late 1960s. But the key to producing the play now – more than thirty years after it was first produced – is to acknowledge that it is rooted in the culture of the late 1960s and, simultaneously, to mine those cultural references for contemporary relevance to the society we inhabit now. Our television screens may no longer offer us images of aristocrats dressed as hippies, and endless speculation about the criminal misconduct of the land-owning gentry, but authority itself, and the inherently contradictory nature of our responses to it, have changed little.

If Strehler's achievement with *The Cherry Orchard* was to fuse 'the psychological (or naturalistic), the socio-political (or epic) and the poetic (or lyrical)' (Hirst, 1993, p. 28), Barnes's is to fashion plays which demand to be read as simultaneously comic and serious; metaphoric and metonymic, shockingly cruel and profoundly humane. Given the exuberance of his imagination and the density of his language, it is surprising that Barnes' critics have so often been unable to see beyond the immediate surface, reading his plays with a dogged literalness, when they demand to be read metaphorically. The problem of balancing social specificity and broader examinations of mortality and abjection, authority and acquiescence is no less evident in the plays which follow *The Ruling Class*. The Royal family in *The Bewitched*, like the aristocratic Gurneys, are an incestuous lot, raddled with inbreeding. But that is not the subject matter of the play, nor the target of its satire, any more than Venetian justice is the target of Ben Jonson's satire in *Volpone*. *The Bewitched* only has real meaning if we read it not as an archaeological excavation in search of some kind of 'truth' about seventeenth-century Spain, but as a play that speaks directly to us about our own 'bewitchment' by authority, procedure, privilege and superstition. *Laughter!* is more difficult to consider in this way. The two parts are set in periods of history nearly four hundred years apart: the first, *Tsar*, in 1575, in the torture chambers of Ivan the Terrible; the second, *Auschwitz*, in 1942, in an office in Berlin – before the action switches for a short Epilogue to the concentration camp at Auschwitz itself. The exploration of humour in *Laughter!* may be considered in the terms I have outlined above, but the immediacy of the legacy of the Holocaust makes it difficult to read in metaphorical or abstract ways. If the strategy of writing history plays is at least partly to give audiences room in which to consider the most appalling events – the Black Death, the Spanish Inquisition, the Wars of the Roses – from strange perspectives, encouraging us to reflect on how these dramas are 'plays for today', then *Auschwitz*, if not *Tsar*, is perhaps too close to allow the curious state of alertness (alternating between engagement and quizzical distance) that Barnes' most successful work achieves. It is nevertheless a remarkable play; I have not only devoted an entire chapter to it, but have returned to a detailed examination of the play's Epilogue in the final chapter of the book.

'Total Theatre'

It is perhaps inevitable that Artaud's theories about cruelty in the theatre should be invoked in relation to Barnes, and especially in connection with *Laughter!*[21] Artaud proposed a form of 'total theatre' that would 'engage the spectator in creating his own power to change, not only himself, but society as a whole.'[22] He sought a theatre and a style of performance 'in the manner of unforgettable soul therapy'.[23] In short, for Artaud, where violence, brutality and cruelty are present in the theatre they should serve a distinct moral purpose. Although Barnes has rarely written about cruelty per se in his theatre, he is very clear that he has sought to produce:

> Writing which has a moral purpose in the service of politics; not politics as propaganda but, rather, teaching by example.
>
> (1986, p. 118)

Barnes's is a 'total theatre' in that it contains elements of spectacle, grotesque physical comedy, circus, music hall, vaudeville, song, dance, lyricism, rhetoric and poetry – a theatre to be experienced, echoing Artaud's belief that 'the proper use of all the languages of theatre would instil in audiences enriching experiences of metaphysical insight.' (Cave, 1995, p. 165) Barnes's is also a theatre which does not shirk from presenting its audience with images of the most extreme cruelty. Furthermore, Artaud and Barnes each use English renaissance theatre as a reference point from which to develop their own theatre. But the connection with Artaud is as useful for the warnings it offers as it is for the insights it gives into Barnes. The dangers of presenting cruelty on stage are that it becomes either voyeuristic, gratuitous and potentially appealing to sadistic impulses, or so shocking that it repels and, rather than engaging us, the spectators, in ethical questioning, disengages and disgusts without asking us to reflect on our responses. For Artaud, cruelty in the theatre should be morally chastening and essentially reflexive. If Barnes occasionally encourages us to laugh at cruelty, he does so with a clear moral purpose. His examination of cruelty is in terms of the social, rather than the individual, psychology that gives rise to it. Laughter in the theatre is an audible and a visible social response. When Barnes deploys comedy at moments of extreme cruelty he is forcing us to reflect not only upon our own individual responses to events on stage, but also upon the collective, social response of the audience. If we laugh, does that make us complicit in the cruelty, or do we laugh in nervous, shocked detachment? Either way, we will be conscious (in a way that we are never made conscious in the 'serious' theatre) of the different responses of others around us and, furthermore, that even for those whose visible and audible reactions seem the same as ours, their responses may be very differently motivated. The strategy of juxtaposing comedy and cruelty seeks to prevent us from standing in disdainful judgement of characters from whom we are distanced by the historical context in which they are presented. But this is also an extremely risky strategy; and the danger is that in the hands of an insensitive director these juxtapositions become merely shocking, without ever provoking us into a consideration of *why* we find them so shocking. In Barnes' finest work the disparate elements of his total theatre are integrated into a montage of attractions which is characterised by its purposeful tonal instability. As I argue in Chapters 8 and 9, this instability is both disconcerting and richly productive of meaning; it also one of the means by which Barnes seeks to ensure that spectators at his plays are made aware of their own active participation in the theatrical event. When he presents us with cruelty or comedy, he ask us to interrogate our own responses, and to ask ourselves not simply 'Why are we shocked?' or 'Why do we laugh?' but 'What were the moral bases for our responses?'

Talking about Ben Jonson, Barnes declared that 'On stage, his

. . . verse unfolds like a Japanese paper flower in water. It is a wonder and a mystery. He *works* in the theatre.'[24] Although Barnes does not write in verse, it would be good to be able to claim the same of his plays, for however fascinating and stimulating they may be when read from the page, they are essentially and vigorously theatrical. Regrettably, however, they have been staged so infrequently that while I make this claim with great confidence, I have less direct evidence to support my assertion than I would wish for. Hopefully, this reappraisal of Barnes' drama (only the second book to be devoted to it)[25] will generate renewed interest in his work, both critically and, more importantly, in the theatre, where the plays demand to be experienced as well as read. I hope that in writing this book I have been able to convey some of the rich diversity of Barnes' work, and to have given a sense that while his plays are frequently provocative and challenging, they are also immensely pleasurable; and that I am able to communicate something to the reader of my own pleasure in working on such fine plays. I look forward in hopeful anticipation to the production of the unproduced plays and to theatrical revivals of at least some of those discussed in this book.

PART TWO
All the Best Lies
Five Stage Plays

The Ruling Class
The Bewitched
Laughter!
Red Noses
Dreaming

1

The Ruling Class

When *The Ruling Class* was first performed it was greeted with
critical amazement. Here was a play that seemed, at least on the
surface, to come from nowhere and to defy then current notions
of theatrical good behaviour. Harold Hobson (the highly influential drama critic of the *Sunday Times*) considered it 'a turning
point in the drama of the second half of the twentieth century',
comparing it directly with Beckett's *Waiting for Godot*,
Osborne's *Look Back in Anger* and Pinter's *The Birthday Party*,
and hailing Barnes as 'an entirely new talent of a very high
order'.[1] Although Hobson and others had never heard of Peter
Barnes, *The Ruling Class* was not Barnes' first play.[2] *The Time of
the Barracudas* had played in San Francisco and Los Angeles in
1963; and *Sclerosis* had opened in June 1965 for a short run at
the Traverse Theatre Club, Edinburgh (though when the RSC
brought the play to London they could find only one Sunday-
night 'club' performance for it at the Aldwych Theatre). In 1966
Barnes had written *Clap Hands Here Comes Charlie*, but as yet
the play has not received a professional production.[3]

Thus, although Barnes should not have been completely unknown to the theatrical establishment, it was perhaps to be
expected that *The Ruling Class* would take people by surprise. It
was certainly the play in which Barnes clearly established his own

theatrical voice. Directed by Stuart Burge (who later collaborated with Barnes on several further projects), it opened at Nottingham Playhouse on 6 November 1968, transferring to the Piccadilly Theatre, London, on 26 February 1969. Ronald Bryden shared Hobson's enthusiasm for the play, describing it as 'one of those pivotal plays . . . in which you can feel the theatre changing direction'.[4] Theirs was not, however, the general view, and although the play won two major awards for Barnes, many reviewers were far more negative, and the production did not run for long in the commercial theatre of London's West End. This reception set a pattern which has become typical of the divided and contrasting responses to most of his major plays. The polarised response to *The Ruling Class* is not surprising, considering its uncompromising mixture of Grand Guignol, high spectacle, eclectic and self-conscious theatricality and its acerbic (at times vitriolic) attack on the relationships between the vested interests of Church and state, money and power. Given the title of the play, it is to be expected that much criticism has read it as a satirical attack on the English class system, characterising Barnes as a theatrical equivalent of Hogarth or Gillray. But although the play's comic caricature of a very particular kind of English aristocrat is as precise and as detailed as a Hogarth cartoon, to view it in this way is to take a narrow view. The play examines authority and although it does not offer as comprehensive an analysis as some of the later plays, much of the territory in which Barnes would work in subsequent plays is established here: the means by which individuals and social groups develop control over others – sexual control, social control, political control – and the ways in which people at all levels in society collude in their own repression.

The play opens with an extraordinary *coup de théâtre*: a Prologue in which the 13th Earl of Gurney, returning from making a passionate speech about the necessity for capital punishment, dresses up in a tutu ballet skirt, straps a ceremonial sword to his side and accidentally hangs himself in a masochistic game of auto-erotic asphyxiation. The irony of this is compounded when we discover that the earl was himself a judge who has condemned many others to death by hanging.[5] The shift from the Prologue to the first scene of Act One has a strongly cinematic feel to it. The Prologue ends with Tucker, the earl's manservant, seeing the earl's body hanging dead. 'Bleeding bloody hell!' he cries (p. 11)[6] and we cut to Bishop Lampton chanting (over thunderous organ music): 'I am the Resurrection and the Life' (p. 15). After a reading from the 1662 Book of Prayer,[7] there is the theatrical equivalent of a cross-fade from the church to the Gurney country house, and the bishop leads the mourners in a rendition of 'All Things Bright and Beautiful' (p. 15): ' "The rich man in his castle, the poor man at his gate. God made them high and lowly, and ordered their estate . . ." '

The incantation of the well-known hymn at this point clearly expresses the close relationships between the political establishment, the Church of England and social stratification that are amongst the central concerns of the play.[8] It is not long before we discover that Bishop Lampton is himself a Gurney (he is Jack's uncle). Although, in the next scene, he expresses some minor reservations about having conducted a church service for someone 'who may have laid violent hands upon himself' (p. 16), he is rarely troubled about possible conflicts of duty between his religion, his social position and the politics of the family; he clearly believes that the function of the Church of England is to legitimise the most extreme reactionary politics.

Although the thirteenth earl has had four sons, only Jack has survived; and he duly becomes the fourteenth Earl of Gurney – much to the horror of the rest of the family, who regard him as mad and dangerous. His 'madness' manifests itself as a belief that he is 'Lord Jesus come again in my body to save the sick, the troubled, the ignorant' (p. 25). Jack argues that this is entirely rational: 'When I pray to Him I find I'm talking to myself' (p. 26). It is not, however, his paranoid delusions of grandeur that concern the family, but his wholehearted espousal of the anti-materialist hippy ideology of the late 1960s that poses such a threat: he sees himself as a 'God of Love' (p. 22) and refers to himself as 'J.C. Mark II', and takes the teachings of 'J. Christ Mark I' far too seriously for the Establishment (in which, as the play explicitly states, the Church is a very active partner). 'Pomp and riches, pride and property will have to be lopped off,' he pronounces. 'All men are brothers. Love makes all equal' (p. 28). Although there is more than a hint of irony about this, given that the aristocracy as presented here are so determined to keep everything 'in the family', it is Jack's liberalism, his espousal of the notion of social equality, that catalyses the family into action against him. Sir Charles Gurney, Jack's uncle, is ruthlessly deter-mined to consign Jack to an asylum, thereby disinheriting him and preventing him from taking up his seat in the House of Lords, where he will be an embarrassment – and clearly a threat – to all. In order for Sir Charles' plan to work, Jack has to have a son to whom Charles can act as guardian.

The first act of the play dramatises this twin-pronged attempt by Sir Charles to counter the threat posed by J.C. Mark II and assume his nephew's inherited authority by taking on the role of guardian of the planned infant. He contrives a wedding between Jack and his own mistress, Grace Shelley, a fertile young woman; and he enlists the assistance of a psychiatrist, Dr Paul Herder, in having Jack committed to an asylum. Herder, however, thinks he is being taken for a fool, and he determines to cure Jack. But therein hangs the brilliance of Sir Charles' (and Barnes') plotting, for whatever Herder does, his actions will serve the interests of the ruling class. If Herder fails, Jack will be rendered powerless, branded a lunatic with paranoid delusions, isolated from society and prevented from subverting authority; if he succeeds (convincing Jack that he is not a second Jesus Christ, that he is not a god of love), then society will deem him harmless – and he will be able to take his seat in the House of Lords. The play thus uses the logic of farce to examine the mechanisms of power.

In the final scene of the first act Herder confronts Jack with a rival madman, McKyle, who regards himself as something of a cross between a god of anger and vengeance (the Old Testament Jehovah) and Dr Frankenstein's monster from a Hammer horror movie: 'Ach, who else has electricity streaming fraw his fingers and eyeballs? I'm the High Voltage Messiah' (p. 68). At the climactic moment the earl/Jack/J.C. Mark II *'wrestles in an epileptic fit . . . twisting from the force of the imaginary electrical charge'* and a *'monstrous eight-feet beast bursts in . . . dressed incongruously in high Victorian fashion'* (pp. 73–4). No one else in the room sees the beast, which attacks Jack, shaking him violently, and only leaves after slamming him across its knee and tossing him to the floor. As he comes round he feebly voices his name: 'Jack. My name's Jack . . .' (p. 74), and slowly it dawns on Herder that the earl no longer thinks of himself as J.C. As Jack voices his name with ever greater strength and confidence, Sir Charles bursts in to announce that Grace Shelley has given birth to a boy. The status quo has been firmly re-established – but at what cost?

As the second act begins it seems that Jack has indeed reverted 'back to normal'. But normality becomes increasingly uncomfortable as he develops another persona. Abandoning the garb and manners of the hippy transcendentalist, he now *'wears an old-fashioned dark suit with waistcoat and stiff collar'* (p. 78), apologises for his earlier behaviour and determines to 'learn the rules of the game' (p. 79). But it seems that the 'rules of the game' demand that he adopt ever more reactionary attitudes; and he embraces these enthusiastically. In the tradition of the blackest of farces, the logic of this new-found illiberalism is pushed to the extreme – and Jack reveals himself to the audience (and to his female victims) as 'Jack from Hell, trade-name Jack the Ripper!' (p. 90). Having killed and got away with it, he duly takes up his seat in the House of Lords where the Lords ('*two tiers of mouldering dummies*') loudly applaud his inaugural speech, in which he insists: 'The strong MUST manipulate the weak. That's the first law of the Universe – was and ever shall be world without end' (p. 118).

Tucker

This account of the play makes scant mention of Tucker, the thirteenth earl's manservant who is inherited by Jack (in much the way that serfs in nineteenth-century Russia belonged to land-owning families);[9] but although his role in the play is tangential to the plot, he is a highly significant character. When the thirteenth earl's will is read, and Tucker learns that he has inherited twenty thousand pounds, he jumps '*clumsily into the air . . . clicking his heels together . . . Flinging open the door . . . he leaps raggedly out, arms held high*' (p. 19). When we meet Tucker later, he is warning the fourteenth earl that the family is 'back there plotting against you like mad . . . I've seen 'em at work a'fore. They got the power and they made the rules' (p. 30). The earl does not want to hear this, which he calls 'negativism'. Urging Tucker to 'Resist it' (p. 31), the earl leaves Tucker alone – with only the audience for company. Although Tucker is an unreliable narrator, his subsequent speech is very revealing. Firstly he tells us that his inheritance leaves him untouched by the earl's rejection of his confidences – 'Tried to help, you stupid old fool' – because he is about to leave for the South of France: 'Just pack a tooth-brush and a French letter'. Then the tone shifts. 'What's keeping you then, Dan?' he asks himself. The answer comes all too quickly: 'Fear.' He characterises this as an English condition: 'Very first thing an Englishman does, straight from his mother's womb, is touch his forelock . . . *Me*, this tired old creeping servant, I'm the real England, not beef-eating Johnny Bullshit' (p. 31). But are we to read this as an easy swipe at English subservience? Certainly, in this play (and in *The Bewitched, Laughter!* and *Dreaming*) Barnes is as concerned with the mechanisms of acquiescence and complicity as he is with the workings of authority and power; but whereas Tucker identifies his Englishness as the root of his problem, the play is not so simplistic. Tucker may be self-deluding, attempting to absolve himself of responsibility for his own timidity, but he is at least aware of his obsequiousness: 'You get into the habit of serving. Born a servant, see, son of a servant. Family of servants. From a nation of servants' (p. 31). His tendency is to retreat into broader and broader social groups, blaming his father, his family and his nation for the behaviour that he so dislikes in himself. This is echoed in the Gurneys' appeal to 'human nature' as justification for their own monstrous behaviour.

Tucker is not the only character in the play to make use of the concept of an 'English' national character: for the Gurney family, and for Truscott (the 'Master in Lunacy' who is required in Act Two to give Jack a clean bill of health), being English is always a sign of the satisfactory. 'Families like ours set the tone,' announces Sir Charles. 'Doesn't help poking and prying into personal lives. The strength of the English people lies in their inhibitions' (p. 61). And anyone who is not English is suspect. As Truscott explains to Jack: 'Dr Herder says you're nearly back to normal. Of course, he *is* a foreigner and his idea of normal may not be mine' (p. 86). This contestation of the qualities of Englishness is one of many indications that the play is richer and more complex than is allowed by the assertion that it is 'out of its time, tilting at windmills such as the aristocracy, the church, the House of Lords . . . symbols of Old England' (Christie, 2001).[10] Certainly, the play critiques xenophobic, reactionary attitudes; but it satirises attitudes to nationhood and patriotism, rather than taking sideswipes at the soft target of the English aristocracy. If, as Samuel Johnson claimed, patriotism is indeed the last refuge of scoundrels, then those very scoundrels can take great comfort from Tucker's inverted patriotism, which, by his own account, assigns him his role in life as definitively as God ordering His estate.

  I want to return briefly to Tucker's speech near the beginning of the play. Having pronounced that he is the 'real England', that he is 'just old faithful Tucker', he asks us: 'Know who I really am?' He again answers himself: 'Alexei Kronstadt. Number 243. Anarchist – Trotskyist – Communist – Revolutionary. I'm a cell! All these years I've been working for the Revolution' (p. 31). Although the idea that he is a 'sleeper' gives Tucker a comfort blanket – it again justifies his deference to the family – it is unlikely that an audience believes this for longer than a moment. He undermines any credibility he might have as a revolutionary by confiding in us that his tactics have been 'spitting in the hot soup, peeing on the Wedgwood dinner plates' (p. 31). I discuss Barnes' narrative methods in detail in Chapter 8, 'A Montage of Attractions', but it is worth briefly noting here that Tucker's speech is structured in such a way that each assertion he makes, each attitude he adopts, casts doubt on a previous position – not only one that he has taken, but also that we, an audience, have taken in relation to him. Immediately before he proclaims his revolutionary credentials, he asks us directly: 'Didn't think I was like that, eh? [i.e. servile] . . . Give doggy boney. Just 'ere for comic relief.' The device takes Tucker briefly out of the fictional world, as he becomes an observer of his place in the Gurney family, and asks us to consider his function in the play.

Metatheatre

Tucker does, of course, provide 'comic relief' – both for us and for the Gurney family. But the moment of metatheatre might push us further, provoking a broader consideration of the functions and purpose of humour in this play: a play which seems, at least superficially, to bear such a strong resemblance to familiar theatrical forms, such as the country house murder mystery and Whitehall farce. Tucker's question might even lead us to query how our perception of Tucker as 'comic relief' might coincide with the Gurneys', for the manservant provides us with a distraction. Any subversive threat that he might pose to the Gurneys is either contained by his own history of obsequiousness or permitted because he is regarded as no more dangerous than a licensed buffoon. When he is thoroughly disrespectful (as in Act One, Scene 13), referring to the guests at the late earl's wedding as 'Lords of conspicuous consumption' (p. 60), he is simply ignored because the true nature of his 'Revolution' is a rebellious but mild-mannered retreat from good manners to heavy drinking. Tucker's twists and turns to avoid responsibility for his own actions are woven into the play like a running gag. The final irony for Tucker, however, and a measure of the play's darkness, is that when he finds himself in a position to dish the dirt on the family, he becomes a serious threat; and his empty boasts of being a radical are turned against him.

In Act Two, Scene 6 we realise just how dangerous Jack, the fourteenth Earl of Gurney, is in his new guise as Old Testament

God of vengeance and defender of (the Gurney) family values. Lady Claire finds him very attractive and sets out to seduce him; this triggers something terrible in Jack.

> CLAIRE   Tell me I'm fairer than the evening star. Clad in the beauty of a thousand nights . . .
> EARL OF GURNEY   The sword of the Lord is filled with blood.
> CLAIRE (*trembling violently*)   Stop talking, Jack, and make me immortal with a kiss.
>
> *. . . he pulls her close, forcing her head back with a kiss. Taking out his knife, he flicks it open, and plunges it into her stomach.*
>
> (p. 99)

Tucker appears '*swaying and singing*' and stumbles, even more drunk than usual, across Lady Claire's dead body. The next scene seems like a cross between *An Inspector Calls* and an episode of *The Goon Show*.[11] When Tucker first sees the body, he assumes Lady Claire is 'Stoned'. He bends over her to help, and only then does he realise that she is dead: '*He gives a great rasping intake of breath . . . and stands mumbling in shock.*' Then, in a notable comic moment, he shouts out manically, 'One less! One less!' (p. 99) But his glee is short-lived. Jack, to whom Tucker has remained personally loyal, in spite of his protestations to the audience that he is a revolutionary, emerges from the darkness and accuses him of the murder. Sir Charles, who has hitherto ignored Tucker, turns on him, accusing him of being a 'brainwashed thug' (p. 106). But although Charles is correct, Tucker has been 'brainwashed' into acquiescence and complicity by the Gurney family and, by extension, the ideology of the English class system – not by the Communist Party. Tucker has used his 'communism' in the way that many people now use the lottery: it fuels his fantasies; it gives him a way of convincing himself that he can escape his existence as a pathetic servant to a dysfunctional, manipulative family. And it is only now, now that he is finally safe in the certainty of his own destitution, that he accuses the family of being 'Upper-class excrement' (p. 107). Tucker rants against the aristocracy; but no evidence is produced to prove him guilty of Lady Claire's murder. For Inspector Brockett, however, his political rage is proof enough: 'Sorry you heard all that . . . but I had to let him rave on. The more they talk, the more they convict themselves' (p. 108).

Rhythm

Any production of *The Ruling Class* needs to be aware of the complexity of internal rhythms within the play.[12] Act Two, Scene 7 ends with Tucker removed and the bishop left alone with the earl. After Tucker's ravings, the ending of the scene is calm and ironically reassuring. The bishop tells Jack (whom we now know to be a psychopath): 'You've become a great source of strength to me, Jack . . . You were the instrument that restored my faith . . . Now let me walk humbly with my God' (p. 108). And they exit quietly together: the bishop with the man who claims to be the Old Testament God of fear and vengeance.

Not only does this confirm the bishop's naivety and his collusion in the savage brutality that characterises the Gurney family, but in structural terms it also creates a telling contrast with the ending of the previous scene, where Sir Charles rushes over to Lady Claire's corpse and

*stares in disbelief, unable to find words to express himself. Finally
he turns and explodes indignantly at the audience:*

SIR CHARLES   All right, who's the impudent clown
responsible for this?'

(p. 100)

His response to his wife's murder is to implicate the audience, as
a public school teacher might accuse *all* the boys in a class of a
practical joke. The accusation is, in its way, wonderfully comic.
We expect Charles's outrage, but turning against the audience is
unexpected. It is a gesture both of his own exasperation – he cannot find words to express his indignation within the constraints
of the fictional world – and also an indication of his inclination
to cast blame on outsiders, on those who are 'not one of us'. In
their different ways, the behaviour of Bishop Lampton, seeking
solace with his demented relative, and Charles, turning against
the audience, are two sides of the same coin. The positioning of
these moments at the end of consecutive scenes draws attention
to the relationship between them.

Barnes' use of structure to create meaning is explored in
greater depth in Chapter 8; before moving on I want to consider
Charles's question a little further. Although there is no doubt
what the character intends at this point – 'who's . . . responsible
for this?' clearly refers to Lady Claire's murder – within the overall context of the play, however, the question is loaded with other
meanings. 'Who *is* responsible for this?' – 'this' being Jack's state
of mind, or 'this' being the socio-political system that permits
the ruling class such unfettered power and privilege? These are the
questions that the play ultimately asks us. A consideration of
the structure and rhythms of the play reinforces the point. In Act
Two, Scene 5 (the scene that immediately precedes Claire's

murder), Mrs Treadwell and Mrs Piggot-Jones, staunch bastions of the local Conservative Party, who had been so horrified by the earl's apparent socialism in the first act (Scene 6), are now won over by his 'blend of God-given arrogance and condescension' (p. 96). Their deference to such qualities empowers the earl; and the play is unequivocal in its mockery of the claim that any human characteristics are 'God-given'. Jack considers himself to be God. If he is arrogant and condescending, these are qualities he has given himself.

The scene with the two women echoes and contrasts with its first-act equivalent in a number of ways. Whereas in the first, Jack terrifies them with his claim that 'God is love', here he reassures them that 'the Hangman holds society together. He is the symbol of the Great Chastiser. He built this world on punishment and fear' (p. 93). And they are mightily impressed by this, remarking on his 'natural dignity' (p. 95). In formal terms, what is distinctive about both this scene and the earlier one is the use of song: in Act Two, Scene 5 the earl's tirade about fear, punishment and certainty metamorphoses from a sadomasochistic fantasy into a parody of a well-known gospel song:

EARL OF GURNEY   Bring back fear . . . When [the
  Executioner] stood on the gallows, stripped to the waist,
  tight breeches, black hood, you knew God was in his heaven
  . . . The punishment for blaspheming was to be broken on
  the wheel. First the fibula . . . Cr-a-a-ck. Then the tibia,
  patella and femur. *Crack, crack, crack* . . . 'Disconnect dem
  bones, dem dry bones, Disconnect dem bones dem dry
  bones. Now hear the word of the Lord.'

Irresistibly the two women join in.

(p. 94)

This metatheatrical device is entertaining in its own right, but it also has a function as metaphor. If we find ourselves caught up in the song, then our response relates closely to that of the two women, who are beguiled by the earl's charisma and, taken over by the catchiness of the routine, join in with it in spite of themselves. In the first scene with the two women, the song can just about be read diegetically – when the earl breaks into 'The Varsity Drag' it could be attributed to his exuberant exhibitionism – but the reprise, described above, demands to be read in more complex ways. Barnes' use of popular song in *The Ruling Class* was highly innovative, anticipating Dennis Potter's use of it in the following decade.[13] It is part of the overall freewheeling, genre-bending style that Barnes developed, and can be seen as contributing to the 'montage of attractions' (see Chapter 8). Its 'meaning', however, is elusive. At one level the song is a diversion, an entertaining device that takes us briefly out of the drama, allowing or encouraging us to reflect on the action of the scene. The specific choice of song here is itself significant: a gospel song, a song once used as a means of asserting solidarity amongst Southern slaves in the face of overwhelming forces of oppression. But here, in *The Ruling Class*, it is appropriated by the Earl of Gurney, whose intentions are precisely the opposite: in his slightly altered version he would *disconnect* 'dem bones' as a punishment for blaspheming against the word of the Lord. And the song sweeps up the women, who remain apparently oblivious to what it is they are subscribing to. As a further wry irony, we do indeed 'hear the word of the Lord', for by the earl's own account they are all singing His song. As so often in Barnes' work, what seems to be a moment of light-hearted, almost whimsical entertainment is provocative and disconcerting. The song is simultaneously comic and serious, engaging and distancing. It asks us to consider several different positions about the play at the same time.

And the earl, a peer of the realm, an aristocratic lord, considers himself to be the Lord. Thus the play interrogates the relationship between Christianity's choice of worldly, political terminology to describe the ineffable, and the hierarchy itself. In Christian terms the earl is himself blaspheming by claiming to be God, but the vocabulary encourages it: 'hear the word of the Lord' . . . 'the rich man in his castle, the poor man at his gate' (p. 15).

Contradictions and Schizophrenia

The play frequently asks us to reconsider that which we might think of as opposites, representing them as two sides of the same coin. The most obvious example of this is the earl himself. That Jesus Christ Mark II and Jack the Ripper are presented as alternate personae of the fourteenth Earl of Gurney is both comic and disturbing (indeed, it is comic because it is disturbing); but the juxtaposition of the two asks us whether some of the characteristics that turn Jack into the Ripper are already present in J.C. Mark II. Whereas the one considers it his right to take life, the other assumes he has the right to sanction sex. Each assumes an authority over others; it is this authority which the play exposes as the heart of the madness. The contradictions reveal Barnes' working methods in this play and in much of his subsequent work. In a short piece entitled 'Notes',[14] he wrote that he wanted to create

A drama of extremes, trying to illuminate the truth as contradictory. Instead of eliminating those contradictions as untrue, they are emphasised; melancholy and joy, tragedy and comedy, the bathetic and the sublime are placed side by side. The similarity of such opposites is shown by such juxtapositions.

In *The Ruling Class*, the personal contradictions may be explicable through psychoanalysis (although Dr Herder's attempts to do so within the play itself are essentially comic – the stuff of horror movies – and his strategy of confronting Jack with the maniacal McKyle effectively pushes a genial fool into dangerous psychosis), but their function within the play is to reveal the exploitative brutality of the society which the Gurney family strive to perpetuate and within which they can rule 'not by superior force or skill / But by sheer presence.' (Prologue, p. 7) In this context, J.C. Mark II and his hippy philosophy is as ineffectual as Jack the Ripper is terrifying. For all his vague tirades against materialism, J.C. Mark II's preaching (like that of the Ranters of the English Revolution, with which it bears a striking similarity) can only license libertarianism. The threat that this poses to the Establishment is contained with relative ease. Indeed, there is a sense in which the play's juxtaposition of the two sides of the Earl of Gurney's character exemplifies Barnes' claim that 'The similarity of . . . [apparent] opposites is shown by such juxtapositions', revealing an uncomfortable proximity between mysticism and fascism.

In the Epilogue to the play, Grace appears in a black nightdress and sings: 'You'd meet him on the street and never notice him . . . / But his form and face, his manly grace. Makes me – *thrill* . . . I love him' (p. 119). The lyrics derive from a song in the Kern and Hammerstein musical, *Show Boat*, but in this context they alert us again to the potential dangers of charismatics. As Grace sings, Jack draws her close. They kiss passionately and, as the lights fade, '*a single scream of fear and agony*' is heard in the darkness. The threat posed by Jack and the Gurney family is invisible. And what makes their power so insidious is that their victims find it so attractive: a theme that Barnes would go on to develop more forcefully in *The Bewitched* and *Laughter!*

2

The Bewitched

Of all Barnes' plays, *The Bewitched* is probably the most demanding to a theatre management. It has a cast of thirty-four speaking roles and thirty separate scenes (including a Prologue and an Epilogue), many of which are conceived of as grand spectacle. First produced by the RSC, directed by Terry Hands, it opened at the Aldwych Theatre in May 1974.[1] The play is set in the Spanish court at the end of the seventeenth century.

As in *The Ruling Class*, the Prologue is a masterpiece in its own right, a *coup de théâtre* that heralds the major themes of the play, establishes the basic situation and sets the (highly unstable) tone for what follows. It begins with the following stage directions: '*Darkness. A funeral bell tolls*' (p. 192).[2] Courtiers are mourning the death of Philip IV's young son, 'that most blessed infant, Prince Felipé . . . heir t' the throne o' Spain' (p. 192). Philip is old and desperately decayed, '*His gnarled body is painfully twisted, his arms and legs pock-marked with sores*' (p. 193), and yet he must produce a male heir for the benefit of Church and state to ensure succession: 'A King who dies w'out an heir betrays his kingdom and his God' (p. 195). Watched by his courtiers as he is ritually undressed (it takes three grandees and two attendants to manage this), he is prepared for 'sheet-duty wi' the Queen. One last assault on Eve's custom house'

43

(p. 195). Monks enter the bedchamber to the sound of the Magnificat; holy water is sprinkled over the decrepit king and his young wife; *'Massive wheels and screws turn laboriously and ancient pistons start pounding'* (p. 197). The frantic coupling is metonymic of the convoluted machinery of Church and state. A woman screams, and *'The scream turns into staccato cries of a woman in childbirth . . . and the floor . . . splits apart'* (p. 197). From this crack a shapeless body appears. Wrapped in a pale pink membrane, it *'slithers painfully towards the throne'* (p. 197). When Philip sees the deformed body that bursts through the membrane he dies in shock. He has been succeeded by the deformed and monstrously ugly Carlos.

This is a spectacular scene, and to realise it as the stage directions request would tax the resources of even the best-funded subsidised theatre company. Barnes has, however, frequently stated that he offers a virtually free hand to producers and directors who want to edit or cut his plays: 'I expect the texts for all the major plays, with the possible exception of *The Ruling Class*, to be cut. But the cuts for each new production will be different' (Barnes, 1993, p. xiii). Although his assessment of theatrical budgets may be pragmatic, it is worth considering what the functions of the spectacle are here. The Prologue powerfully establishes the difference between the aspirations of the court – with all its pomp and formality – and the sexual inadequacy of Philip; it highlights the importance of succession; and it sets up the enormous expectations that ride on the 'success' of the sexual act – which is thus equated with performance in both a literal and a metaphorical sense. Set against the decadent splendour of the court, Philip has to be undressed by attendants (the apparatus of the state does not allow him to undress himself). And while the act of procreation has enormous significance for the royal family and for the state,

Philip's speech simultaneously reveals both his obsession with and his profoundly misogynist disgust for sex: 'No sin in't for 't will be no pleasure' (p. 195). The scene is as monstrous in its content as it is in the demands it appears to make on theatrical resources. The key to staging it, however, is not financial, but an understanding of the contrasts and contradictions it contains: its juxtaposition of ritualised excess and human frailty; the confusion and brutal conflation of private relations with public exhibition, of personal identity with the self-perpetuating demands of the state. Almost incidentally, the Prologue also alerts us to the sheer scale of the play's ambition: birth and death; brutality, suffering and abjection. I use the term abjection here with caution, but it is appropriate both in the common usage of the term and in the more complex theoretical sense established by Julia Kristeva.[3]

The Prologue is certainly grotesque and disturbing, but it does not really prepare an audience for the humour that is characteristic of most of the rest of the play. Act One jumps forward in time some thirty years and, taking its cue from Ben Jonson's opening of *The Alchemist*, begins with a furious argument between Ana, the queen to King Carlos; and Mariana, Carlos's mother.[4] As in Jonson's play, the argument is both entertaining in itself and revealing of plot. Carlos is an imbecile who has been physically incapable of producing an heir. As Ana says: 'You casn't produce an heir wi' the usual instrument so you must use pen and ink.' Mariana turns this against Ana, accusing her of barrenness: 'O' course you're not impotent Carlos . . . every night [of nineteen years of marriage] you've performed thy duty. That's o'er 6,000 performances, wi'out success. Carlos you're not concentrating! . . . Cast her off, Carlos. She's sterile' (p. 201).

The quarrel becomes ever fiercer and vituperative, culminating in a sequence of cursing, which grows increasingly irrational until the point at which their fulmination seems to turn them into animals:

> ANA   Toads gnaw thy flesh and the little devils laugh *hee-hee-hee*, they laugh *hee-hee-hee*.
> MARIANA   I hear thy screams *aaarrhh*, mercy, mercy *aaarhh aaarhh*.

(p. 202)

And then, as the lights flicker, '*They howl and hiss with increasing fury*' and all three let out loud cries and '*fall into epileptic fits*' (p. 202). Language itself has broken down. If the early parts of the scene are at least in some way humorous, the ending is shocking, cruel and frightening, but characteristic of the way that the play constantly shifts in tone and style. The apparition of the king, the queen and the queen mother in paroxysms functions in several ways: the convulsions of epilepsy are symptomatic of inbreeding within the royal family, indicative of the extent to which each of them (and especially Carlos) is dependent upon others for their own survival, and to perpetuate their political power. In dramatic terms, the grotesque physical convulsions also allow each of the characters to give extreme bodily expression to the painful contortions of their own identities:

> CARLOS*'s head rotates and his tongue lolls out as he whirls round on his own axis, limbs thrashing wildly.* MARIANA*'s legs kick convulsively while her arms thrust bolt upright, fingers clutching the air, her teeth bared in a fixed grin.* ANA*'s body jerks up and down as she tears her dress and hits her crotch in excitement.*

(p. 202)

Carlos's aimless, directionless expression of frustration compares with the terrible tensions between his mother's upper and lower body; Mariana is a woman who is, as we will see as the play develops, in a constant state of turmoil: at the mercy of her resentment and her hatred for Ana, whose own sexual frustration and rage can only vent themselves in violence.

Henceforth, the narrative of the play concerns itself with Carlos's attempts to beget an heir, to ensure the continuity of the Hapsburg line.[5] But Carlos is even more deformed and incapable than his father, and even if he is not impotent, he is certainly prone to epilepsy. This results in the key contradiction that underpins the play: if he succeeds in fathering an heir, Hapsburg inbreeding will almost certainly make the resulting progeny even more incapable and grotesque than Carlos; if he fails, it will be a 'heresy 'gainst the Church who anointed him' (p. 319). As in Brecht's theatre, the contradictions reveal the absurdity of the social and political structures which give rise to them – in this instance exemplified by the conflation of religious conviction, superstition, political hegemony and patriarchal repression.

Dramatic Strategies and Thematic Concerns

One of the great achievements of *The Bewitched* is the way in which it successfully integrates such a wide range of dramatic strategies and such large thematic concerns. Scene 3 of Act One exemplifies several of these achievements. It is set in 'The Council Chamber . . . dominated by a huge map of the Spanish Empire' – echoing the dramatic technique of the Prologue by contrasting the grandiose aspirations and the enormous political power of the assembly with the absurdity of its procedures and proceedings. The scene starts with a discussion of whether the king is conscious, and how anybody might know for certain. The participants take the debate very seriously but it is clearly comic in effect. Pontocarrero, the Jesuit Cardinal-Archbishop of Toledo, interrupts to insist that they '*must* recommend an heir t' the throne. All decisions wait on this, wi'out 't Spain's impotent' (p. 206). Carlos's impotence is Spain's impotence. The king is not merely the titular head of state; his physical condition becomes metonymic for Spain's self-destructive internal convulsions. But before the discussion can get under way, Alba interjects to demand they address his concerns about the undermining of his privileges: 'When His Majesty was convulsed last night, Attendants placed the distemper stick 'tween his teeth. All know that privilege's been reserved f' the de Albas since the Moorish Conquest!' (p. 206). That he was five hours away at the time, and that the king could have died had the attendants not intervened, is not important to Alba: 'Take away one privilege 'cause 'tisn't convenient, others follow. Wi'out privileges no man knows his worth' (p. 207).

The problem of the heir is of acute importance to the court (and is temporarily resolved by Motilla's announcement towards the end of the scene that Queen Ana is pregnant); but within the Council Chamber issues of privilege and personal worth at least temporarily oust this central problem. In such a society, personal worth is so closely tied up with social, hierarchical position as to make individuals worth less than the social position they hold. It is worth noting that historically the very notion of the individual 'subject' was much more contentious and problematic in the period in which *The Bewitched* is set than it is now; but the play is not satirising late seventeenth- and early eighteenth-century attitudes. Barnes uses history in *The Bewitched* (and in his other history plays) in much the same way that Jonathan Swift used geography in *Gulliver's Travels*: he is much less interested in historical authenticity (whatever that might be) than in the parallels we might draw and the associations we might make. Barnes perceives of himself as a populist. His own cultural preferences are demotic: he is immersed in popular film, music hall, vaudeville. His work bounces off associations and expectations generated by popular culture. Thus his versions of the Spanish court in *The Bewitched* and in *Bye Bye Columbus* draw as much from *Carry On* films and Hammer horror movies as they do from the detailed historical research he undertook while writing these plays.

Before moving on from this early scene, it is worth briefly drawing attention to a moment in the scene which interrupts the flow of action and debate, and which exemplifies a significant and characteristic feature of the theatrical methodology that Barnes adopts in his mature work. After Pontocarrero has wrested attention away from Alba and back to the question of who shall be named as Carlos's heir, it comes down to a vote. Mariana has championed the king's choice, José of Bavaria (because he would be 'pliable'), but is outvoted by the council four to one in favour of Charles of Austria. At which point there emerges, from out of the shadows, a '*carbuncled* OLD MAN'. He '*hobbles towards her . . . She gasps in agony as the* OLD MAN *deliberately squeezes her breast*'. (She watches him) '*exiting . . . wheezing and scratching himself. He has left a silver crab-brooch pinned to her breast*' (pp. 210–11). What is worth noting in this is the way that we as an audience are positioned. We do not know who the Old Man is, what his status is within the fictional world of the play. When he first appears we do not even know which characters can see him and which cannot. Is he a beggar who has talked his way into the court, an assassin or a messenger? We experience these events from Mariana's point of view. She does not know who he is, or what he is doing here. Our momentary confusion is her confusion: it is not until the Old Man has left the stage that we, and she, realise that she is the only character to have seen him, although all respond to her gasp of agony as he squeezes her breast. This complicates our perspective of events. While we are never encouraged to 'identify' with Mariana – it is debatable whether the play has a central character in the traditional sense – this close positioning with her complicates our response to what follows. We know she has cancer, although she never mentions anything about it, and, given a degree of familiarity with dramatic conventions, we can be fairly certain that she will die before the end of the play; but she is constructed as something of a villain. No sooner has the Old Man left the stage than Motilla, the royal confessor, arrives to announce that Queen Ana is pregnant. Mariana's response to this is immediate: 'A lie! . . . She's barren' (p. 211). If we have briefly seen events through Mariana's eyes, we are now encouraged to be suspicious of her – and also of our own responses to events. Such 'interruptions' to the flow of our responses occur frequently, and are an important formal structuring element in the play, echoing some of the various functions that humour serves. Our relationship with events on the stage is constantly changing – sometimes because, as here, our perspective on a scene moves between characters; sometimes because we might laugh at something we know we should not find humorous; sometimes because of the shifts in tone and style. And this makes us very alert to our own responses. This self-consciousness in an audience, which the play encourages, bears some resemblance to the effect that Brecht intended with his strategy of *Verfremdungseffekt* (discussed at some length in Chapter 7).

The rivalry between Ana and Mariana runs throughout the play from this point onward, their mutual hatred fuelled by their involvement with Carlos: Mariana is bitterly jealous of her daughter-in-law, and goes to great lengths to prove that it is Ana who is sterile rather than Carlos who is impotent; Ana is bitterly resentful of the queen mother's constant interference in her rela-

tionship with Carlos. Although *The Bewitched* is most certainly
not a play in which characters are psychologised in a naturalistic
sense, Mariana's loathing is psychologically complex. It is evident
that she feels in some way ashamed of and personally responsible
for Carlos's condition (although she never states as much ver-
bally), and the intensity of her hatred of Ana is at least partly a
manifestation of guilt and self-destructiveness. This is evident in
Act One, Scene 5, where Mariana is praying. She begins: 'Lord
God, let my son live and his son live as Thy son lives, eternally'
(p. 216). But she then '*thrusts out her neck and speaks in a hysterical parrot-like croak*'; and she conducts a dialogue with herself in which the 'normal' self, the respectable self, voices what
she should say while the parrot-like alter ego gives voice to
repressed rancour and darkest terrors. 'I pray, let Carlos live!' she
demands, only for the parrot self to respond: '*But he's half-dead,
clod back t' clod, his child'll die, I'd six die so why shouldst his live
. . . let the donkey-dick stink and die, let me breathe again*'
(pp. 216–17). In the crucible of guilt and racking pain ('*I'm
staked out daily, pain like as a wedge*') Carlos's survival and
Mariana's pain are smelted together. Cause and effect become
inextricable, just as, by the end of this short scene, her rational
self and the parrot self have become one:

> But he's my flesh. I bore him *and he bores me* . . . God's the
> answer, *what's the question? CRRAH. CRRAH.* I ask, I sweat,
> I wonder. I swallow the world i' a yawn. (*Gasping
> asthmatically.*) Aiai . . . Aiai . . . Aiai . . . (*Violently.*) GRRRRX
> CRRAH CRRAH.

> *Jamming the Bible into her mouth she flaps her arms desperately
> as her Spot goes out to the sound of singing.*

> (p. 217)

It is significant that the 'real' parrot, named Joey, that appears in the play belongs to Queen Ana. It is a wise old bird, occasionally assuming the role of a narrator and commentator. Act Two opens with the parrot observing:

> *O impotence, where is thy sting? Nothing's changed. Carlos sits i'*
> *the dust anointing his penis-stick wi' goat's grease and the*
> *Queen's still barren . . . So what else's new? . . . the poor still*
> *starve. Men don't get results, only consequences.*

(p. 274)

In her 'normal' state of mind Mariana detests the parrot, partly because it can remain an insightful and disinterested observer of the monstrous goings-on at court and partly because it belongs to Ana – so for Mariana to assume the parrot's identity in this scene is indicative of her self-destructiveness as well as her inner turmoil. The scene which opens Act Two ends with Mariana strangling the parrot. The schizophrenic symptoms that Mariana exhibits in the scene where she is at prayer echo the convulsive tensions between the upper and lower body that we saw in her at the end of the first scene of Act One. The grotesque extremes of such scenes are characteristic of the play, but although Barnes' use of Grand Guignol effects carries with it the risk of distracting an audience, they are highly productive in meaning. There is no more place in the court for emotional integrity than there is for reason. Both the individual and the state are tearing themselves apart.

At the time when *The Bewitched* and *The Ruling Class* were written, 'madness' was in vogue as a subject for films, television and the stage, but Barnes does not follow fashion.[6] The madness in both *The Ruling Class* and *The Bewitched* is collective; if Mariana and the Earl of Gurney are 'mad', their actions and behaviour are symptomatic and metonymic. For each of them, their individual madness is both a response to the insanity of the worlds in which they live and a significant contributor to it.

Nowhere is this physicalised expression of a collective madness more evident than in an extraordinary sequence (Act One, Scene 4) in which Antonio, the royal dancing master, attempts to teach Carlos the Pavan:

ANTONIO Your Majesty, the dance is a remedy f' all natural ills . . . The perfect harmony o' the dance glorifies the perfect harmony o' God's universe . . . Today, Sire, we practise the 'Pavan', again . . . 'Tis . . . the courtliest o' all court dances . . . its natural authority mirroring the natural authority o' its dancers . . .

CARLOS's left foot skids forward and his right knee buckles . . . and keels over onto the floor with a crash . . . The **COURTIERS** *murmur approval . . .*
CARLOS gets up . . . reverses and skids about in a series of extraordinary spastic lurches, arms and legs jerking uncontrollably and ending once again on the floor . . .

TORRES Your Majesty hath a natural sense o' rhythm . . .
CARLOS KINGS aaaaren't subject t' rules, decrees . . . I dance f' joy na-aaa i' thy cold French way.
ANTONIO 'Tis . . . 'er, magnificent, Your Majesty, but, 'er 'tisn't the 'Pavan'.
CARLOS No, 'tis 'The Carlos'! . . .

[The courtiers and grandees] make reverence . . . and they dance Down Stage following **CARLOS**'s *grotesque jerkings exactly . . . With their* **MAJESTIES** *in the lead, they wobble, lurch, do the splits, skid and spin with poker-faced dignity . . . in their*

*grotesque cavortings. The music grows faster, until the climax is
reached with the male dancers all simultaneously keeling over
onto the floor with a crash.*

(pp. 214–16)

As Christopher Innes observes: 'dance was a traditional image
of aristocratic ideals. So Carlos' epileptic fit is both a burlesque
of hierarchical order, and an expression of its true nature' (1992,
p. 301). And the response of the court, flattering him and taking
their lead from his disjointed contortions, is a display of their
willingness to yield all reason to an authority that is both absurd
and terrifying.

Pleasure and Sin

At several points in the play (from Philip's proud boast in the
Prologue onwards) we are reminded of the superstitious connections that this society makes between pleasure and sin; sin and
disease. Such 'old-fashioned' beliefs might be construed as easy
targets for satire, and the play is certainly wholehearted in its
mockery of sexual repression; but the real target here is not the
familiar conflation of sexuality, pleasure, sin and disease, but the
attempt to separate emotion, sexuality, intellect and physicality.
This is exemplified in the scene (Act One, Scene 11) where
Almirante, who has been persuaded by Motilla that 'God wants
[him] t' mutton-monger the Queen' in order to ensure that she
really is pregnant, visits Ana in her bedchamber. Motilla urges
Almirante (disguised as a lady-in-waiting to the queen): 'What's
t' be done must be done quickly' (p. 243). The prosaic parody
of *Macbeth* echoes the original in that Almirante will also take the
place of a king.[7] As Dukore has argued (1981, p. 52), there is

54

also an indirect equation of sex and death, with Almirante's imagined *petite mort* replacing Duncan's *grande mort* in *Macbeth*. But it is Motilla's setting of rules, entwining authority and the prohibition of pleasure with sin and sexuality, which exposes the deranged logic that underpins the actions and rituals of the court. He prescribes in some detail precisely what kind of noises can accompany the sexual act, for 'there can't be one jot o' pleasure in't.'

> I'll be listening hard f' sinful love-cries, sobs, gasps, squeaks, heavy breathing. All 're an anathema . . . I'll permit grunts that betoken honest effort, *ugh*, but not grunts o' joy, *ugghh* . . . There must be no undue familiarity 'twixt you that could give rise t' scandal. Only bodily contacts're permitted and that but o' vile necessity.
>
> (pp. 243–4)

The exigencies of procuring an heir for Carlos demand measures so extraordinary that the Church's usual teaching is reversed. '*Only* bodily contacts [my italics]' presumably means that there is to be no emotional contact, no human connection; Motilla would clearly prefer it if the only contact were of reproductive organs. Behind the grotesquerie of comic excess lies an insistence upon separating human behaviour into constituent parts; thus language is separated from action, sexuality from desire, pleasure from work – a satirical sideswipe at the Church's separation of love and lust. As Ana and Almirante draw the curtains of the four-poster bed behind them and get to work (or whatever it is to be) and Motilla busies himself with eavesdropping, there is a '*loud knocking on the door*' (p. 245) and the scene shifts in tone and style to farce. First Carlos arrives, followed soon after by Rafael (the king's dwarf and fool). Motilla insists that they both kneel and pray with their eyes closed, while he leads them all in prayers, which are encoded instructions to Ana and Almirante. Before Almirante can make his getaway, however, there is another knock on the door. It is Mariana; and now Carlos and Rafael (as well as Almirante) all have to find themselves a hiding place to avoid the wrath of the queen mother. This is high-energy bedroom farce: the chase in semi-darkness, with everybody changing hiding places, culminates in Mariana opening the door to the wardrobe and finding Ana, who falls in a faint. This brings Carlos out from behind the bed curtains, which outrages Mariana: 'Carlos, I want t' know; what were you doing in your wife's bed?!' (p. 250). The scene is driven by the crazy internal logic of farce; but unlike conventional farce, in which there is a tendency to contain linguistic misuse within the fiction,[8] these inversions of conventional morality are a visible consequence of moral and ideological systems which connect our own world rather disconcertingly to that of the play.

Ana seizes the opportunity to blame Mariana for her miscarriage – 'That witch hath frighted him [her child] away' (p. 250) – and when Carlos then *'starts to throttle'* Mariana, Rafael intercedes: 'Sire, you'll do thyself an injury' (p. 251). Carlos has an epileptic fit; as elsewhere in the play, Barnes uses the state that follows, described in the stage directions as a *'post-epileptic automation'*, to allow Carlos lucid speech. His distress at the death of his child drives him into ranting against God:

> CARLOS I'll . . . drag that tit-face tyrant, God,
> Down by his greasy locks, f' taking back my child . . .
> There's no difference 'tween prayers and curses,
> He's long since fled.
> Heaven's as empty as her [Ana's] belly;
> *There is no God.*

Thunder, a streak of lightning and a great voice booms:

GOD'S VOICE   YES THERE IS.
CARLOS   I've prayed t' you. Where's my son?

Another streak of lightning.

GOD'S VOICE (*wearily*)   NO SON – ONLY LIGHTNING.

(pp. 252–3)

The God whose existence Carlos would like to deny is capable only of quick puns and theatrical special effects, not miracles. This would be a cheap (meta)theatrical joke indeed, if it were taken out of context. But the object of Carlos's wrath is not a generalised Judaeo-Christian God, but rather the specific God and the concomitant ideological package invoked by Motilla in the very next scene (Act One, Scene 12). The scene changes and 'MOTILLA *appears in the Spot behind* CARLOS', who asks: 'WWWWWhy do I suffer?' To which Motilla replies: ''Cause thou art a man.' Motilla equates healing with pain and loss, arguing that if we suffer in this life it is because we are guilty: 'Can a damned soul be brought t' salvation wi'out the healing pain? . . . God shows His mercy only by punishing us i' this world where pain hath an end, rather than the next, where 'tis everlasting' (pp. 253–4). The scene has strong links with the Earl of Gurney's invocation of fear as a basic ideological principle in *The Ruling Class* – and it sets in motion the wheels of the Inquisition, which provides the background against which most of the rest of the drama is played out.

Wisdom in Unlikely Places

It could be argued that the three wisest characters in the play are Rafael (the court jester), the parrot and, intermittently, as we have seen, Carlos himself. Rafael is very much in the tradition of the Shakespearean fool, offering insults and wisdom in equal measure (and often in the same breath):[9]

> **CARLOS**   Honour's ccccome the very peak o' fashion.
>
> **RAFAEL**   Aye, Sire, thieves steal 'cause they're too honourable
> t' beg and beggars beg 'cause they're too honourable t'
> steal. All have 't, but I've ne'er truly seen 't. As a friend
> (*To* **ALBA**.) show me thy honour, my lord.
>
> **ALBA** (*clasping sword*)   I'll show you my weapon, Sir!
>
> **RAFAEL**   If 'tis as flexible as thy honour, I'll've nothing t' fear
> . . . I'm court magician and t' amuse His Majesty, I've
> changed water into wine, frogs into footmen, beetles into
> bailiffs and made grandees out o' gobbley turkey-cocks . . .
> Dry water? Here . . . (*He mimes pouring*.) An honourable
> courtier? That's impossible even f' a great magician.
>
> (p. 213)

Rafael might be seen as an agent of rebellion and subversiveness. His pricking of the grandees' self-importance operates in a spirit of aggressive carnivalesque unruliness, refusing to acknowledge any inherent value in the social hierarchy. He is, however, politically ineffectual, an echo of Tucker in *The Ruling Class*, ranting and constantly challenging the court but more as a hostile irritant than an instrument of change. His approach is scattergun: 'You've no need o' emetics . . . Sire. Jus' look around you' (p. 276). Even though he kills Almirante in a duel,[10] he is tolerated, and survives until very nearly the end of the play. He dies in the torture chambers of the Inquisition, not because he is seen in any way as an enemy of the state, but rather because Theresa Diego, the head washerwoman, has been charged with sniffing out witches. One by one she identifies those she dislikes. Prejudice and privilege go hand in hand in this society. When she turns on Rafael, announcing '*This buffoon's suspect*', Father Froylan, assistant to the Archbishop of Toledo, quickly adds: 'Sire, laughter's a true mark o' Lucifer . . . We follow Satan when we laugh' (p. 313). And although it would be unwise to overstate the specific importance of Rafael in the play, this condemnation is highly significant. Those who claim a personal relationship with God are themselves agents of suffering and torture on such a scale that Alcala (the chief torturer) and Valladares (the inquisitor-general) both complain that the torture chambers are overcrowded (pp. 314–16).

For one of the priests who have instigated this regime of persecution to claim that laughter leads us to Satan might be taken as an indication that even if laughter cannot effect political change, it is, however briefly, life-enhancing; but the logic of this position is flawed. Although *The Bewitched* does not specifically examine the social functions of humour and laughter, its formal structure – juxtaposing a wide range of comic forms alongside theatrical forms, such as expressionism, that normally ask to be taken very seriously – uses comedy both to engage and deliberately to distance an audience from the events of the play. This poses troublesome questions about comedy and makes it difficult to know how to respond: and this, surely, is precisely the intended effect. If, as an audience, we are uncertain of our own responses, we are likely to be very alert – both to the nuances of the theatrical event, and to our own relationship with it. The strategy is, however, inherently risky. Create too much distance between the theatrical event and the audience, and people are likely to leave the auditorium. In his next major play, *Laughter!* (first produced four years after *The Bewitched*), Barnes would deliberately set out to interrogate the notion of laughter as intrinsically positive and beneficial, asking whether laughter is the 'ally of tyrants' (p. 343). It is evident, however, that *The Bewitched* is already exploring many of the concerns that drive the later play.

Authority, Possession and Bewitchment

Towards the end of the first act of the play Motilla, the royal confessor, warns Carlos about the connections between desire and sin: 'Diseases're sins made manifest, passed down generation t' generation. Sire, we stink and putrify from the sins o' our fathers' (p. 253). Motilla is more accurate than he knows, for Carlos's diseases and privations are the product of generations of incestuous couplings, many determined years of 'keeping it in the family'. It is precisely the determination to keep the royal line pure, to keep the grip on power, which results in Carlos's impotence. To admit as much would be ideologically impossible, and later in the play (Act Two, Scene 8), when Carlos still hasn't got himself an heir, the new royal confessor, Froylan, is forced to announce that the King's impotence 'isn't physical, but magical . . . You're bewitched . . . 'Tis magic that frustrates us, not brute reality' (p. 301). Although we recognise the absurdity of this hypothesis, it is, paradoxically, profoundly accurate: it is the willingness to believe in 'magic' that is at the root of their problems. In the ensuing attempt to root out the witchcraft that Froylan claims is the cause of Carlos's impotence, so many are thrown into the prison that Alcala, the chief torturer, insists that he hasn't

enough men to do a decent job. In spite of the extensive programme of torture and execution, Carlos remains as impotent as
ever. Pontecarrero (Archbishop of Toledo) argues that Carlos
must therefore be possessed from within and not bewitched. A
spectacular exorcism ensues, at the end of which Carlos falls into
an epileptic fit. When this passes (in another state of post-epileptic automation) he again becomes uncharacteristically and elo-
quently lucid, denouncing authority itself:

> Authority's the Basilisk, the crowned dragon,
> Scaly, beaked and toothsome . . .
> 'Twill make a desert o' this world
> While there's still one man left t' gi' commands
> And another who'll obey 'em

(p. 327)

Ana's ecstatic trance-like response culminates in a cry of
' ". . . love, love, love" . . . / Christ comes t' gather up our flowers
o' love!' (p. 327). And she starts singing ' "Clap-a-yo' hands!
Slap-a-yo' thigh!" ' She is rapidly joined by others, and we are
treated to the bizarre spectacle of the whole court raising a
gospel-like chorus – a spectacular clap-happy parody of a revival-
ist prayer meeting. The parody is complete when one after
another of the courtiers (those still alive after the ravages of the
Inquisition joined by the dead, who *'join in with even more
strength and liveliness than the living'*) step forward to bear
witness, each of them corrupting Carlos's vision with their own
egotistical take on it. Monterrey, for example: 'I thank him . . .
f' showing me that riches're a wax shield 'gainst the sword o'
State. Money must be made the very woof and weave o' society
so whoso'er attacks a rich man attacks society' (p. 328). The
collective hysteria of the prayer meeting continues until Carlos

proclaims that he will 'Drop my sceptre, renounce my crown, vacate my throne.' And the living all flee, leaving Carlos threatened by the dead. His '*bout of post-epileptic automatism*' ends, and '*He collapses. The* DEAD *retreat slowly backwards from him into the darkness. A funeral bell tolls once.* CARLOS *is dying*' (p. 329). The scene is characteristic of the theatrical method that Barnes adopts in his mature work. When Monterrey speaks up it seems initially that he is attacking materialism, when he is actually bemoaning the fact that he does not live in an advanced capitalist state. The scene is also indicative of the richness of the play's title: at the heart of the play is an examination of what it means to be 'bewitched'. When Froylan announces that the king is 'bewitched', he sets in motion a monstrous hunt for scapegoats; persecuting 'witches' is an obscene attempt to ensure the survival of a hierarchy. Carlos, however, is as bewitched by his courtiers, by the sycophants who vie for power around him, as they are by their own superstitious belief in divine right. But the bewitchment does not stop there: the courtiers, the priests, the torturers, the aristocracy, the councillors, at every level those who exert authority, are bewitched by their own self-importance; the people are not only bewitched by authority but also by their own habitual acquiescence and, ultimately, terrified by the possibility of authority's absence, by the potential of their own freedom.

The Bewitched is a profoundly unsettling play – not least because it is essentially a farce. A dark, dark, bitter farce, certainly, but nonetheless a very funny play, and all the more disturbing for the laughter it rouses in an audience. It is a play which makes great use of theatre's visual possibilities – often spectacular, occasionally Grand Guignol. It frequently seems like a series of comic routines, an end-of-the-pier revue, a surrealist music hall. This circus-like quality might detract from the play's very serious themes, were it not such an integral part of the structure. To present the Spanish court as a circus is at least partially a mischievously anarchic act of historical debunking; it is also a means of focusing on the performative qualities of the court. Royalty, courtiers, priests, inquisitors, jesters and washerwomen – they all perform versions of themselves for each other. The play is about performance, in many senses. The question which is constantly on everyone's lips, but is never actually spoken, is whether Carlos has 'performed' sexually and, indeed, whether he *can* perform. The sexual act can rarely have been so carefully scrutinised. By creating a visual spectacle which is frequently reminiscent of those most ostentatiously performative of entertainment forms, Barnes forces us to be alert to our own responses, to ask ourselves how we too might be bewitched by social, political and ideological systems we accept as necessary and determined.

3

Laughter!

*As long as I am obedient to the power of the state, of Church,
or public opinion I feel safe and protected.*

Erich Fromm[1]

The way to rise is to obey and please.
He that will thrive in state, he must neglect
The trodden paths that truth and right respect . . .

Ben Jonson[2]

The Bewitched is a dangerous play – a play which challenges both
reactionary and liberal attitudes. Of all Barnes' plays, however,
the most controversial has undoubtedly been *Laughter!* Com-
prising two distinct parts, with no shared characters and set
chronologically nearly four hundred years apart, this is nevertheless a coherent play and not a double bill, as it is sometimes considered. It was first performed at the Royal Court Theatre,
London, on 25 January 1978 under the direction of Charles
Marowitz,[3] who had previously worked with Barnes on
Leonardo's Last Supper and *Noonday Demons*. The first part, *Tsar*,
is set in Moscow 1573, the second part, *Auschwitz*, in a minor
bureaucrat's office in Berlin 1942 – until the Epilogue, when the
action shifts briefly to the concentration camp. The play exam-

ines Ivan the Terrible's personalised reign of terror and measures it against the depersonalised bureaucracy that underpinned the Nazi extermination machine. It shares some of the formal strategies of *The Bewitched* – the use of elements of the grotesque, an Artaudian interest in cruelty, a critical examination of uses and abuses of humour in both social and psychological terms – while developing the earlier play's interest in the mechanisms of authority and complicity. Complicity with authority (on whatever basis that authority is claimed) enables people to deny responsibility for their own actions and for the socio-political structures of the world they inhabit. This theme reverberates between the two parts of the play. In *Tsar*, for example, Ivan spears the foot of his courtier, Shibanov, to the floor. It is apparently an act of gratuitous cruelty, but when Ivan asks him why he doesn't unpin himself, Shibanov answers: 'You've not given me permission, Sire . . . You've the authority o' blood, Sire . . . It gi'es our world a permanence which men need . . . You gi'e us certainty Sire, which is better than goodness' (p. 351).[4] The violence of the scene is darkly comic, but the argument is echoed in *Auschwitz* when Cranach (a minor bureaucrat obsessed with regulations and administrative thoroughness) insists that 'The German people've always preferred strong government to self-government . . . We've had enough choices. We chose well because all choices're made for us' (p. 376). Through the two parts of the play Barnes explores the relationship between these attitudes and the Holocaust, while subjecting the social and psychological functions of laughter to intense scrutiny.

The play opens with a Prologue, in which a character named Author attempts to give a brief lecture on the inadequacy of laughter. His argument is that laughter, and by extension comedy, is by its nature politically naive at best, reactionary at worst:

Comedy itself is the enemy . . . A sense of humour's no remedy
for evil . . . Laughter's the ally of tyrants. It softens our hatred.
An excuse to change nothing, for nothing needs changing when
it's all a joke.

(p. 343)

As he speaks, however, he is interrupted by a custard pie suddenly thrown into his face from the wings of the stage, his bow
tie starts spinning randomly out of control, a carnation in his
button hole spurts water, and finally his trousers fall down to
reveal spangled underpants. His irritation at these ever more
humiliating distractions (he angrily pulls off the bow tie, tears off
the carnation) implies that they are out of his control. He is
undermined by his own appearance, by his own attempts to
impress; and yet he is the Author, it is he who is the author of his
own humiliation. And therein lies one of the central paradoxes of
the play. The Author is by definition a figure of authority; he is
trying to impose on the audience a single-minded view of
humour and history (for this is a history play), yet his own
'vision' is made to look ridiculous. Our laughter (if there is any)
not only subverts his argument but also undermines his authority. If this complex dialectic carries any kind of a 'message', it is
that authorial 'messages' are not to be trusted.

The play constantly tests itself with similarly unruly comic dis-
ruptions which, in the hands of a sympathetic director, are
potentially extremely challenging to an audience. If an audience
laughs it becomes complicit in the horrors of the drama. As
Christopher Innes has noted in a short but very perceptive essay
on Barnes: 'If the basis of comedy is the perception of incongruity . . . then Barnes has accentuated this principle to the point
where it becomes reversed. In his work incongruities deny the
validity of laughter in order to generate perception' (1992,

p. 305). In all of Barnes' work this is nowhere so explicit as in the Epilogue to *Laughter!*, when the scene shifts to Auschwitz itself and '*two hollow-eyed comics*' (p. 410) appear in a spotlight in what is announced as 'the climax of this Extermination Camp Christmas Concert, the farewell appearance of the Boffo Boys of Birkenau'. The act proceeds as a music-hall turn – until '*The music has faded out imperceptibly into a hissing sound*' and the two comedians cough and stagger.

> **BIEBERSTEIN** I could be wrong but I think this act is dying.
>
> **BIMKO** The way to beat hydro-cyanide gas is by holding your breath for five minutes. It's just a question of mind over matter. They don't mind and we don't matter.
>
> (p. 411)

The Epilogue is, of, course, in extremely bad taste and potentially deeply offensive; and it is certainly amongst the most shocking and distressing scenes in any Barnes play. Whether it works in the theatre as Barnes intends it to, however, is a different matter.[5] Whether it alienates audiences to such an extent that they refuse to see the play as anything other than an assault is open to question. Certainly, critics (both academic and journalistic) have been divided on this issue. As one might expect, there are numerous accounts of audience hostility to *Laughter!*[6] On the other hand, Irving Wardle (writing in *The Times* in January 1978) asserted: 'Nothing is more exciting in the theatre than a moment of genuine stylistic change: when . . . one sees a playwright not merely writing a play but reinventing what a play ought to be.'[7] Barnes considered the play an experiment, a deliberate attempt to push the boundaries of what is possible in theatre, to explore the relationship between the laughter which heals divisions and alleviates suffering, and the laughter which compounds injustice and misery. The camp comedians' routine is so profoundly discomforting because it presents us with the disturbingly familiar picture of victims turning 'jokes' against themselves, but in a context which poses painfully difficult questions about the function of humour. Is it a courageous token of resistance, the only kind of resistance available to them? Or by trivialising their own plight do they deny their oppressors triumph? Is it a form of resignation to, or even collaboration with, the most obscenely inhumane regime – a regime which the play represents as 'ordinary' and banal, a regime which the bureaucrats insist is part of 'A benevolent brotherhood of man' (p. 409)? By denying their own plight do they trivialise their own oppression?[8]

This questioning of complicity runs throughout both parts of the play, although each part deals with it in rather different ways. Of the other concerns which underpin the two parts, perhaps the most central is the issue of identity. In *Tsar*, Ivan is presented as an aggressive pantomimic villain, in rivalry with everybody he encounters. When *Tsar* opens we are greeted with an image of Odoevsky impaled on a sharpened stake '*covered with congealed blood like candle grease*' (p. 344). Although Odoevsky cannot speak, can only utter excruciating howls of pain, Ivan argues that he suffers more, that his own sin, and therefore his pain, is greater. When his own son wants to take command of the army, Ivan insists that he is not ready for it, that he, the tsar, is, and always has been, more suspicious, more devious, more malignant, that he feels more anger and more hatred, though (even as he kills him) he argues that he loves him. His competitiveness even extends to Samael, the Angel of Death, whom he fights – and appears to beat. This unrelenting competition is presented comically, but it indicates an inability to come to terms with himself, to acknowledge the contradictions of his own identity. His existence is predicated on his insistence that he is different from others; and thus his sense of self becomes entirely dependent upon others, even if it is expressed as an insistence of his supremacy over them. In *Auschwitz*, Cranach's unquestioning obedience to the state seems the polar opposite of Ivan's terrible egotism. He constructs his own identity in terms of the work that he does; his meticulousness and attention to administrative minutiae protect him from having to confront any sense that his actions have consequences. Because the state makes decisions on his behalf he feels strength in being part of the power of the state. He does not see his actions as having consequences, because he sees the state as making decisions on his behalf. Thus the desolate, lonely man perceives himself as not alone. But his, too, is a refusal to come to terms with who he is.

Parallels and Contrasts

Given the truly horrific content of *Tsar*, it is perhaps initially surprising that this first part of the play aroused little offence when *Laughter!* was first staged. This is partly because the horrors of *Tsar* are upstaged by those of *Auschwitz*, but I suspect it is also because the Holocaust is still relatively recent; regardless of the intelligence and integrity (or for that matter the tastelessness and insensitivity) of Barnes' play, the subject matter of the Nazi extermination camps is taboo as material for comic writing. But if that is the case, it begs the question why this should be so. Why is it taboo to make attitudes to the extermination camps the subject matter of a comic investigation? And why then is it not taboo to joke about the hundreds of thousands of deaths caused by Ivan? Is it because we may personally know relatives of those who were victims of the Nazi camps? Is it because of some collective guilt that we do not fully understand? Or is it because such questions force us to consider the possibility of our own complicity in similar circumstances? Such questions as these are central to the play's interrogation of the functions of comedy. *Tsar* and *Auschwitz* each function independently of the other, but *Laughter!* as a whole demands that we reflect on and compare our responses to each part of the play.

The two parts of *Laughter!* are rather different in tone. *Tsar* invites us to mock Ivan. He may be terrible, in every sense of that word, but the presentation of the character makes his brutal persecution of everybody around him pantomimic, absurdist. The setting for *Auschwitz* is far removed from the torture chambers of sixteenth-century Russia: an office in Berlin in 1942. The juxtaposition of the two, however, asks an audience to make links between them. The connection between the two parts is made in the final moments of *Tsar*, where a statue of Ivan is unveiled and a loudspeaker announces the dedication

> to the memory of Ivan IV, Tsar of Russia . . . Out of . . . chaos
> . . . he created the first centralized, multi-national State in the
> West and proved an inspiration for those who followed . . . The
> title 'Terrible' was due to an unfortunate mistranslation; it was
> more accurately 'Ivan the Awe-Inspiring'.
>
> (p. 367)

This rewriting of history strongly resembles the propaganda put out by tyrants such as Stalin and Hitler; although it is Ivan's voice that we hear making the dedication over the loudspeaker system, the language of the dedication is that of bureaucratic officialdom; and in *Auschwitz* it is minor officials who are seen to sanitise and trivialise tyranny. But the motif of bureaucracy has already appeared in *Tsar*. When Shibanov, the ever obedient courtier, is asked to intervene in the ferocious argument between

Ivan and his son, the Tsarevitch, his response brilliantly caricatures the bureaucrat's position. Tsarevitch insists that he is ready
to take command of the army and asks Shibanov to confirm this.

> **SHIBANOV** You're ready, Sire.
>
> **IVAN** Shibanov confirm the truth, he's not.
>
> **SHIBANOV** He's not ready, Sire. Anyone who doesn't
> contradict himself's a dogmatist. Sires, I twist in the wind.
> You're my now and future Tsars. I can cringe, lick boots wi'
> a sycophant's rankling tongue . . . But I casn't speak truth
> that's true f' you both. As a loyal, two-faced courtier Sires, I
> mustn't be pinned down.
>
> (p. 357)

The twisted logic of this confirms the truth of his own position: he
does as he is told, and cannot be held responsible for actions, as he
always defers to those he considers his superiors. In many ways
Shibanov prefigures Cranach in *Auschwitz*; but the more direct parallels are with Samael, the Angel of Death, who first appears
'*dressed in a worn, double-breasted, blue serge suit, starched collar,
waistcoat and stainless-steel framed spectacles*' (p. 363). When Ivan
cannot believe he is who he claims to be, Samael complains: 'with
the relentless progress of civilisation I've changed from being a
stately angel to an over-worked head-clerk . . . I keep accounts . . .
In the end all accounts must be closed. It's a matter of good book-
keeping' (p. 364). Samael's subsequent prediction that

> In the coming years they'll institutionalize it, take the passion
> out of killing, turn men into numbers and the slaughter'll be so
> vast no one mind'll grasp it, no heart'll break 'cause of it. Ah,
> what an age that'll be
>
> (p. 365)

is deeply ominous in its own right; but it also connects Samael directly with Cranach and informs the second part of the play. Cranach (the small-minded bureaucrat who, like Shibanov, is determined to deny his personal responsibilities) is an Angel of Death.[9]

The change in styles of humour between *Tsar* and *Auschwitz* is worth noting in more detail. *Tsar* demands a playing style that is grotesque and extreme. It contains scenes of gruesome slapstick, and grotesque expressionist nightmare. Although *Auschwitz* contains numerous jokes, the humour shifts in tone and style as the second part of the play moves through various different phases. To start with it is an exaggerated, distorted version of office humour, a relentless series of jokes about the ordinariness of life under Hitler:

> I don't mince words. I've always believed in calling a CF/83 a CF/83.
>
> (p. 369)

> I know the first step's hard, but once you've tried it you'll enjoy using commas.
>
> (p. 370)

> No one understands the arbitrary terror we all live under nowadays in the Third Reich – redundancy, compulsory retirement with loss of pension rights!
>
> (pp. 372–3)

> I like my coffee weak but this is helpless.
>
> (p. 374)

This humour becomes increasingly disturbing as the play develops, and the office workers' sense of their own ordinariness is revealed as a determination to isolate themselves from the political contexts in which they work. The first reference to Auschwitz itself is oblique. Cranach boasts that 'We're now dealing with an estimated 74,000 administrative units in the three complexes in Upper Silesia alone' (p. 371). The terminology is not so much a euphemism as a denial – as becomes clear in the final minutes of the play. Six pages further in, however, Cranach still refers to '622.75 units per day . . . transported from all over Europe to Upper Silesia' (p. 377). The first threat to their steadfast ignorance arrives in the shape of Gottleb, an ardent admirer of Hitler and passionate Party man, who argues that 'Our work here's a crusade or it's nothing' (p. 379). He is determined to get rid of the bureaucrats, seeing them as undermining the purity of his, and the Party's, vision. The action of much of the rest of the play is driven by his desire to oust them: he detests their pettiness, their refusal to share publicly in his open celebration of what he considers to be the triumphant achievements of the Third Reich, the most notable of which is, for him, the camp at Auschwitz.

There is, however, something of an interlude before Gottleb launches a full-scale assault on the bureaucrats and the audience. Georg Wochner appears out of nowhere (*'No one has noticed . . . a young man in a long, weighed-down overcoat'*) (p. 381). He starts by selling them black-market schnapps, and then offers a range of black-market goods including 'Confiscated wedding rings' and 'Hammer-and-sickle badges. Every one guaranteed taken by hand from the body of a dead Russian soldier' (p. 383). For Wochner, everything is a commercial transaction – which Cranach and Gottleb both find appalling.

> CRANACH   We raise our eyes to the hills; the soul, the soul,
>   the German soul! And you talk of money, credit ratings.

74

GOTTLEB Materialistic filth! People spending money they
haven't earned, to buy things they don't need . . .

(pp. 386–7)

We might share something of their self-righteous indignation at Wochner's entrepreneurial opportunism were it not for
their own lack of moral credibility; although *Laughter!* was
written before the first Thatcher government was elected,
there is more than a hint of the arguments that were to take
place within the Conservative Party as Cranach and Gottleb
fiercely debate the true nature of National Socialism. While the
former declares that 'National Socialism is part of the great
conservative tradition . . . based on solid middle-class values'
(p. 385), Gottleb aggressively conflates brutality, the need for
self-sacrifice, national pride and mysticism. This is not to argue
that Thatcher's version of English conservatism should be
equated with German fascism, but that for all the grotesque
knockabout in Barnes' play, there is a core of serious political
debate about the relationships between conservatism, unfettered capitalism and nationalism.

Entrapment

Gradually, however, as they get increasingly drunk on Wochner's
schnapps, their dialogue begins to take the form of a series of
competing stories, anecdotes and jokes, and they become
increasingly disrespectful of those at the top of the Nazi hierarchy, mocking Ribbentrop, Goering and Goebbels. '*Their laughter quickly grows louder and more hysterical*' until Cranach tops
everything:

CRANACH   Listen, listen, what do you call someone who
sticks his finger up the Führer's arse?!
GOTTLEB   Heroic.
CRANACH   No, a brain surgeon!
CRANACH, ELSE *and* STROOP *collapse in hysterical laughter.*
But it dies away as they become aware that a suddenly sober
GOTTLEB *is staring balefully at them.*

(pp. 395–6)

Gottleb has caught them out, using laughter to entrap them:
'Death's mandatory for all jokes . . . about our beloved Führer'
(p. 396). Laughter has made their own disrespect seem safe,
momentarily giving them a false sense of security in an illusion of
comradeship. Whatever inhibitions normally protect them from
rash criticism of the Party, the ephemeral community created by
their laughter sanctions the erosion of those inhibitions. But
their mockery of the Nazi hierarchy is as gestural as Tucker's self-
styled and self-deceiving sedition is in *The Ruling Class*: no
sooner does Gottleb spring his trap than the office workers deny
having ever made the joke. Cranach claims: 'You've been drinking, Gottleb! I never tell jokes. Everyone knows I've no sense of
humour' (p. 396). Then Gottleb produces a primitive tape
recorder which he has secretly used to record them. When played
back, however, it yields nothing more than distortion of their
laughter: '*a cacophony of high-pitched screeches, muffled squawks
and clicks*' (p. 397). Gottleb and Cranach compete for the testi-
mony of Stroop and Else. Gottleb tries to bribe them with the
promise of promotion: 'Stroop, if you tell the truth and say you
hear Cranach's voice on the tape, you take over his position . . .
And you Fräulein, from Acting Secretary Grade III (Admin) to
Permanent Secretary Grade I' (pp. 398–9). Eventually they
repeat the joke – but only after Gottleb has had to dictate it back

to them personally. Cranach, however, knows his own, knows
that their need for routine is greater than their desire for prefer-
ment: 'Sometimes you're bored, but never anxious for you
know tomorrow'll be the same as today. If you denounce me
it'll never be the same again, only the same as outside, full of
choice and change' (p. 400). And this is the deciding factor.
Stroop and Else turn against Gottleb, accusing him of having
told the joke. I have examined this moment in detail because it
is pivotal within the play – both in terms of narrative and in the
way that it explores jokes and laughter. The joke becomes a
matter of life and death. The laughter, however, not only
provides an illusory sense of fellowship, but also a means of
concealing the 'truth'. The tape recorder does not yield evidence,
but 'noise'. The meaning of the laughter is entirely dependent
upon interpretation; meaning and interpretation are open to
manipulation.

Throughout this section, for all its underlying threats – when
Gottleb thinks he has caught Cranach, he proudly boasts he'll be
'sentenced and hanging from piano wire by the end of the week'
(p. 396) – the tone is humorous and light. This now suddenly
turns very dark: darker, indeed, and more shocking than anything to be found in any Barnes play. Outfoxed by Cranach,
Gottleb loses patience: 'we should find room for you in one of
our complexes in Upper Silesia: Birkenau, Monowitz or
Auschwitz . . . working with people . . . Dealing with flesh and
blood, not deadly abstractions' (p. 401). He confronts Cranach,
Stroop and Else with the consequences of their paper-pushing,
delivering the most hideous account of the realities of
Auschwitz, hitherto referred to innocuously as one of the 'complexes' in Upper Silesia. The office workers vigorously resist this
onslaught:

ELSE   I only type and file . . .

STROOP   We only deal in concrete . . . what's CP3(m) to do
with life and death in Upper Silesia? . . .

GOTTLEB   CP3(m) described in regulation E(5) is the new
concrete flue for the crematoriums.

(p. 401)

To which the office workers chorus as one: 'We don't know that.'
But Gottleb is as relentless as the play itself: 'You help build 'em
so you should be able to see 'em plain' (p. 403). The logic is
meticulous. Gottleb's harangue becomes an assault on the audience, from which there is no escape: if we try to shut it out, we
are, according to the logic of the play, as culpable as Cranach,
Stroop and Else, whose own response is ultimately to shout
together: 'We don't see! We don't see!' (p. 404). Until this
moment, Gottleb's attack has been purely verbal, and the shock
of the speech has arisen from the power of the imagery. When the
bureaucrats cry out that they do not see (perhaps also articulat-
ing an audience's resistance), Gottleb ensures that they, and we,
do:

> *As the sound of the gas-chamber door being opened reverberates, the*
> *whole of the filing section Up Stage slowly splits . . . to reveal . . . a*
> *vast mound of filthy, wet straw dummies . . . numbers tattooed on*
> *their left arms.*
>
> *. . . two monstrous figures appear out of the vapour . . .*

(pp. 404–5)

These figures are Sanitation Men. And we, the audience, watch
an on-stage audience of office workers, themselves watching in
horror as the Sanitation Men 'recover' what Gottleb describes as

'strategic war material for the Reich' (p. 405): wedding rings, gold teeth, glass eyes. And while Gottleb exalts in the work of the Sanitation Squad, the bureaucrats remain as voyeuristic, passive observers, refusing to acknowledge their own connection with this 'work':

> CRANACH   I see it! I can't fight 'em . . . This isn't the time
> to say 'no'. I've just taken out a second mortgage!
> ELSE   I see it too! But what can I do? . . . This isn't a good
> time for me either to say 'no'. Mother's just bought a new
> suite of furniture!
> STROOP   Yes, I see it! But . . . I'm an old man. You can't
> expect me to say 'no' . . . I'm retiring next year.
>
>   (pp. 405–6)

Gottleb, however, has not been asking them to say no. Although there is no indication that their justifications are addressed directly to the audience, it is the theatre audience with whom they are trying to exonerate themselves, as if aware that the theatre audience is likely to want to cast blame on them. At this point, however, the play twists again. Cranach succeeds in fighting back – not preventing the horrors of Auschwitz, but shutting out everything, dissociating their own work from that of Gottleb and the Sanitation Squad. His speech is worth quoting from at length because it is so important in developing an interpretation of the play.

> CRANACH   We're Civil Servants, words on paper, not
> pictures in the mind . . . Writers write, builders build, potters
> potter, book-keepers keep books . . . 'Gas-chambers', 'fire-
> ovens', ramps', he's using words to make us see images,
> words to create meanings, not contained in them; then

nothing means what it says and our world dissolves . . . We
merely operate policies embodied in existing legislation and
implement decisions of higher authority . . . hard facts leave
nothing to the imagination. We're trained to kill imagination
before it kills us.

The steel door of the gas chamber is heard slowly closing and the
two sections of the filing cabinet . . . begin to slide back into
position . . . blocking off the dummies and the SANITATION
MEN.

(pp. 406–7)

Filing the Metaphors

The filing cabinet thus becomes a potent metaphor; it becomes
clear that the decision to centre the action in the office is not
because the satirical target is office workers, but because the
actions of Cranach, Stroop and Else are themselves metonymic
of a tendency to compartmentalise lives, filing people as data, as
'administrative units'.

Given that the play is insistently aggressive in its onslaught on
the audience, its moral complexity is perhaps surprising. The
principle of merit, for example, is vigorously attacked by Gottleb:
'We . . . didn't fight in the streets, gutters filled with our dead, to
build a world based on merit' (p. 377). Barnes knows his essentially liberal audience well enough to realise that they are likely to
subscribe to the principle of merit, and that the denunciation will
briefly shift sympathies towards the bureaucrats.

In the final moments of the play (prior to the Epilogue)
Cranach proudly turns to Else and glories in their achievements:
'In centuries to come when our complexes at Auschwitz're

empty ruins . . . tourist attractions, they'll ask . . . what kind of men built . . . these extraordinary structures. They'll find it hard to believe they weren't heroic visionaries . . . but ordinary people, people who liked people, people like them [i.e. the audience], you, me, us' (p. 409).

It is difficult to write about this final section of the play without still feeling shaken, such is its power. It might be said that the argument implied by Cranach's final speech, that the horrors of the Holocaust could only have come about with the complicity of 'ordinary people', is naive and overfamiliar. It might further be argued, by extension, that the play does little to examine the notion of evil.[10] But Cranach's ironic claim for glory is not the play's argument any more than it is Barnes' 'message'. Gottleb and Ivan are monstrously inhumane, certainly, but as dramatic characters they are pantomimic villains. While they may represent evil, the play is not concerned with how they come to be the way they are, but rather with others' responses to evil. If we are shocked by the play's assertion that one of these responses is to laugh in the face of it, then so be it; but we delude ourselves if we deny that jokes seem to emerge from the rubble of even the most extreme horrors. Even if we do not do it ourselves, it is a common response. Humour seems to be a way of asserting that one is in control, of gaining reassurance in the notion that 'life goes on'. It represents an attempt to put on a brave face. As such, it can be seen as a performance of optimism. But *Laughter!* interrogates all these assumptions, confronting us with laughter as a performance of disengagement.

If the play were an analytical, academic essay, it would balance these possibilities through reasoned argument; but *Laughter!* is not rational. Its dialectics are not situated in the stable positions of rationality, but in the shifting instabilities of an audience's involuntary responses to humour.

Christopher Innes maintains that 'Barnes seems to have extended comedy into a *cul-de-sac* . . . violence becomes increasingly graphic, while physical deformity, extremes of suffering, or even genocide are presented as objects of humour . . . But as a propaganda tactic, alienating the audience is self-defeating' (1992, pp. 305, 307–8). I would counter this by arguing that although *Laughter!* refuses an audience any ultimate sanctuary, it is not a piece of propaganda and its use of humour is far more complex than Innes allows. Genocide and violence are not presented as objects of humour per se. Rather, humour is presented in a variety of forms – from grotesque slapstick, through flawed sophistry (in which the humour arises from the audience's ability to see through false logic), to racist self-mockery. Each of these forms is familiar and recognisable to an audience – but in other contexts. The moment when Ivan (in *Tsar*) spears Shibanov's foot to the floor and the courtier reads a letter 'His voice . . . calm, but his body twist[ing] grotesquely in pain' (p. 349) could come straight from a *Monty Python* sketch. Cranach's joke about the finger up Hitler's arse is generic. Tell the joke to a friend or colleague, and they will almost certainly have heard a variation of it. Similarly, the final routine of the 'Boffo Boys of Birkenau' might be obscene, but it is all too recognisable as a form of racist self-deprecation. What Innes refers to as 'alienating' is more accurately described as 'distancing', provoking an audience into a more reflective mode than narrative engagement allows.

Laughter! is not, however, as relentlessly distancing and tormenting as some of its critics have maintained, but it is structured in such a way that its final fifteen minutes are, indeed, deeply distressing and disturbing. In spite of its subject matter – until the moment when Gottleb turns on the office workers and forces them to hear and see the implications of their work – it is surprisingly light in tone. I should qualify that: it is written in such a way as to allow for the possibility of lightness in the playing. The play has been even less successful in England than Barnes' other major works. It has not received a professional revival in England[11] since the 1978 Royal Court premiere – a production which Michael Billington felt was seriously compromised by Charles Marowitz's direction, which he referred to as 'heavy as lead'.[12] There is no doubt that Barnes' plays demand sympathetic productions in the theatre, and equally little doubt that in the 'wrong' hands they tend to become crass and heavy-handed. In the case of a play as dangerous and as risky as *Laughter!*, this tendency is likely to be intensified. But however *Laughter!* is played, it is the work of a writer determined to push himself and his audience to the limits. Its implied relationship between the spectator and the performance is both aggressive and confrontational. In this sense, then, it certainly draws on Artaud's theories of a 'Theatre of Cruelty' and, indirectly, on some of Peter Brook's investigations into Artaud's ideas. There is also a tendency in many of Barnes' plays to pursue the aim of creating a 'total theatre', a theatre in which the spoken word has to be 'read' as a sign system alongside many other interacting signifiers – visual, audible and even visceral. In this sense, too, the play can be thought of as Artaudian. And there is another way in which the play can be seen as a response to the Brook/Marowitz experiments with Artaud's urgings and provocations: the 'Theatre of Cruelty' season became part of a wider tendency to question the 'authority' of the dramatist. In spite of its self-reflexive Prologue, and its active encouragement of the audience to question the role of the author, it does not seek to substitute the director for the playwright as the dominant authorial voice.[13] Billington's 'heavy as lead' description of Marowitz's direction of *Laughter!* implies that the director attempted to impose his own authority on the play, to place emphasis where it is not needed, to draw unnecessary attention to those horrific juxtapositions that pervade the play. This not only underestimates an audience's ability to make its own connections, to shape its own meanings, but also undermines Barnes' dramatic method, which requires a light directorial touch. Barnes' theatre seeks an active audience, an audience which becomes gradually and uncomfortably aware of its own responses to the theatrical event – but not of a director's interventionist hand in that event.

In the 1930s Vsevolod Meyerhold commented to Aleksandr Gladkov: 'If everyone praises your production, almost certainly it is rubbish. If everyone abuses it, then perhaps there is something in it. But if some praise and others abuse it, if you split the audience in half, then for sure it is a good production. Sarah Bernhardt . . . maintained that the worst thing of all was a production accepted by everyone. It is a polite form of indifference.' (Gladkov, 1997, p. 165). Whatever else *Laughter!* achieves, it is unlikely to meet with indifference.

What becomes clear, when looking at Barnes' plays as a body of work, is that *Laughter!* was a necessary play for the playwright: a means of exploring his and our understanding of the functions and limitations of humour and laughter.

4

Red Noses

Each of the plays examined so far is concerned in some way with uses and abuses of religion. In *The Ruling Class* Jack claims to be God; in *The Bewitched* religion is used to justify the Inquisition; and the action of *Tsar*, the first part of *Laughter!*, for all its grotesque expressionism, is underpinned by some surprisingly cerebral philosophical debate about the function of priests and relations between Church and state. In each case, however, religion is characterised as being a sanctuary for social inadequates, charlatans, schizophrenics or psychopaths; religious belief is represented as a manifestation of ignorant superstition at best, callous exploitation at worst. There are no 'good' characters in these plays. There are, however, plenty of characters with whom we can engage, whose point of view we occasionally share, and there are some with whom we are undoubtedly encouraged to sympathise (Carlos in *The Bewitched*, for example), but none with whom we might identify. This is partly because in such harsh satire, to present us with a figure of unproblematic sympathy would offer us far too easy a way out; partly because the metatheatrical devices and formal structures destabilise our relationship (as an audience) with the theatrical event, continually forcing us to shift our point of view and reassess our own responses to what we experience.

Red Noses marks a significant change in Barnes' work. Whereas hitherto religion had been presented in an almost wholly negative light, *Red Noses* is concerned with spirituality in the broadest sense. I have argued that *The Bewitched* and *Laughter!* are dangerous, risky plays; the boldness of *Red Noses* is not that it is set during the Black Death, but that it dares to explore goodness, virtue and hope. It is a play which uses a theatrical form that might loosely be described as materialist modernism, but which not only interrogates social, political and cultural hegemony but also examines the interaction between material needs, social organisation and spiritual impulses. If *Laughter!* was an experiment in pushing boundaries to interrogate the darkest extremes of humour, then *Red Noses* is one of the products of that experiment. The dramatic methods – the relentless barrage of one-liners, the puns, the sustained knockabout slapstick, the juxtaposition of humour and horror, the montage effects – may be familiar from the earlier work, but the tone of *Red Noses* allows us at least occasional moments of joy. Barnes wrote the play seven years before it was first produced – in 1985. His introduction to the published edition of the play claims that 'It's a letter wishing you good thoughts, but chiefly, good feelings.'[1] He adds that if the play had been written in 1985 it would have been 'much less optimistic'. It is, however, hardly an optimistic play; rather, and most unusually, it is one that explores the possibilities of optimism. In much the same way that *Laughter!* is not a funny play, but one that explores the boundaries and social functions of humour, so *Red Noses* poses a series of intriguing conundrums about relationships between optimism, social change and the redistribution of social resources and power. It is one of Barnes' most entertaining plays, and is frequently revived by amateur groups with remarkable success – giving the lie to the notion that his plays require spectacular special effects and enormous budgets to match.[2]

Billington's comments on *Laughter!* (noted above) become particularly enlightening when compared with his review of *Red Noses*, which opened in July 1985 in an RSC production at the Barbican Theatre, London. It is 'a brilliant play,' he wrote, 'a play . . . [which] presents us, unsentimentally, with a vision of love and hope . . . and . . . [has] broken the petty rules by which we judge plays.'[3] The play is set in France in 1348 and 1349, with the Black Death rampant throughout Europe, affecting rich and poor, young and old, male and female alike. The Black Death has become a leveller, in which traditional sites of power and privilege – the Church, the state, the medical and legal professions – are denied their authority. The title, *Red Noses*, is itself a pun, being both an early symptom of the plague and the name that Father Flote gives to his 'brotherhood of joy, Christ's Clowns, God's Zanies' (p. 15) whose mission is to 'cheer the hearts of men' (p. 14).[4] Every member of the group wears a clown's red nose, and they are known by this name or as 'Floties'.

As the Black Death continues its relentless destruction of humanity, two other groups contend for popular influence. The Black Ravens, former slaves who have earned their freedom by burying the dead, welcome the plague, seeing it as an apocalypse which opens possibilities for revolution and the establishment of a new social order. As Scarron, their leader, says, 'War, famine, pestilence, the world's dying only to be born again . . . Salvation's built on putrefaction' (p. 12). The Black Ravens come to represent a kind of amoral entrepreneurial anarchism. The third group vying for power and influence is the Flagellants. They too aim to change the world – by taking what they perceive to be its sins upon themselves. 'Let our penitential scourging take away God's pestilential wrath,' cries Grez, the master flagellant (p. 7), claiming that divinity lies within every human being, and thereby undermining the power of centrally organised religion (their beliefs echoing the heretical anti-authoritarian elements of Gnosticism and of the Cathars). Each of these groups has the potential to subvert existing power structures, but none can achieve lasting social change unless it collaborates with the others. Subversive ideologies are depicted as prone to the paralysis of dogma as authority from on high.

Informing the play is an exploration of laughter and comedy as a social force. At the beginning of the play Flote's aim is to cheer people up, to distract them from the horrors of their lives, to help them bear their troubles. By the end he is determined that 'Every jest should be a small revolution' (p. 119). While the plague threatens social disruption, Flote's band of Red Noses is sanctioned by the Church, in the person of Pope Clement VI; once the threat from plague has passed, the Church needs to re-establish control and the Noses are destroyed. In spite of this bleak conclusion, the play is neither desolate nor melancholy. The final scene is followed by a curious Epilogue in which '*The ghostly voices of* FLOTE *and the others are heard in snatches of conversation and sounds from the past*' (p. 118). 'Curious' because its effect is the antithesis of most epilogues: here, these snatches of dialogue, and recapitulations of arguments, function as a way of refusing the closure that Flote's death seems to imply. In the Epilogue, Toulon's voice is heard to say to Father Flote: 'we're about to be ushered into the Creator's presence' (p. 119). But if we are momentarily encouraged to read the scene as set before the Pearly Gates, such a neat ending is problematised by the broader context: at one time Toulon had been a spy for Archbishop Monselet, a 'zealot's zealot' (p. 96). He, and indeed each of the characters, brings to the Epilogue their own history and their own desires. The conclusion of the scene, the final moments of the play, takes us not to a religious epiphany, but to a refrain from the song that has come to characterise the Noses' ideological resistance to first the Black Death and then the Church: '"Join together. No weak link. Must keep trying. Else we sink. Join together all of you. Pierre Frapper and blind Le Grue"' (p. 120).

The song has first been heard in Act One, Scene 4, when the Noses expand their numbers, welcoming Le Grue, Bembo, Frapper and the Boutros Brothers, all of them unlikely entertainers; and again in Act Two, Scene 2, when they hear that 'The plague is over! . . . *the* FLOTIES, FLAGELLANTS *and* BLACK RAVENS *find themselves hugging each other in a spontaneous explosion of joy* . . .' and Father Flote urges that 'All forms of rebellion must come together.' He sings: '"Join together, that's the plan. It's the secret. Man helps man"' (p. 85). The song has powerful echoes of the quotation from *The Brotherhood of Man* at the end of *Auschwitz*. But whereas in *Laughter!* the sentiment that the 'brotherhood of man' is a 'noble tie that binds, all human hearts and minds' (p. 409) is deeply ironic, here in *Red Noses* the exhortation to collective action, the celebration of community, is genuine – which is not to say that it is either sentimental or unproblematic. The form of the play ensures that an audience retains its critical distance from anything that smacks of doctrine or political sloganeering.

Open Texts

I have argued above that *The Ruling Class, The Bewitched* and *Laughter!* are all more open texts than they at first seem. *Red Noses* develops this openness in new directions. This is achieved, as before, through the use of humour, structural rhymes and rhythms, all of which serve to destabilise an audience's response. The dialectics of *Red Noses* are, however, more complex than we have seen in the earlier plays. And this, in its turn, is also because although *Red Noses* seems to be situated in the same territory as *The Bewitched* (a history play set in a time of catastrophe, with the threat of an immensely powerful Church lurking in the background), it is not primarily a satire. Although the Church is again seen as corrupt, opportunistic and inhumane, and the Church has the Floties executed, the emphasis of the play is on the struggle of the band of 'God's Zanies'. In structural terms, the Church (Pope Clement and his archbishop, Monselet) takes on a relatively minor role as one of several antagonists to Father Flote, the others being the Black Ravens, the Flagellants and the Black Death itself. Each of these groups (even Death, who appears as a character in the play that the Noses perform in Act One, Scene 7) comes to embody facets of the central dialectics, creating oppositional tensions between hope and experience, humour and seriousness, evasion and responsibility, spirituality and materialism, and the twin plagues of pestilential disease and human oppression. Each of these oppositions informs the others; it is impossible to extricate any one of them and discuss how it works within the play without invoking the others.

The jokey one-liners that pervade most (but not all) of the scenes can give the impression that the philosophical and political discourses that underpin the play are conducted in rather superficial terms. But while some of the dialogue has an aphoristic quality, the use of such aphorisms is woven into the fabric of the theatrical dialectic. In Act One, Scene 4, for example, a number of 'new recruits' seek to join the Floties. Toulon is highly sceptical about their abilities and their motivation: 'Every halfwit and quarterwit left breathing . . . The dull-eyed and hopeless. They come for free food and lodging not for love of God' (pp. 34–5). Flote is more generous, arguing that it is not their business to judge, but 'to see if Christ can use them'. One after another, the new recruits go through a series of routines which are comic in their awfulness and inappropriateness: Le Grue, a blind man, attempts to juggle three heavy wooden clubs. He '*throws the clubs into the air and misses them. They fall on his head and he slumps down with a groan*' (p. 36). Pierre Frapper, announced as a 'quick wit and stand-up jibster', has a stutter so bad that, even if he could remember his opening line, he would not be able to complete it. And the Boutros Brothers make a woeful attempt to tap-dance – on crutches. Toulon is angry, accusing them of 'Satanic pride'. He states: 'It's God's judgement that the blind, dumb and crippled stay so, till prayer and repentance change it. They're guilty and must accept their punishments' (p. 57). But Flote sees their 'acts' quite differently: 'It wasn't pride but hope, hope shining anew despite of every discouragement . . . Brother Toulon, we just saw the very apotheosis of Christianity: the triumph of hope over experience.' But although Flote is a central character, and he is a far more sympathetic character than any we have encountered in the plays discussed hitherto, his opinions and points of view are always qualified by the context in which they are offered. What the 'performers' hope for here is not that their acts will be recognised, but that they might receive 'free food and lodging' (p. 35). If hope is the antithesis of experience, then they will know the world as a profoundly cruel place; the real irony in Flote's aphorism is that although they find sanctuary, it is not with a Christian fraternity. Although Flote claims that the 'triumph of hope' is an essential Christian quality, his organisation of the Noses draws more on humanist than Christian principles. The recurring hymn never once mentions Christ or God. The spirituality of the group comes from its insistence that 'Man helps Man' and from Flote's refusal to despair: 'I know that the real sin of the Israelites in the desert was not their rebellion against God but their despair' (p. 12). It is also possible to read the aphorism more cynically – as an attack on Christianity for offering false hopes. But while this reading is Father Toulon's – 'A definition [of Christianity that] – the Supreme Pontiff will be most interested to hear' (p. 37) – and it is the most readily available to an audience because it is the most comic, it is further qualified by subsequent events in the play. In spite of all the attacks on it, Flote's optimism becomes a positive force, a means of surviving; his determination to laugh at the miseries and horrors of the plague is not, however, a Panglossian denial of reality – for Flote, hope and laughter are the means of dealing with experience, not denying it.

Beneath the laughter, however, there lie two profound contradictions. The first of these is that the Floties' determination to avoid despair, characterised by the dogged insistence of their humour and laughter, reveals a deep sense of the absurdity of existence. As Grez (the leader of the Flagellants) says as he burns to death on the stake in the final scene of the play: 'You were right, friend Flote. God's a joker' (p. 107). The group's dramatisation of *Everyman* (at the end of Act One) may allow Everyman to win the shirt off Death's back (p. 64), but Toulon (appearing as God in the play) voices what they all know: 'Death will come again'. Although Brodin's response is defiant, it recognises that Death is an indiscriminate leveller: 'Whether dying in a privy or marble halls, green field or white bed . . . don't do Death's job for him. Don't start dying before you die' (p. 65). The second of these contradictions is that although the group's humanism sees them through the depredations of the plague, it offers no protection against the oppression of the Church. As Flote himself acknowledges: 'In the days of pestilence we could be funny but now we're back to normal, life is too serious to be funny.' In the face of the despotism of the 'Supreme Pontiff', he comes closest to despair:

I tried to lift Creation from bondage with mirth. Wrong. Our humour was a way of evading truth, avoiding responsibility. Our mirth was used to divert attention while the strong ones slunk back to their thrones and palaces . . .

(p. 113)

This concern with the socio-political functions of humour echoes *Laughter!*, though ultimately *Red Noses* is far more defiant than the earlier play. Although the pope has the Black Ravens and the Flagellants executed, he is willing to let the Noses continue, providing they remove all political content from their shows; he invites Flote to submit to the Church as a licensing authority: 'I must give your company strict rules and orders . . . Please the populace with passing shows . . . meringues, jellies and whipped cream. But give them no meat to chew on' (p. 109). Although Flote tries to accede, he cannot; and in the Epilogue his disembodied voice calls for 'Not the mirth born of anxiety and fear but the mirth of children and sages, the laughter of compassion and joy' (p. 119). There is more than a touch of sentimentality in the notion that the 'mirth of children' is devoid of anxiety and fear, but what is significant here is that the debate about the differing functions of laughter and humour echoes around the play like yodelling in a mountain valley.

Metamorphosis and Carnival

Flote's refusal to submit to the demands of the Church marks his own transformation – not only in the way he is viewed by the authorities, but also in his self-perception. During the plague he has been useful to the Church. With the plague passed, and the Flagellants and Black Ravens willing to join with the Noses, he becomes an agent of subversion. Unusually for a play which is constructed around dramatic types rather than psychologised characters, several of the characters undergo major shifts in perception and attitude. That these are not psychologically motivated changes does not lessen their significance. The general tendencies of these changes are positive: Toulon, sent to spy on Flote by the pope, becomes wholly committed to the group, willing to die rather than return to the religious establishment; Brodin, a ruthless mercenary, gives up killing and adopts a moral position; Grez, the Flagellant, bitterly opposed to the Noses until the final scene, recants publicly – 'We embraced pain when we should've tried to eliminate it . . . God . . . doesn't want our suffering' (p. 107); and Frapper, who suffers from a crippling stutter when he first arrives, becomes highly articulate, gleefully reciting tongue-twisters. These metamorphoses might be dismissed as merely emblematic; I would rather think of them as metaphorical, representing various possibilities of change: political, ideological, emotional, physiological. All bar one of these metamorphoses take place during the Black Death; the exception is Grez, the Flagellant, who undergoes his 'conversion' in a reaction against the refusal of the Church to allow independent thought (in its own terms, heresy). The days of pestilence thus create a kind of liminal space in which established authority is challenged and change becomes possible. Although it might seem that the only certainty in this chaos is death itself, the randomness of death destabilises all. Change is thus not only possible, but necessary if (to paraphrase Brodin) they are not to start dying before they die.

Barnes' work has sometimes been termed 'carnivalesque'. And he himself alludes in these terms to his childhood in Clacton-on-Sea, where his parents ran amusement stalls on the pier.[5] There are certainly elements of the carnivalesque in *Red Noses*. The interlude of pestilential horror during which the Noses give their world a glimpse of 'otherness', a means of social organisation that encourages independent thought and refuses the authority of the Church, comes to an end as soon as the Church fears independent thought more than it fears the Black Death. While still working in the service of the pope, Toulon gives voice to the argument that carnival is a political force: 'Laughter produces freedom. It's against all authority, ripping off the public mask to show the idiot face beneath . . . [We] glimpse the world as it could be' (p. 50). But the pope gives a licence to the Noses because, as we later hear, Flote has 'helped keep unrest down to a minimum; made men more readily accept their miserable lot' (p. 95). To develop the analogy, the end of the plague is marked as if it is the end of a holiday; indeed, the original meaning of the word 'holiday' is alluded to in the death of Sonnerie in Act Two, Scene 2. Toulon, by now wholly committed to the Floties, eulogises: 'All those who saw his holy dancing were changed, for in their hearts he worked both weeping and rapture in one' (p. 87).

There are, however, significant differences between familiar notions of carnival and the unstable world of *Red Noses*. Father Flote and his 'Zanies' take opportunistic advantage of catastrophic social upheaval to create a glimpse of benevolent anarchy, but their success in creating an alternative to the monolithic central authority of the Church is as dependent upon the absence of Archbishop Monselet (who flees to the hills to avoid contact with his plague-ridden flock) as it is upon the sanction of the pope, who has 'no healthy clerics left for the important work of collecting taxes and drafting new laws' (p. 48). Furthermore, in carnival, when the world turns right-side-up again, all go back to their places; the fool, who was king for a day, resumes his lowly status. In *Red Noses*, however, the Floties refuse the pope's offer of a licence; death is better than denial of the spirit of collectivity that the group has found. Toulon, formerly the pope's agent, articulates it thus: 'I'd rather rot, lose my life than your friendship. Though I'm no dancer, I'm dancing with you' (p. 114). Although Toulon expresses this in personal terms, Flote's friendship has engendered a group dynamic in which dance signifies both an emotional and a spiritual connection between the members.

Dancing Bells

Throughout the play Sonnerie never uses the spoken word. Although his appearance (in the very first scene) is never explained, he arrives at exactly the moment when Flote is praying for companionship:

> Must I cross the river alone? Solitude is welcome but loneliness is hard to bear . . . (*There is the sound of tiny bells.*) Bells? Who asked for bells? Since when did God speak with bells? (**SONNERIE** *enters . . . his costume covered with tiny silver bells which ring gently. He crosses to* **FLOTE** *and bows gracefully.*) And good day to you too . . . (**SONNERIE** *shakes his right leg.*) Yes, it is quite common nowadays . . . Who are you? (**SONNERIE** *jumps, shaking his left leg.*) Ah yes, a beautiful name . . .
>
> (pp. 12–13)

Sonnerie's use of his bells allows space for others to make meaning, to read his shaking in their own terms. I am put in mind of Rouben Mamoulian asking Greta Garbo to 'think of her face as a blank piece of paper that audiences would sign'.[6] Whether intentionally or not, Mamoulian's use of the word 'sign' here is doubly rich: it is the audience who creates the sign, which it then reads; and it is the audience that inscribes the face – or, in the case of Sonnerie, his dance. For Sonnerie's language is a joyous language of dance and music of the whole body; a dance which is open to interpretation, and which glories in the possibility of difference and otherness. He and his dance are open texts; and his audience is both on the stage and in the theatre auditorium.

In contrast, the Church uses language to limit and constrain, to define meaning and coerce into conformity. Where Sonnerie, a Harpo Marx-like character, brings warmth, joy and love to those around him, Pope Clement embalms the 'sacred texts' of the Bible, refusing the openness of metaphor and symbol, labelling anything except the most rigid literalism as heresy. The restrictions imposed by the Church, in the person of Pope Clement, are callous and brutal, driven by that insistence on literalism and a refusal to read 'the word' as metaphor or symbol which characterises all fundamentalism. Although the end of the 'carnival' occurs when the Church re-establishes control, dramatically it is Sonnerie's death that marks the turning point, confirming the character as embodying opposition to the establishment Church's mechanisms of oppression.

Metatheatre

Almost all of Barnes' plays contain elements of the metatheatrical. Occasionally the strategy offers us little more than a brief witty self-referential interlude, as when characters acknowledge their metonymic role in a social drama – for example Toulon saying 'A man of my moral inflexibility would be welcomed with open arms in any religious community' (p. 17) – but more often metatheatricality is used to distance an audience from the narrative and provoke reflection. The game (for that is what it is) depends greatly on the skill of the actors, for it frequently implies stepping briefly out of role and at least acknowledging the audience in the auditorium as well as the on-stage audience, if not engaging in full-blown direct address. Reminding us of the difference and separation between the actor, the character and the role may not of itself be particularly provocative; but at its most interesting the game also calls into question the roles of author and audience. Consider, for example, the moment when the First Attendant complains: 'I've only just been born and now I have to die. All the fault of writers . . . writing stories where some characters are important and others just disposable stock – First Attendant, Second Peasant, Third Guard. Stories're easier when 'tisn't possible to care for everyone equal' (pp. 15–16). This rant against writers is jokey and might even be said to be facetious, but it is not a distraction from a play which is concerned with social equality; and it parallels the authority of the invisible playwright with those random interventions ascribed to God that strike down all and sundry with the plague.

Red Noses pushes the game still further, for it is structured around two on-stage performances by the Noses, each of the two plays within the play coming at the end of an act. The second act culminates in the performance of the Noses' subversive rendering of *The Nativity*, echoing their version of *Everyman* at the end of Act One. The rhythmic positioning of these two plays, the structural rhyme, draws attention to the similarities and differences between the two. *Everyman* is celebratory; on stage Everyman plays dice with Death and wins, taking the shirt off Death's back. *The Nativity*, which is usually performed to celebrate Christ's birth, results in the death of Flote and the Noses. In both cases the intervention of the on-stage audience is highly significant: during the *Everyman* performance there is the constant good-natured banter between audience and performers that characterises what Peter Brook has referred to as 'Rough Theatre'.[7] When Flote first appears, dressed as Death, Scarron shouts out 'Death? Another lie. That's your red-nosed sallow-pate, Flote. We Ravens know about death' (p. 58). Scarron's refusal to accept the theatrical conventions has numerous well-known theatrical antecedents; perhaps the most relevant here is not the arguments amongst the 'rude mechanicals' in *A Midsummer Night's Dream* but Zeal-of-the-Land Busy's authoritarian outrage at the puppet show in Ben Jonson's *Bartholomew Fair*. Scarron shares with Busy an inability to distinguish between role-playing and deceit, between the performer and the role. But in the world of *Red Noses* everyone knows about death. By drawing attention to Flote's shabby disguise, Scarron confirms the on-stage audience's willingness to participate in the theatrical game. But the doubts that Scarron expresses from outside the drama are echoed within it by Everyman's wife (played by Marguerite). Flote is by now '*dressed in a long black cloak and gloves and carrying a scythe. The* AUDIENCE *gasps:* "It's Death. Death's amongst us!"' and Flote announces: 'Prepare thyself, Everyman. I'm Death.' But Everyman's wife is not convinced: 'It's some stark pimp, a straw-in-the-hair moon-loon.' To which Everyman counters: 'If he says he's Death, he's Death. He looks like Death' (p. 59). Although, within the world of the fiction, Scarron is outside the play and Marguerite is within it, each is concerned with their own ability to recognise death and both are attempting to match what they think they know of death with Flote's iconic representation. When Rochfort, playing Good Fellowship, encounters Death, the banter continues in the same vein: 'Death? Did you say Death? *This* is Death . . .? I thought you'd be thinner' (p. 61). This spirited mockery of Death's appearance develops into something of a running gag – until the metatheatrical 'game' takes a further metaphysical turn when Mother Metz starts laughing at the way that Everyman seems to be outwitting death and '(*As her laughter grows louder she suddenly slumps down.*) I'm Mother Metz and earth is in my ears. I relaxed and dusty death's slipped in through the cracks' (p. 63). And she dies laughing. Although '*The* AUDIENCE *shrinks back*' as it loses one of its own, the play is more important. Druce (one of the Black Ravens) wants 'to see what happens next', and '*The playlet continues*' (p. 63).

The light-hearted knockabout of this scene contains two grave paradoxes: Mother Metz's laughter is at once both the cause of her death and an act of defiance, a refusal to accept the misery of death; and Father Flote, the leader of 'Christ's Clowns', mocks Death through his impersonation, while death, in the 'real world', takes Mother Metz while she is laughing at Everyman's defiance. Bernard Dukore's claim that 'The Everyman parody diverts people's minds from the reality of death' (1981, p. 43) may be accurate, but the play makes it clear that this can only happen because this Death is an undiscriminating killer who shares a home with Disease and Natural Disaster, not a vengeful and malicious force of repression. That such diversions are inappropriate in the face of human agencies is made abundantly clear in the second playlet.

The performance of *The Nativity* at the end of Act Two develops the interaction between on-stage performers and spectators along paths that are darker and more political. While Lefranc's insistence that 'That stuttering simikin's not Joseph and that licentious nun's never been a mother or a virgin' (p. 106) echoes Scarron's comment in the earlier scene, Archbishop Monselet reads the performance as scurrilous, seditious and blasphemous. What Monselet really objects to is that the playlet makes a laughing stock of Herod: 'You mock God. For the authority of kings, yea even Herod's, comes from God, and in mocking them you mock Him' (p. 106). They are indeed mocking 'the authority of kings', but it is Monselet's reading which turns this into an attack on the concept of divine right, and thence against his highly politicised construction of God Himself. After the pope's subsequent intervention, the Noses are allowed to proceed with the playlet providing they agree to remove all political content from their shows – until Sabine and Patris (members of the on-stage audience) urge Herod's guards, about to massacre the innocents, to 'Stop! . . . Spit on your orders!' (p. 112). Again the boundaries between spectators and performers are broken down, but now it is the audience's engagement in the morality of the performance which damns the Noses. For the Church to sanction their activities, theatre should function as an anaesthetic, numbing moral outrage, not inciting it. As, one after another, the Floties stand in solidarity with Father Flote, refusing to comply with clerical authority and rejecting passivity, their resistance gives new meaning to Everyman's plea to the audience at the end of the earlier play: 'don't do Death's job for him. Don't start dying before you die' (p. 65). Barnes contrives to blur the boundaries between on- and off-stage morality; for all who participate in the metatheatrical game, it is passivity which is the real enemy.

Community

As noted above, Act 2, Scene Two of *Red Noses* is a turning point within the play. The scene begins with a communal meal, an opportunity for all the Floties to share in each other's pleasures. This modest gathering is effectively the zenith of the group's achievement. It becomes a 'last supper'. They have survived by supporting each other, by offering a viable alternative to the anguished guilt of the Flagellants, the entrepreneurial exploitation of the Black Ravens and the repressive orthodoxies of the Church. This simple scene becomes genuinely celebratory – culminating in a '*spontaneous explosion of joy*' as news arrives that 'The plague is over'. Unfortunately the announcement is premature: no sooner has Flote declared that 'It's time to cast off old ways, old thoughts' (p. 85) and the Flagellants and Black Ravens seem to have set aside their differences, than Sonnerie dies. The death of Sonnerie, as we have seen, marks a significant turning point in the play. With the cruellest of ironies, where the Floties have been able to resist the depredations of the plague to flourish in the resulting anarchy, they are about to be destroyed by the Church.

Red Noses has been described as an oblique account of a period in the late 1960s,[8] a period which was characterised by a refusal of authority on behalf of the young (student movements) and intellectuals, and various previously disenfranchised and/or marginalised minority groups. For those who felt themselves to be part of these groups, it was a time when collective action was seen as a viable alternative to central authority. Although Barnes does not acknowledge that he was consciously exploring aspects of 1960s cultures, the play is concerned with the development and survival of an essentially pacifist independent group. Furthermore, in the arts, one of the characteristic phenomena of the period in Europe and America was the emergence of 'alternative' theatre groups. Theatre is essentially a community experience; the more radical of these theatre companies saw communities of actors as a paradigm for communality – as a political statement about ways of living lives, ways of *being* as well as performing.[9] Although the various groups differed greatly in their aims and in their methodologies, what they all had in common was a commitment to the collective, a belief in the power of theatre as a force for change. In that respect, the Noses bear a strong resemblance to some of these radical theatre groups – at least in their commitment to the power of popular entertainment as a means of creating a sense of community, if not in the pompous self-righteousness that characterised some of the 'manifestos' produced by their twentieth-century equivalents. The play can unquestionably be read as a metaphorical examination of the movements and urges that occur at moments of massive social upheaval. But the problem with drawing specific analogies is that it tends to tie the play down, presenting it as an allegorical parable – when it is far more open than that. Certainly, the play is informed by the social changes that took place in the 1960s, and by Establishment responses to those changes; but it is no more 'about' the 1960s than it is 'about' the Black Death.

Perhaps the greatest achievement of *Red Noses* is that in exploring the possibilities of optimism in the darkest of times, it creates moments of genuine joy while, for the most part, avoiding sentimentality, creating powerful dialectics which place the possibilities of personal change in increasingly complex political contexts.

5

Dreaming

Bid him remember of this unstable world.

Sir Thomas Malory[1]

Dreaming opened at the Manchester Royal Exchange Theatre in March 1999. It was the first major production of a Peter Barnes play since *Sunsets and Glories*[2] at the West Yorkshire Playhouse in 1990. The play and the production were hailed by the critics of several national newspapers: 'This is a major play and it gets a major production' (Lyn Gardner, *Guardian*, 31 March 1999); 'No other British dramatist attempts themes of this huge scale' (Jeremy Kingston, *The Times*, 27 March 1999). A revival of the play was mounted for a five-week run at the Queen's Theatre, Shaftesbury Avenue, in June and July 1999.[3] Peter Barnes himself directed the revival. In London the play received remarkably mixed notices. This was, nevertheless, a significant theatrical event: the first production of a major Peter Barnes play to be seen in London since *Red Noses* at the Barbican in 1985.

As many newspaper critics observed, however, since *The Ruling Class*, Barnes' relationships with both the institutional and the academic wings of the theatrical establishment have been erratic at best, frosty and dismissive at worst. Almost all the reviews of *Dreaming* noted the apparent inconsistency of the play, its constant shifts in tone and style and its apparently arbitrary (and often 'tasteless') uses of humour. What is remarkable about these notices is that even the more insightful and positive of them failed to relate the 'freewheeling' form of the play to its content; and very few of them related the subject matter of the play – the dispossessed seeking safety during brutal civil war – to contemporary events in the Balkans.

Set in the 'bloody aftermath of the Wars of the Roses', the play follows a small band of refugees and their struggles to survive. While the themes and theatrical methods are familiar from Barnes' earlier work (the wonderful use of song and dance; metatheatrical devices, such as Richard, Duke of Gloucester, misquoting from Shakespeare's *Richard III*; the iconoclastic humour), the play marks new developments in Barnes' work. There are ways in which *Dreaming* reprises *Red Noses*: its episodic, picaresque journey structure; the irreverent appropriation of a historical context; the interrogation of the functions of humour and laughter; the small band of oddballs who congregate around an eccentric leader (with several of the characters echoing some of those seen in *Red Noses*). But *Dreaming* is a darker play and Mallory is a more complex and ambivalent figure than Father Flote. Again the play is concerned with issues of authority, liberty, leadership and the power of the group. But whereas in *Red Noses*, Flote is as near as one gets in Barnes' theatre to a character who is an unequivocally 'good' man, in *Dreaming*, Mallory, although engaging, is flawed, and the play problematises the charismatic qualities of leadership, while examining relations between the group and its constituent members.

The play opens as the Wars of the Roses come to a bloody end. Mallory, a killing machine grown sick of war, is determined to return to his family and something he can call home. During the wars, however, a small but diverse group has gathered around

106

him: Bess, whose blend of warmth and worldly cynicism echoes that of Marguerite in *Red Noses*, still searches for love; Davy, the mercenary, who openly boasts that 'Gold is friendship, beauty, wit, courage, honour, reason for living' (p. 4);[4] the melancholic Skelton, who craves death but somehow always manages to avoid it, much to his own continuing disappointment. Accompanied by this small band of war-weary mercenaries, who look to him for leadership, Mallory finds the farmhouse that had been his home, and dreams that Sarah and Anna, his wife and daughter, are safe in domestic peace; but he wakes to find that his farm is a ruin and his family is buried nearby in makeshift graves beneath crude wooden crosses. Thereafter he vows to 'make them live again' (p. 25) and the group sets off again in search of 'home' – Mallory's home. The play then episodically follows them as they struggle to survive in the aftermath of war. As they wander through the war-ravaged landscape, they encounter various other survivors: peasants who want a leader, cut-throats who want to rob them, blind beggars who attack them for food. They are joined by Jethro Kell, an insightful, though sceptical, priest; and Susan, a distraught young woman betrothed to Percy Beaufort (whose throat has been slit by Davy on Mallory's orders in the first scene of the play). Mallory insists that she is his wife, Sarah, although he knows Sarah to be dead. He (re)marries Susan/Sarah in a wedding service conducted by the godless priest, Kell, and she too joins the group. But this makes an enemy of Richard of Gloucester, who, having murdered all the Beauforts, wants Mallory to hand Susan/Sarah over to him. As the last of the Beauforts, she has a claim on the estates that Richard has taken for himself. One by one the members of the group are killed, until finally only Mallory, Susan/Sarah and their memories survive. In the final scene it seems that, although the 'home' they have found is itself a burnt-out ruin, Mallory and Susan/Sarah have found some kind of reconciliation and can die in peace. By the time Richard and his men have caught up with them they have frozen to death in each other's arms.

Contradictions

Several journalist critics referred to *Dreaming* as 'uneven'. Their intention was clearly to damn the play for inconsistencies. The charge would be indefensible – were it worth entering into a debate about the play on those terms. I would, however, prefer to argue that it is more productive to consider these inconsistencies as inherent contradictions which destabilise an audience's response to the narrative. And, certainly, *Dreaming* is replete with contradictions. Barnes has always been interested in contradictions of style and tone. In a short piece entitled 'Notes', he wrote that he sought to create 'A drama of extremes, trying to illuminate the truth as contradictory. Instead of eliminating . . . contradictions as untrue, they are emphasised; melancholy and joy, tragedy and comedy, the bathetic and the sublime are placed side by side. The similarity of such opposites is shown by such juxtapositions' (p. 113).[5] *Dreaming*'s contradictions are both structural and dialectical. Although the play boasts a strong linear narrative, that narrative is highly fragmented. The central concerns of the play, for example the discourses about visionary inspiration, leadership, authority, heroism and identity, are presented in such a way as to refuse resolution. The major characters are all 'contradictory' in some way: Mallory, who searches for home, while acknowledging that 'home is no longer a place' (p. 26); Skelton, who seeks the release of death and yet is himself an extremely efficient killer; Davy, who claims that he is only ever motivated by the desire for profit, and yet sacrifices his own life to save Susan; Susan, who accepts the identity that Mallory imposes on her as Sarah, yet always remains Susan; and Bess, the formidably independent Mother Courage-like figure, who seeks the warmth of a bed with the godless priest Kell.

Barnes has sometimes been compared with Brecht (many of the reviews of *Dreaming* noted the play's resemblance to *Mother Courage*), and he has acknowledged Brecht as one of several significant influences on his work.[6] Indeed, the starting point for *Dreaming* might well have been Galileo's 'Unglücklich das Land, das Helden nötig hat' ('Unhappy the land that is in need of heroes').[7] But whereas in Brecht contradictions are sought and used as a means of exposing the social and political structures that give rise to those apparent contradictions, in Barnes' work they are used to create meaning through unfamiliar and unexpected juxtaposition – in ways which recall the work of the Russian directors Vsevolod Meyerhold[8] and Sergei Eisenstein and the more politically motivated amongst the surrealists.[9] What all these have in common, however, is their use of dramatic strategies to activate an audience, to create in an audience a sense of 'rational detachment', of making the familiar seem strange,[10] of challenging the inevitability of history.

Chapter 8 considers ways in which the concept of the 'montage of attractions' (a term coined by Eisenstein, but developed by him in collaboration with Meyerhold) can usefully be seen to inform Barnes' work. I shall not, therefore, discuss the connections with Meyerhold here, but it is worth examining the way that the montage structure of the play itself creates meaning. *Dreaming* is built up as a series of vaudeville-like 'turns' with strong rhythmic relationships, all of which reflect upon and inflect the central concerns of the play. A close examination of the opening sequence of five scenes gives some indication of Barnes' method. The play opens with a wordless Prologue: a short expressionist evocation of the Battle of Tewkesbury, in which giant crows strut around the battlefield.[11] Although the scene creates a grotesque sense that the only beneficiaries of war are scavengers, it does not directly advance the narrative. The first scene with dialogue (Act One, Scene 1) is longer than most, and is one of the more conventional episodes in that it establishes characters and offers basic narrative information: Richard of Gloucester claims the war is over, and tries to persuade Mallory to join him: 'I need your cold sword and colder heart . . . to help me keep what we steal. I've a high destiny and I'll pull you up in my wake. Power and money, Mallory, beyond your dreams . . . take what's real' (p. 8). Meanwhile, Bess has given Skelton plates to spin (presumably to distract him from his melancholy, though, as I shall examine in greater detail shortly, the motive for this is never made clear); and when everybody looks at Mallory to see what his response will be to Richard, 'SKELTON *stops shaking the canes and the plates fall with a loud crash*' (p. 8). Mallory rejects Richard, whose offer of security and 'reality' is as illusory as any patron's in time of war. Thus Mallory and his small group of mercenaries become outcasts, refugees who know what they are fleeing from but have little idea (save Mallory's dream of home) of where they might be headed. The crashing of the plates punctuates the narrative, and the circus-like routine reinforces the notion that the demands made on individual participants in a war become ever more frenetic and absurd. The next scene (Act One, Scene 2) is a short and beautifully contradictory little meditation by Mallory on the harshness of the universe and his euphoria at his belief that he thinks he is 'sailing home!' (p. 9). This is immediately followed by a scene in which Mallory confronts a priest leading a group of demoralised peasants bemoaning their losses. The priest offers them the promise of Christ's blessing in heaven. Mallory rounds on them: 'You're being

blessed in another universe. Here and now you're being crushed.
Send your crushers into the dark!' The peasants seem embold-
ened by Mallory's vision and urge him to be their leader, to 'Be
a true hero' (p. 10). He chastises them, insisting that 'Nothing's
sacred or powerful unless you make it so.' The peasants assure
him: 'We won't crawl!' Mallory retorts: 'Then you can do without me, I'm going home!' And as soon as Mallory has gone, the
priest claims the peasants back for himself and they *'resume
singing the "Dies Irae"'* (p. 11). The scene is short and light in
tone; it has the feel of a sketch. When the peasants (whom we do
not meet again after this scene) resume their singing it is like the
punchline of a music-hall routine, yet the content of the scene is
serious. Brecht might have given it a title: 'The Peasants Seek a
Hero'. The wit of the scene lies in its exposure of contradictions
and contrariness: the peasants will even agree not to be led if only
they have a strong leader to help them renounce leadership. And
the scene comments (indirectly, by association) on Mallory's
leadership of his own motley crew.

The peasant scene is followed by an encounter between
Mallory and Pedlar Cobett and his two teenaged children.[12] The
scene offers another take on the *Mother Courage* motif. Cobett
pushes his handcart full of goods for barter and announces:

> The name's Cobett, Pedlar Cobett, and there are my two bur-
> dens, Joanna and Edward Cobett . . . You want t' buy a bunch
> of dusty blue ribbons or a gallon of rot-gut? We'll sell you any-
> thing under heaven.
>
> (p. 17)

When Cobett admonishes his son, Edward – 'Haven't I taught
you, make money where you can' (p. 17) – it could almost be
Mother Courage herself speaking. Cobett is harsh, exploitative,

cynical and very drunk; and yet he saves the lives of his children by drinking from the poisoned bottle that he had offered to Mallory. He is, however, no hero. As he dies he exhorts his children to 'Strive to be the very best murdering cut-throats' (p. 20). There is more than postmodern playfulness and whimsical irony about the reference to *Mother Courage*. Whereas Mother Courage is furious when Kattrin dresses up in Yvette's clothes because it will make her attractive to men, Cobett has no compunction about offering his own daughter to Mallory: 'She lays well, like a soft plover' (p. 18). The scene may be fleeting, but it emphasises the instability and amorality of the world in which Mallory and his followers are trying to survive – partly in its own terms, and partly by its points of comparison with Mother Courage, whose behaviour is not moral in absolute terms, but who is trying to do right for her children in a corrupt and dangerous world. Cobett, too, is trying to 'do right' for his family; but to protect them he first offers his daughter as a sexual lure, and, when that fails, drinks his own poison. When he collapses, his daughter questions him:

JOANNA   Why did you drink it, father?
COBETT   He'd've killed you two, then me. I saw it in his eyes
    I had years of killing, like knows like . . .
EDWARD   We could've cut him down.
COBETT   We weren't good enough. I couldn't see you both
    die. We're a family.

(p. 19)

The scene is a variation on a theme, a sketch of the play as a whole, in which Mallory's dream of home becomes conflated with his desire for family. In musical terms the rhythm of these scenes is more like syncopated jazz than the symphonic score that Meyerhold emulated, but as in any montage, each of these scenes creates meaning in itself and simultaneously derives meaning from its relationships with the others. Meaning created in this way is, elusive, though not difficult to approximate. Circus and music-hall routines are interposed with scenes of harsh violence and cynical exploitation; 'sketches' such as the peasants' routine and the encounter with the Cobett family are simultaneously whimsical and serious. They reach across into the worlds of popular culture and more mainstream theatrical practice, and in doing so they create a sense of anarchy and arbitrariness. It is ironic that Brecht proposed a theatre that was rooted in popular culture – cabaret, music hall, popular song – and yet a play like *Mother Courage* has become the staple fare of the mainstream, 'high cultural' repertoire.

With its heady eclecticism, richness of language and theatrical imagery, and fragmented narrative, *Dreaming* is an invitingly open text; but although it is at least partly concerned with arbitrary cruelty, horrific brutality and the dehumanising effects of war, it is far from arbitrary in its form. The scenes that immediately follow Act One, Scene 1 may do little to move forward the narrative of the play, but their function is to set up the contexts within which the play operates, and to begin to tease out some of the central tensions. Each of the scenes discussed above is driven by an acceptance or refusal of authority, by tensions between tendencies to self-transcendence and self-assertion.

In *Red Noses*, Father Flote's merry band of Floties is unproblematically constituted as a supportive collective; Flote's leadership is challenged neither by members of the Noses, nor by the play. In *Dreaming*, however, Mallory's dream of returning home becomes inextricably coupled with an examination of the relationships between group and individual identity. The interrogation of these is woven into almost every scene of the play at some level. I want to consider in detail two particular scenes which draw attention to the play's treatment of this tension. The first of these is the conclusion of Act One,[13] where Mallory recognises that Sarah and Anna (his wife and daughter) are dead, and that his former home is now nothing but a ruined shed:

He bends down and reads the names carved on the crosses.

'Anna, daughter of John Mallory' . . . 'Sarah, wife of John Mallory' . . . (*He lets out a great howl.*) *Ahhhhhhh* . . . Lord God, reverse the river of time, suck them back for me. Lucifer . . .

I'll tear out my soul, only make them live again . . .

(p. 25)

Bess, Skelton and Davy commiserate and attempt to help Mallory deal with his loss. The exchange is emotive and moving, but we are not allowed to stay in this mode for long. In the space of four lines of dialogue the emotional exchange turns into a beautifully executed sand dance:

SKELTON   So move on, life is a journey.
DAVY   Life is a race.
BESS   No, life is a dance.

She takes a handful of sand, throws it across the ground and dances a soft-shoe/sand-dance on it . . .

Don't you hear life pour away/Every second of the day? . . . /
   All the things we've ever done/They're all written down in
   sand . . .
BESS/SKELTON/DAVY (*singing*)   All blown away like
   sand/Tiny grains of sand . . .

(p. 26)

Although the exchange is light-hearted, each character offers an apparently simple metaphor for their basic attitude to life; and, in doing so, each states their difference. Bess's metaphor, 'life is a dance', however, is the most complex – both in itself, and in the performance of the sand dance. Resonating throughout the play, it performs a number of functions simultaneously: it is Bess's rebuke to Skelton and Davy – in a sand dance the dancers appear to be moving forward together, but end up going nowhere, and certainly not racing each other – it is her way of taking Mallory out of his melancholic reflection on the deaths of his wife and daughter. At the same time as Bess entertains Mallory, Dilys Laye, who played Bess in the original production, entertains the theatre audience. Thus we are simultaneously meant to enjoy the actor's performance as character, as music-hall entertainer and as wry Brechtian commentator on the action of the scene and the play. If life is a sand dance, then Mallory's dream of finding home is itself likely to become a repeated step – forward and back, forward and back, forever making your mark, only to scuff it out – with your companion(s) the most significant thing in your life. Davy '*then* SKELTON *join* [BESS] *as they dance softly on the sand*', and then '*MALLORY finally gets up. The four join hands, sand-dancing and singing gently round the graves*' (p. 26). The group is seen not only to tolerate difference but also to honour it; and individuals within it are seen to gain strength from each other.

The scene contrasts with Act Two, Scene Five, where Mallory marries Susan, insisting that she is Sarah.

KELL Mallory insists on a wedding. He's convinced Susan she's here for their marriage and cast us as her family.

(p. 37)

Kell is to be Susan/Sarah's father; Bess her mother; Skelton her brother; Davy her son from her first marriage. Each of them is aware of the role-playing that is required of them: Mallory asks them to play the roles of family in order to 'normalise' the wedding, to make it seem more domestic, to reinforce his sense of coming home. The metaphor of being 'caught in a story that isn't our story, minor characters, pushed to the edge . . . only part of Mallory's dream' (p. 37) is one with which most of us can identify. But it is particularly apposite for refugees in wartime. For the majority of those fleeing Kosovo or Serbia in the early summer of 1999 (when *Dreaming* was produced in London) it was a very precise metaphor. War, as *Dreaming* reminds us, heightens the differences between assertive leaders and an acquiescent majority, between those who impose particular versions of history on to others and those who accept these narratives without questioning whether their own interests are really served by the claims that are made on their behalf. In this wedding scene, everybody has to play a role that Mallory has cast them in: even Christ Himself. The stage is set very simply, '*a life-size crucifix . . . behind an altar*' suggesting a church. As Kell begins to intone

> *the marriage service . . . the figure of Christ . . . stirs and then comes down off the cross . . .* KELL *silently mouths the words of the marriage service while Christ stretches and talks directly to* SUSAN . . .'

(p. 38)

Christ tells Susan and the theatre audience a series of jokes. The routine ends as he returns to the cross and asks Susan if she thinks his last joke is better than those that have gone before. 'I do!' she says, to which Kell announces:

... By the power vested in me I now pronounce you man and wife!

SUSAN *bursts out laughing at* CHRIST*'s joke and the lights snap out quickly.*

(p. 39)

The scene is constructed as a 'turn', presenting the marriage service as a ritual in which a woman, well aware of the joke, agrees to participate in a male narrative because it is amusing. Or is she tricked by Christ into agreeing to the marriage? The next scene (in which Susan and Mallory are in bed together) indicates that she is aware, but resentful that she has been tricked:

MALLORY   Why did you dream my dream?
SUSAN   I need a protector.
MALLORY   I need a wife and family.
SUSAN   I hate needing you.

(p. 40)

The price that Susan pays for protection by Mallory and incorporation into the group is the loss of her identity. Susan's shifting, negotiated identity is the background against which subsequent scenes take place – until the final scene of the play when we find Mallory and Susan, '*on a mountain top, biting winds and swirling snow . . . where they rest*' (pp. 70–1). He takes off his coat and puts it around her. And a strange reversal takes place:

SUSAN   The name's Sarah, Sarah! We've been married long
   enough for you to know that, John . . . I've risen from the
   dead to be with you, John . . . Sarah, let me hear you say,
   Sarah.

117

MALLORY Sarah.
SUSAN We're home, John! It's what you wanted, isn't it? . . .
MALLORY We're home, Sarah.

. . . they sit huddled together in the freezing cold . . .

SUSAN We're here in our own home, safe and warm.
MALLORY I made enough sacrifices to make it real. Davy,
  Bess, Kell, Skelton, all gone, died hard on the hoof . . .

(p. 71)

This is a deeply ambivalent moment. Mallory has protected
Susan from Richard of Gloucester. Their marriage has become as
stable as anything can be in such a profoundly unstable world.
Defying Richard to the end, they die together, yet death does not
part them. His dream has become her dream. But the price that
they have paid for it, Mallory's 'sacrifices', are the lives of those
who looked to him for leadership.

The Dream of Home

Mallory's dream is at once the driving force that holds the group
together, and an imposition on the other members of the group.
The fragmentation of the narrative, and the frequent 'sidesteps'
into dance, song and metatheatrical, self-referential humour all
serve to problematise the primacy of Mallory's narrative and
indeed the very notion of 'returning home'. In times of extreme
social upheaval home can only be a dream, a dream not of future
possibilities but of past certainties. The only home that Mallory's
band of refugees can enjoy is companionship; and, for them, the
antonym for home becomes isolation.

If the play is at least partly exploring notions of 'home' and family, it is crucially concerned with dreaming. In the two 1999 productions of the play, the set had strong connotations of Bosch and Brueghel.[14] In her review of the play, Lyn Gardner described the set for the Royal Exchange production: 'Stephen Brimson Lewis has designed a glass circle for the floor of Manchester's Royal Exchange under which piles of the slaughtered lie with their bones twisted in the agonies of death. It is like looking into the pit of Hell. At night the skulls glow like phosphorus.'[15]

This set makes visible the nightmare world in which all the action of the play takes place. Mallory's dream of home is haunted by killing and suffering. Wherever they go, whatever they do, death is close at hand. *Dreaming* is as much a contemporary nightmare and an apocalyptic vision of the future as it is a history play. The play is much less interested in personality than it is in relationships between the dreamer's vision and the effect that this vision has on others. The 'pit of Hell' that Mallory and his tattered band of followers walk across, skate over and dance upon is the product of the Wars of the Roses. It is the only certainty they know. And, as the opening scenes of the play make clear, it is the product of wars which originate in the ruthless 'visions' of kings and queens and would-be kings. Though Richard, Duke of Gloucester, is presented in a parodic, humorous way,[16] he stalks the play, an insidious and ever present threat to Mallory's group. Mallory's dream is simultaneously visionary, liberating and dangerous: by refusing Richard's request to hand over Susan/Sarah, he leads his group not just into danger but to their deaths. The final exchange between Mallory and Susan (who has by now willingly accepted her role as Sarah, Mallory's long-dead wife) is a whimsical reflection on this:

MALLORY Why did they follow my dream, Sarah?

SUSAN You're the hero of this story, my love.

MALLORY Some kind of hero, me, with a sliver of ice in the heart. Not a hero's heart. So why did they follow my dream?

SUSAN Most lives're matter-of-fact . . . You gave us something else.

MALLORY But I was never sure what it was.

SUSAN But you believed it, that's enough!

MALLORY I failed.

SUSAN No, you let us glimpse another world.

(pp. 71–2)

This may be lighter in tone than the horrific nightmares of some of *The Bewitched* and *Laughter!*, where complicity with tyranny is seen in the context of the Spanish Inquisition and the Holocaust, but beneath her light-hearted banter, Susan is dividing people into those who seek leaders and those who lead. Mallory is the leader because he lets his followers 'glimpse another world'. He is not an orator; he makes no effort to convert them to his cause. As witnesses to his hallucination in the first act, when he conjures his wife and daughter from the ruins of their former home (Act One, Scene 8), they know his dream is illusory. He does not need to exhort or bewitch his followers; he simply allows them a glimpse of 'another world'. And, whereas in *Laughter!* the 'other world' for Cranach is the certainty that rigid bureaucratic hierarchy provides, in *Dreaming* the glimpse of otherness is more transitory, more intangible than in the earlier plays. Mallory inspires those who stick with him, he gives meaning to their lives, and yet he is no hero; his drive and determination motivate them, but also create a kind of dependence and ultimately lead them to their deaths.

Late in the play, Davy goes missing. 'We must wait for him,' says Susan.

KELL   Unless we get through the swamp, they'll have us. We can't wait too long.

MALLORY   We must. We're going home together. That's what home means. It's not just a fixed point on a map.

(p. 50)

Thus the 'home' that Mallory is determined to find metamorphoses during the course of the play from the concrete and materialist farmstead that is a ruin when he returns, to the ghosts of his wife and daughter, to something more abstract and metaphysical: something whose precise meaning is elusive, but which is akin to the bonding of individuals within a group. Ultimately his vision of home is not geographical but ideological; the glimpse of 'another world' that he offers is a dream of community in which personal difference is both respected and valued. Or is it?

In the final moments of the play, Susan and Mallory huddle closer together on the freezing mountain top.[17] Their last words are:

SUSAN   Mallory?

MALLORY   I'm thinking of another world . . .

(p. 72)

By the time Richard arrives they are frozen. They may be together, but Mallory's reverie is enigmatic; and we are not allowed to know whether Susan shares his dreams in death. In performance, such uncertainties could be resolved by a look of anxiety, or the briefest of smiles, or perhaps even a wry, shared joke between them; my own inclination as a director would be to leave it open to the audience, for that, increasingly, is the direction that Barnes himself has taken as a playwright.

121

While I have argued above that reading *The Ruling Class* as exclusively satirising the idiocies of English class structures is to take an inappropriately narrow view of the play, it is certainly a play which is not as open to interpretation as those which follow it. The richness of *Dreaming* is that it is at once enigmatic and elliptic, yet also profoundly moving and relevant to the present day. In *Luna Park Eclipses*, examined in Chapter 9, Barnes seeks to develop this openness still further, creating a text which would be as open to audience interpretation as an abstract painting.

PART THREE

Confessing Our Selves

Plays for Radio and Television

6

Bright Lights in Dark Rooms

The plays discussed in Part One have made a major contribution to British theatre, but Barnes' significance as a dramatist needs also to be measured in terms of the large number of plays he has written for radio and television. Even discounting the major stage plays, he demands consideration as an innovator with a radical voice of his own.

The Radio Plays – Barnes' People

Barnes' People is a set of monologues, each lasting about ten minutes, all but one of which were broadcast on BBC Radio 3 in 1981. The series was successful and a further series was commissioned. But rather than write a second series of monologues, lapsing into a pattern of writing that he felt risked becoming formulaic, Barnes wrote *Barnes' People II* as a series of seven duologues, and a third series, *Barnes' People III* (first broadcast by BBC Radio 3 in 1986), as a set of eight three-handers. *Barnes' People II* and *III* were published in small separate volumes, the three-handers going out under the title *The Real Long John Silver and Other Plays*. They have not yet been included in any of the volumes of collected plays. *Worms* and *Acting Exercise* were subsequently used in a revue entitled *Somersaults* (produced at Leicester in 1981); and *Acting Exercise* reappeared in *Corpsing*, a programme of four one-act plays by Barnes produced at the Tristan Bates Theatre, London, in 1996. In 1989 the BBC commissioned a further set of six monologues. They were broadcast under the title *More Barnes' People* on BBC Radio 3 in 1989 and 1990. They were published with *The Spirit of Man* in the volume of that name.

In Britain the medium of radio has often provided dramatists with opportunities to experiment with areas of work that would be deemed too risky in theatre or television. However else one might describe Barnes' theatre work, it is far from 'safe', so it is interesting to reflect on what attracted him to writing for radio, especially given that these twenty-nine plays amount to a very substantial body of work. In the 1970s Barnes had undertaken several major adaptations for BBC Radio 3. As can be seen in the complete list of these adaptations, which appears in full in the bibliography, these included versions of Early Modern plays by Jonson, Marston, Middleton and a compilation of work by Brecht and Wedekind. Barnes was well known to BBC producers and his work for radio was much admired. It is worth noting that at that time the BBC allowed its producers a great deal more freedom, particularly on radio, than they enjoy now. He was asked if he wanted to write a play of his own for radio. His own account of his decision to explore the monologue format was that he 'wanted to prove something to myself'.[1] It had been three years since the production of *Laughter!*, and although he had completed *Red Noses*, no theatrical management was willing to take a risk on it.[2] It must have seemed at that time that *Laughter!* had made him into something of a *persona non grata* in the English theatre. The large casts of his major work for theatre also create considerable financial problems for theatre

management, and I suspect that in writing a series of monologues he was not the only person to whom he wanted to prove
things.

One of the characteristics of these series of plays ('miniatures',
as Barnes calls them)[3] is their remarkable casting. The first series
featured performances by some of the best-known and highly
regarded actors in British theatre, including Alec Guinness, Leo
McKern, Peggy Ashcroft, John Gielgud and Judi Dench. The
casts for the subsequent series read like a *Who's Who* of British
theatre, and included Peter Ustinov, Joan Plowright, Paul
Scofield, Harry Andrews, Trevor Howard, Ian McKellen, Sean
Connery and John Hurt. Barnes speaks almost self-deprecatingly
of the success of the first series, anecdotally suggesting that the
stellar cast came on board once Alec Guinness had agreed to take
part. While there may always be an element of fortune and fashion in the success, or failure, of any drama, and there is no doubt
that with relatively unknown actors in the roles the first series
might not have led to the three that followed, this undervalues
the quality of the monologues, their innovative use of the
medium and their significance in Barnes' own work.

The radio plays share with the stage plays a powerful, rich use
of language, dense visual imagery and a willingness to engage in
major themes. In particular, many of them are dramatically structured around tensions between the materialist and the metaphysical. The characters are distinctive, idiosyncratic, on the
edges of society. And, as befits radio, they are more personal and
more focused on the individual than the major stage plays.

Dukore has observed that 'Surprisingly, the vociferous anti-
naturalist Barnes employs the medium of radio in a realistic
manner. Motivating each of the monologues, he provides legiti-
mate reasons for his people to speak aloud' (1981, p. 146). Alan
Bennett's *Talking Heads* series of monologues for television,

which the *Barnes 'People* series preceded by six years,[4] and with which it invites some comparison, may reasonably be described as naturalistic, but I would argue that Barnes' series defies naturalism. The characters may be 'motivated' to talk to us, but this does not on its own make for naturalism. Barnes makes no attempt to create an illusion of reality; the use of language is self-consciously rich, laden with metaphors and puns; few of the monologues are set in domestic spaces, and where they are there is very little sense of domesticity. The 'motivation' that Dukore writes of is more of a metatheatrical device than a naturalist building block to a rounded character. What is significant about the 'motive' for each of the monologues is that it problematises the audience's position in relation to what it hears. I use the word 'metatheatrical' here in a loose sense, in that the monologues draw attention to their own artifice, consciously exploiting the intensely private relationship that exists between radio and the listener.

In the *Barnes' People* monologues, all of the characters are actors in their own dramas, in that they constantly perform versions of themselves. And the sense of confidentiality between character and listener invites us to question *who* we are, what role we are playing as we listen to this person who is talking directly to us. The Alec Guinness monologue, *Confessions of a Primary Terrestrial Mental Receiver and Communicator: Num III Mark I*, begins: 'You don't know. How could you know?' and ends with the same words. Maybe, as Dukore suggests, Lilly (the speaker) is talking to himself and 'we' are a fly on the wall; but the flies in Barnes' drama tend to be hovering over corpses, not listening in on bizarre monologues and dialogues for purposes of self-edification. In *The End of the World – And After* William Miller addresses himself to the Lord.[5] Are we eavesdropping on the prayer, or is the prayer to us? Anna, the 113-year-old narrator of *Yesterday's News,* addresses herself to a young man who is tape-recording an interview with her in advance of her forth-coming visit from the queen.[6] She boasts of her amoral past, her years as a prostitute, as 'the most notorious madame in London' (p. 450), and proudly talks of living every moment of her 113 years for herself alone: 'I'm still interested in myself. That's what keeps me going' (p. 452). On several occasions she flatters her interviewer – whether this is teasing, an attempted seduction or gentle mockery depends on the delivery of the lines. Finally she gets round to telling her story of the horrible suicide of Mrs Allen, 'a charlady at one of my brothels', who tried to prevent her neighbours from stealing her hat by attaching it to her head with a nail hammered into her skull. But still the young man with the 'lovely hair' remains silent, and Anna's energy begins to drain away: 'The sentences are sounding like a lot of noise now. I'm tired.' She may be 'mean and selfish', but she depends upon an audience; without human interaction, without the shocked response she might have expected, her stories, and indeed her life, become 'Yesterday's news'. She says: 'You've got enough now haven't you? Prostitution, white slavery, drugs, abortion, murder, blackmail . . . it's about as wicked as smoking a cigarette, as interesting as watching celery grow. Yesterday's news' (p. 452). The monologue has cast us as the attractive young man, has written our silence into the very fabric of the drama.

Barnes argues that the duologues, *Barnes' People II,* are 'darker than the first' (1984, p. v), claiming that each of the monologues in the first series 'turned out to be victories of one kind or another' (p. iv). Certainly the second series of plays is dark, and one of them, *Worms,* discussed below, is frighteningly bleak. I want to qualify his appraisal of the first series, however, by noting that each of the 'victories' is, at the least, double-edged. They may champion a spirit of resistance, and celebrate a certain indomitability, but there is a wry ambiguity about the resolution of each. The duologues, and the three-handers in *Barnes' People III*, are wide-ranging in their subject matter, though all of them are in some way concerned with presentation and performance, 'truth' and lying. *Moondog Rogan and the Mighty Hamster* (Betty and Carol) are female wrestlers.[7] As they rehearse their forthcoming wrestling bout they muse on the nature of wrestling as a performance art: 'We should've applied for an Arts Council Grant long ago. It's real Community Theatre' (p. 12). Their dialogue is punctuated by grunts and thuds, gasps and squeaks; the 'stage' directions for the play read as visually as if it had been written for television or the theatre: 'She grunts as Betty places her hand in the shape of a claw over her face and forces her down' (p. 10). Carol (the Mighty Hamster) bemoans the fact that their fights are always fixed; Betty (Moondog) is more pragmatic: 'If you did it for real they'd think it was fixed . . . Wrestling used to be one of the arts of war . . . now it's one of the arts of show-biz . . . That's progress' (pp. 13–14). The sentiment that 'reality' and 'truthfulness' are separate concepts pervades much of Barnes' work. In his aphoristic introductions he presents the issue in simple (and sometimes self-consciously simplistic) terms; but these aphorisms are liberally interwoven with jokes that undercut the authority of the authorial voice. Similarly, the form of *Moondog and the Mighty Hamster* complicates the discourse. If the wrestlers were simply waiting in their dressing room talking about their forthcoming fight, the debate about the 'reality' of the contest might be engagingly witty, but the presentation of their practice session – with its 'real' sound effects – becomes a performance in itself; and although the characters never draw attention to their own performance outside of the wrestling ring, the play becomes as much of an artifice as the wrestling: we are asked to respond to it in a similar way, to enjoy it, to be engaged by it, and to be aware that it, no less than the wrestling bout it rehearses, is simultaneously 'fake' and 'truthful'.

The Three Visions, the last of the plays in the *Barnes' People III* series, also foregrounds the artifice of radio. The play begins with '*The sound of a door opening*' followed by the sounds of '*a forest fire . . . a cricket match . . . a ship's foghorn*' (1986, p. 101). A character named Peter Barnes is sitting in a sound studio in Broadcasting House playing with sound effects.[8] He is interrupted by the sound of a door opening, and a young man enters, soon revealed to be another Peter Barnes, the 31-year-old playwright. This young Peter Barnes and the 55-year-old, who had been musing about the way a listener makes meaning out of sound effects, try to find a rational explanation for what is happening. They agree that one of them is inhabiting the other's dream. 'Will we ever wake from it? . . . One of us will' (p. 104). Just as they seem to have come to terms with this, an 'old man' comes in. He too is Peter Barnes – at the age of 74. Although the play refers to specific personal incidents and achievements (the 55-year-old is in Broadcasting House to record *The Three Visions*; the younger man has come to record the radio talk show *My Ben Jonson*; and the older man talks about breaking his leg and having a replacement knee when he fell off the stage directing *Bartholomew Fair* at the Round House), the play is not autobiographical. Their conversation turns to ageing, ambition, memory and isolation; the radio studio becomes a liminal space, in which the three Barnes characters play out a variation on *Huis clos*, although there is much less direct antagonism between the characters than there is in Sartre's play. Each one of them, none of them incidentally played by Peter Barnes himself,[9] needs the others to confirm his own identity, yet is isolated from them, as uncertain of himself as he is of them. The play ends as it begins

– with the '*sound of the studio door opening in the darkness*' (p. 112). But, as the opening moments have established, 'It's the liar's world of sound . . . (*The sound of applause.*) A hundred men clapping, or one man overlaid a hundred times' (p. 101). The play's use of sound effects makes our reading of them unreliable. Often, as in the opening, they signify the effect, the recorded sound. Thus, in semiotic terms, the '*horse galloping*' is an iconic signifier, signifying not a horse, but the taped sound effect. Elsewhere, sound is used more expressionistically: 'Don't keep quoting me,' says the Young Barnes. 'It's depressing'. We hear '*The sound of a single heartbeat*'. And, on occasions, as when the Young and the Old Barnes arrive, we are to read the sound of the studio door opening as itself rather than an effect. This confusion, begging the question whether any sound on radio can ever be iconic rather than indexical, is never resolved, leaving us with a metatheatrical conundrum about what is real, what is a dream, what is artifice, what *is*?

The playful use of form in the two plays discussed above is a manifestation of a consistent concern throughout Barnes' work: to activate the audience. I use the word 'metatheatricality' advisedly in connection with these plays for radio (and those for television discussed below). Their self-conscious reflexivity draws our attention to three things: the particular formal qualities of the specific medium; the theatrical relationships between performer and spectator/listener; and issues around the nature of performance and self-dramatisation. As listeners, we are constantly being asked to reassess our own relationship with what we are hearing – whether it is in the light-hearted metaphysical terms of *Three Visions* or the much more uneasy shifts of judgement that we are asked to make as we listen to *After the Funeral*.

When *After the Funeral* opens we find ourselves in the company of three men, Harry, Tom and Max,[10] who are mourning the death of Anna – Harry's wife? Or lover? Harry rambles, and his friends console him:

> HARRY   Too late for words, too late for tears . . . What am I going to do now? . . . I come back home and the house is empty; she's not here and the days are blank. Fifteen years together . . .
>
> TOM   You'd better have another drink, these're bad times for you, Harry . . . I can tell you, Anna was the best . . .
>
> MAX   She was like a mother to my three girls . . .
>
> (p. 3)

We seem to be in familiar territory. Gradually, however, we become suspicious of this comfortable reassurance. We are taken into their world, only for it to be revealed as brutally violent and exploitative. The three men are pimps, and Anna was 'the best' of Harry's prostitutes, 'the Queen of the East Acton Red Light District' (p. 5); 'like a mother' not to Max's daughters, but to his own 'stable' of working girls. They talk about their 'flatbackers' with callous indifference; and when Harry tells his story of how he first met Anna in a brothel in Casablanca, he proudly boasts, with a hint of nostalgia, how he dealt with 'Little Mama' the madame: 'She wasn't going to let her best worker go just like that . . . so I shot off her left kneecap. I was younger then . . . Anna and me left hand in hand . . . What started in blood ended in roses . . . Memories, memories' (p. 7). They tell jokes and stories; they discuss how difficult it is going to be to find a replacement for Anna. In short, they are a model of political incorrectness. One might expect Barnes to allow them to redeem themselves as a final twist, but he refuses that. The only concession in that direction is Harry's insistence that

Because Anna isn't earning any more doesn't mean she has no meaning for me. She does; she does . . . Gentlemen, there's no question, like her, I shall be sleeping alone tonight. It's a matter of honour – for my love's sake . . . You can ring Rita first thing tomorrow, Max. I'm sure it's what Anna would've wanted.'

(pp. 10–11)

They may not redeem themselves in any normal sense, but there is an energy and a warmth between them which, while not making them sympathetic characters, does temper any rush to judgement. They are also curiously vulnerable, and their endless storytelling and banter only serve to underline the desolate isolation between them. In his introduction to this volume, Barnes writes: 'The great sin is the complete lack of compassionate vision, the inability to conceive of life existing on any other level than our own limited experience of it' (p. ix). The play takes us on a journey, drawing us in to this alien world, shocking us with its representation of the attitudes of the three men, and then challenging our judgement of them. The method of positioning and repositioning an audience may bear some resemblance to that of naturalism (as we find out more about Ibsen's characters, for example, their behaviour is revealed as determined by the complex interaction of personal history and socio-political environment and, as a result, our response to those characters might be expected to change), but this is not naturalism. We are not encouraged to perceive the characters' actions as being environmentally determined. They support each other by telling jokes and stories to justify themselves, not to explain how they come to be the way they are, but to normalise their behaviour. In this respect, the play is driven by the satirical impulse that nourishes the early stage plays:[11] throughout the play they equate their work with business, with the workings of capitalism. *Silver*

Bridges[12] is full-blown satire, as Barnes describes it, 'a comedy about that perfect symbol of red-meat capitalism, the blood-stained clapped-out Erie Railroad and the monsters who manipulated it' (p. v). Elsewhere, however, the radio plays are not primarily satirical. What they do share in common is a poignant sense of the characters' isolation. This is not, perhaps, surprising in the monologues; it is even more evident in the two- and three-handers. *After the Funeral* is certainly a dark play, in which brutality and abuse are spoken of casually, but it is also a play which examines modes of communication. The three men allow each other space for their own stories; they take consolation from each other. They may speak in what are effectively intersecting monologues, but they are not competitive in the sense that their personal anecdotes do not attempt to dismiss or cap the others' stories.

There is little such optimism in *Worms*, one of the two-handers in *Barnes' People II*. Mary visits a priest to make her confession.[13] Mary is a desperately lonely woman, a homeless bag lady, whose husband left her when her son (Jimmy) was born, who was himself then killed in a car crash (three years before the events of the play). It is only two days since she last came to confession, and yet, when the Priest asks 'What are your sins?' her immediate response is: 'Pride, envy, covetousness, lust, sloth and anger.' What she needs, even more than the temporary physical shelter of the church, is friendship and an attentive listener: somebody to give her the companionship and solace that the three men in *After the Funeral* manage to give to each other. She constructs sins for herself, chastising herself for gluttony, for example, because she wanted two bowls of soup and a plate of chips; and lust, because she 'kipped down in a corner and dreamed of Frank' (p. 27), the husband who abandoned her. The Priest does not respond to what she says; he asks only the most routine of questions: 'What are your sins?' (p. 26), 'Are there any sins in your past life' (p. 27), 'You still believe and do not doubt?' (p. 28). He returns several times to the issue of doubt, but pays very little attention to what she actually says. He dismisses out of hand her brief foray into politics:

> **MARY** He [her son, Jimmy] said that Christians hid behind the clasped hands of their lives and that for two thousand years had worshipped the Cross and made the working class carry it.
> **PRIEST** I have heard that. It is of no consequence.
>
> (p. 28)

She is troubled by Jimmy's atheism, but he pays little attention to this either – until she mentions, in passing, that Jimmy once said that the earth is 'made out of mouldy cheese'. And suddenly the Priest is alert – though not to her. For Mary, Jimmy talking about the Earth being made of mouldy cheese 'was just his fun way of speaking . . . He was working for the Milk Marketing Board at the time, so it was sort of natural' (p. 30). For the Priest this creates an opportunity for him to launch into a sermon about Menocchio's heresy:[14] 'Menocchio believed that in the beginning it was all chaos, that the earth, air, fire and water were all mixed together and out of this mixture, a mass was formed like cheese is formed out of milk.' So insensitive is he to Mary's state (of mind and body) that he says: 'I must speak with your son', before correcting himself and remembering that 'you said he was dead, didn't you' (p. 30).

The only points of contact for Mary and the Priest are this image of cheese and the isolation that each feels, but that he does not allow her to share. And it transpires that his obsession with her doubt is a transference of his own disbelief: 'What if all that's up there to pray to, swaying in the cold winds of space, is a great blind worm?' (p. 31). The priest's obsession with 'certain minor Christian heresies' has a kind of fascination in itself, but in this instance it is destructive, and indicates his failure both to understand and to play his role as a confessor. Indeed, he effectively reverses their roles, expecting Mary to become the healing listener as he expounds his heretical scepticism. This bleak contemporary analysis of the Priest's exploitation of Mary parallels the view of the Church as separate from the people it purports to guide and support that recurs throughout Barnes' work. The Priest uses Mary's misery as an opportunity to indulge his own obsessions and doubts.

The last of the duologues in the *Barnes' People II* series goes under the curious title *Lament for Armenians and Grey Viruses*.[15] In his introduction to the series, Barnes wrote:

> The most interesting play from the writing point of view, if not from the audience's, is *Lament*. I had read somewhere a remark of Flaubert's to the effect that he wished to write a novel about nothing . . . I wondered if it were possible to write a play about nothing . . . I quickly found, however, the task I had set myself was impossible. There was no such thing as nothing. The more I eliminated meaning and significance, the more meaningful and significant it became. I tried not to tell a story but one emerged.[16]
>
> (p. v)

The story that emerges is one of two drunken old beggars rambling around their life stories, each believing they are bedevilled: Joseph blaming his failures and inadequacies on grey viruses and John on Armenians. 'I could've been one of the richest men of this century,' boasts Joseph (p. 52); and for John:

'Armenians . . . never let up. They're with you to the end and then some.' Their monologues intersect; they do not argue – their stories do not even compete – but they do gain some consolation and companionship from each other. Barnes' account of his method of writing this piece closely parallels the way in which the play allows the two men's stories themselves to begin to emerge. It is difficult to make sense of the opening lines of the play: 'Asthma and wet dreams're brought on by cockroaches with leaky feet. My Aunt Sophie got dropsy from wearing tight shoes in a hot kitchen, so I know' (p. 50). It resembles a sketch by Peter Cook as much as it does an absurdist drama.[17] But if Barnes was genuinely trying to 'write a play about nothing', it seems that with this play he lacked the courage of his convictions. The incoherence of their rambling is contextualised as soon as we hear that Joseph (the first speaker) blames 'the drink' as much as he does the 'Grey Viruses'. Later he regrets that 'Drink's been my curse'; and John mournfully hopes that 'someone, someday, listens to our drunken jimjams.' (pp. 57–8). The two men's drinking habits become a dominant signifier, precisely because it 'makes sense' of their incoherence. Certainly, one might speculate about the 'meaning' of grey viruses and Armenians as metaphors; I do not propose to do that here. I am more interested in how the play relates to the body of Barnes' work. I do not wish to take issue with what Barnes intended with the play, for that risks repeating arguments about the authority of the author which I examine elsewhere in this volume.[18] In terms of this play, however, what Barnes articulates as a desire to 'eliminate meaning' might better be expressed as a desire to make the listeners (audience or readers) not merely active, but conscious of their own active role in reading the drama. *Lament for Armenians and Grey Viruses* . . . is indicative of Barnes' relentless desire to experiment. The stage play *Luna Park Eclipses*, discussed in Chapter 9[19]clearly relates closely to *Lament* and pursues this interest in developing texts that are increasingly open to interpretation. If I have given the impression that *Lament* is a cold technical exercise, then I have not done it justice.

As some kind of thread, if not actually coherence, emerges from the stories told by the 'two old, louse-ridden beggars, half-mad, dead-drunk and sitting in a pile of rubbish' (p. 56), the play creates an extraordinary sense of desolation; and yet, rising up out of that desolation, there is optimism. The two men's fantasies about saving the world may be pathetic, but their plea to be listened to is profoundly moving; and it is characteristic of Barnes' best work that form and content are so closely integrated. 'Don't turn away. We're confessing ourselves,' says John in the final moments of the play. 'When a man or woman confesses it doesn't matter how they confess or when or why, truth or lies. Someone should always listen . . . They'll find out such things. Without us confessing, how would anyone ever know about Armenians and grey viruses?' (p. 57). It is we, the listeners, the readers, the audience, who should listen; and 'listening' demands much more of us than stopping whatever we might be doing: it demands that we create meaning, that we make sense of other people's grey viruses.

The Television Plays

Barnes' television work can be divided into the plays (and an adaptation) he has written for British television and the miniseries he has written and/or collaborated on for American companies, such as *Merlin* (1998), *Alice in Wonderland* (1999), *Noah's Ark* (1999), *A Christmas Carol* (1999) and *Arabian Nights* (2000). These American miniseries, for Hallmark and

NBC, are a relatively recent development, involving very large budgets, advanced computer graphics and very starry casts. With the exception of *Merlin* and *Alice*, this material has not been seen in Britain at the time of writing, although, at least in terms of audience figures, it has been extremely successful in America. Although Barnes himself insists that the scripts are 'craft work', something of his spirited anarchism survives the complex process of corporate production, not only in the scripting, but also in the casting: in the *Alice* adaptation, for example, Ken Dodd plays Mouse, with Robbie Coltrane and Gene Wilder as Tweedledum and Tweedledee and Whoopi Goldberg as the Cheshire Cat. His writing for British TV is far closer to his work for radio and the stage; it is that work that I shall focus on here.

The short radio plays and monologues have much in common with three plays he wrote for British television, all of them broadcast in 1989 in what, in retrospect, seems something of a Barnesfest: *Revolutionary Witness*[20] was commissioned and broadcast by BBC TV in July 1989 as part of a season to mark the two-hundredth anniversary of the French Revolution; *The Spirit of Man*[21] was broadcast by BBC TV in August 1989, a delightfully witty trilogy of short 'history plays' in which fundamentalist certainties are defied and ridiculed, and has also been performed as a stage play. *Nobody Here But Us Chickens* (broadcast by Channel 4 in September 1989) had originally been written for the stage, and is again a trilogy of three short plays. Each focuses on an aspect of disability and, unusually for Barnes, is set in the present day. He directed both these trilogies himself, the latter receiving the Royal Television Society Award for the Best Drama of 1989. These television plays may eschew the large casts demanded by his major stage plays, but they share with them an epic quality.

REVOLUTIONARY WITNESS
'What is to be done?'

The four characters who appear in *Revolutionary Witness* (the Butcher, the Patriot, the Preacher and the Amazon) all tell their own story in turn about the Revolution, their part in it, and the effect it has had on them. In an author's note to the 1989 edition of the play,[22] Barnes wrote: 'These monologues – the four seasons of revolution, Spring, Summer, Autumn, Winter – are studies in the way ordinary–extraordinary people make sense of the world and try to change it. They are not studies of typical revolutionaries for I do not believe there is such a thing as a typical revolutionary or a typical reactionary bourgeois for that matter' (p. 2). Although set very specifically in the aftermath of the French Revolution, and based on the stories of historical characters, the play explores privilege and injustice in our contemporary world. I use the singular 'play' advisedly, for there is a far stronger relationship between each of the quartet of monologues than shared setting and thematic commonality. Indeed, there is something almost Chekhovian in the play's allusion to the passing of time;[23] although each monologue can be read independently of the others (the monologues were broadcast sequentially, one per night, over four weekdays), each benefits greatly from its relation with the others, the whole creating something far richer than the sum of the parts.

In *The Patriot*, Patriot Palloy, as he refers to himself, having assumed the name 'Patriot' as his own, is 'selling the Revolution to the world' (p. 161), but his celebration of the Revolution is not some romantic rose-tinted socialism. He has benefited greatly by the Revolution, but not in the way one might expect. The play opens with an image of Palloy standing in front of '*a skeleton, balls and chains, and a set of manacles. All have price tags . . . Elegantly displayed amongst the stones are various expensive gift-cases containing medals, pieces of wood and model replicas of the Bastille. All are priced.*' Although it seems that he is selling relics – 'Why should the old religion have the monopoly of holy relics?' (p. 159) – he is also proselytising for a new 'aristocracy of trade' (p. 160), 'selling the Revolution to the World' (p. 161). He has appropriated the Revolution to his own ends. His 'dream is to build a Monument to the Glory of Liberty' on the site of the Bastille; already he has acquired the sole rights to dismantle it (p. 166). Palloy, however, is a highly unreliable narrator. As his monologue develops, his self-aggrandising hyperbole begins to cast doubts on whether he took any part in the Revolution itself. Although he tells vivid stories of his own participation – 'Volley after volley cut us down. Suddenly there was blood and death all around but we didn't flee or turn tail' (p. 165) – his stories are no less cynical an exploitation of the Revolution than his merchandising of its relics and his ruthless abuse of his own daughter to 'defend' him when he is accused of looting from the Tuileries and 'clapped in prison': 'She was seventeen, wild as a fawn, sweet as maple syrup, as beautiful in the face as any angel could be . . . That bright figure of a girl . . . won all hearts to the truth' (p. 163). As a fully paid-up member of the libertarian right, he is a very modern 'revolutionary'.

His conflation of entrepreneurial verve, self-deception, religious iconography and spiritual liberation is a vigorous example of the way in which an emerging idealism attracts virulent parasites. If this is the 'Spring' of the Revolution, then it is already germinating the seeds of its own corruption. Barnes' characterisation of Palloy's opportunistic exploitation of the Revolution was remarkably prescient. In July 1989, when the play was broadcast in its four parts, Hungary had only recently begun dismantling the barbed wire and minefields on its border with Austria; and it was not until November of that year that the

1. David Neal as Dr Herder, Derek Godfrey as Jack
in *The Ruling Class*, Nottingham, 1968.

2. Rosemary McHale as Queen Ana and Alan Howerd as Carlos in *The Bewitched*, an RSC production, London, 1974.

3. Timothy West as Ivan in the Royal Court
production of *Laughter!*, London, 1978.

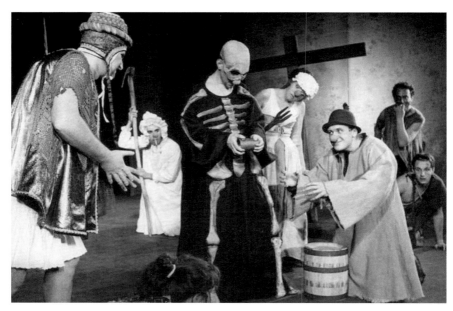

4. and 4a. From a 1994 production of *Red Noses*
(*Czerwone Nosy*) at the Teatr Ludowy, Kraków, Poland.

5. From a production of *Dreaming* at the Queen's Theatre, London, 1999. Christ (Luke Williams) comes down from the cross to talk to Sarah (Kate Isitt).

6. A break from the recording of *After the Funeral*, from the series of radio plays *Barnes People III*, 1986. Front row (left to right): John Hurt, Sean Connery, Donald Pleasance. Back row: members of the production team and Peter Barnes (right).

7. Joan Plowright (Mary) and Paul Scofield (the Priest) preparing for the recording of *Worms* from the series of radio plays *Barnes People II*, 1984.

8. Harriet Walter as Queen Isabella in *Bye Bye Columbus*, a Greenpoint production for BBC Television, 1992.

9. (Left to right) Nicholas Farrell as Hills, David Suchet as Carver, Michael Maloney as Powell in *More Than A Touch of Zen*, Channel 4, London, 1989.

10. The many faces of Peter Barnes.

Berlin Wall was taken down. The mood in those countries under Soviet domination was understandably optimistic. At the time when the play was written and broadcast, although Palloy's descendants were undoubtedly salivating at the prospects of the rich pickings in the free market to come, the 'Russian Mafia' had hardly been heard of outside the Soviet Union.

In spite of its title, *The Butcher* is far more optimistic, though it would be uncharacteristic of Barnes if there were not a sting in the tail. The monologue takes the form of an address by Robert Sauveur to the National Assembly. The address is effectively in two parts: in the first he offers an account of his own moral and emotional development; in the second he pleads to the National Assembly for the Revolution to acknowledge its responsibility for its citizens.

His personal story is a journey of transformation. He never knew his mother, and his father 'was spared old age'; he started butchering at the age of thirteen, 'killed two men by accident . . . and three in brawls but they hardly counted' (p. 168). By his own account he was addicted to excessive drinking, stealing, whoring – until he won a woman in a card game, who stayed with him for six months and then went missing. 'She was hooked out of the Seine a week later. I found her one morning, hung up by her feet along the riverbank with the others' (p. 169). From this point on he gradually transforms himself – a transformation that is catalysed by personal grief but made possible by the changing social circumstances of the Revolution. As Sauveur says: 'To make a man moral you have to make the world he lives in moral too' (p. 172). Although the monologue echoes the struggle for optimism that we have seen in *Red Noses*, and drama-tises potentialities for personal change and social change, it is clear that the one is not possible without the other.

The change in Sauveur is essentially that he becomes responsible for his own actions: 'I had to . . . make myself worthy of the Revolution which remade me' (p. 171). Unlike Palloy, there is never any doubt that Sauveur took a very active part in the Revolution. The culmination of his personal story is the storming of the Bastille, where 'we lost one hundred and fifty good men and women, the defendants only seven . . . We'd won a great victory. But nothing comes free. Winners suffer as well as losers' (pp. 173–4). As a participant and a beneficiary of the Revolution, he now sees it as his responsibility to ensure that the Revolution stays on track: 'I'm here to speak for the winners' (p. 174). But the 'winners' are suffering. His reason for coming to the National Assembly, for telling his own personal story, is to persuade the delegates to pay compensation to the widows of those who died, to help the maimed who 'will probably die from their wounds . . . Crippled they can't work' (p. 174). He has become a highly principled man, a man whose understanding of 'common justice' has been wrought through hardship, whose moral purpose is based on a simple socialism: 'we must cleanse [our old but beautiful world] . . . of all evil, violence and oppression . . . It'll be a long journey to that new world. We must pick up those who fall on the way and carry them with us . . . So, let us honour our debts' (pp. 174–5). His urgent sense of social justice contrasts strongly with Palloy's self-serving claim on patriotism. And the structural correspondence between the two monologues enriches each. Whereas Sauveur tells us, almost in passing, that he has become known as 'Robert the Virtuous Butcher' because of his actions – 'If you can't be good, act it because if you act something you are it' (p. 172) – Palloy seizes his 'Patriot' moniker as part of a sales pitch. For him patriotism is a tag, an advertising slogan; for Sauveur it is the antithesis of the problematic axiom 'my country right or wrong'. He sees that loving the Revolution, and loving his country, carries obligations. His sense of his own accountability demands that he cannot use patriotism as a cover for complicity with a regime that is beginning to betray its own ideals.

The third of the monologues, *The Preacher*, again opens with powerful images – this time of bloody struggle, of religion as an agent of violent change:

> *A priest,* **Jacques Roux,** *in a cassock with a dagger stuck in his belt, speaks from a battered pulpit. Behind him, a broken stained-glass window of an angel with a flaming sword.*

(p. 177)

Jacques Roux's personal account of the Revolution is again vivid and rich in detail; as a self-contained play, however, the monologue is less complex than the other three. Roux's monologue takes the form of a sermon, given from a '*battered pulpit*' on the day before he has to answer to 'the tribunal . . . charged with revolutionary excess' (p. 178). He is proud that he 'renounced [his] alliance to Rome and gave it to France' (p. 179). But although he 'became a constitutional priest, put off the mitred robes of privilege and put on the white robes of Liberty' he has become a fundamentalist zealot, totally convinced of his own righteousness. His journey from church cleric to violent revolutionary leads him to believe that violence is 'the only way to end the greater violence that keeps the majority of mankind in servitude'. This very certainty, the refusal of doubt and the wholehearted espousal of violence, becomes deeply troubling – especially when set against the other monologues of *The Patriot*, *The Butcher* and *The Amazon*. For, although Roux denounces authority in all its forms – the Church, the monarchy and even the revolutionary tribunal – his intense conviction itself assumes authority over anyone who would disagree with him. But this is the 'Autumn' of the Revolution, and in setting before us his personal history and asserting his ideological convictions, Roux paints a picture of a Revolution that is losing its way. The monologue is haunted by imagery from the earlier monologues; the poor are starving and hardship is not being shared: 'We were dying because of filthy bourgeois graft and greed' (p. 182). Sauveur's idealism has lost out to Palloy's self-interest, and there is no need to spell out to us the horrors that this implies because Palloy and Sauveur have done just that. The Preacher leaves turbulence in his wake because his diagnosis of social injustice is as accurate as his solutions are terrifying: 'The Revolution isn't complete, hardly begun. Defend it . . . Without action no life . . . Without perfection no eternal peace and freedom' (p. 184).

The final monologue, Act Four, is entitled *The Amazon*. Théroigne de Méricourt *'sits on a wooden chair in the centre of a bare cell in Salpêtrière Asylum'* (p. 187). What is at stake here is Théroigne's identity and, metonymically, the identity of the Revolution itself. The monologue begins with the repetition of the revolutionary slogan 'Liberty, Equality, Fraternity, Liberty, Equality, Fraternity, Liberty, Equality, Fraternity', but 'the words die, rot, or go mad like me, curtains drawn across my face'. Palloy, Sauveur and Roux tell their stories to an audience: Palloy sells his 'relics' (that are either faked or thieved) and the slogans from which he has stolen all meaning; Sauveur pleads with the National Assembly to honour the spirit of the Revolution that he fears is in danger of breaking faith with those who sacrificed everything for it; and in defending himself against charges of revolutionary excess Roux exhorts his audience to continue the violent struggle. Théroigne's audience is herself. She looks in a hand mirror, but there is no glass in the frame. Her only sense of how she looks is through memory, her only sense of self through story:

Repeat and repeat the story else you'll lose all sense of who you
are and what you've done and your life will drift away down and
you'll become mad. So repeat and repeat though there are only
flickering ghosts who listen out there.

(p. 188)

The inversion that turns us, the television audience, into 'flickering ghosts' may be a wry metatheatrical conceit, but it also
reminds us that our own memory of radicalism and idealism may
be 'flickering'. The story that she tells asserts both her own identity and the changing identity of the Revolution itself.

Born of 'peasant stock', admired for her beauty, Théroigne
rapidly rises through society. Her first love is an Englishman
who 'wanted to give me everything . . . but his family objected
and he obeyed' (p. 187). She tells of many lovers – 'I think I
even had the Prince of Wales', and then a French Marquis. She
becomes a high-class, and very expensive, courtesan; and she
imagines that if she had 'continued in the way of business I
would've ended my days in a chateau in Salpêtrière, not a mouldering asylum' (p. 189). But she prefers 'new errors to old
certainties and is 'burnt to a cinder, first for money and men'.
She does not dwell on her fall: 'I like men but I don't esteem
them. I've been betrayed too often' (p. 189). And then, as the
Bastille falls, she finds herself 'illuminated by visions, ideas,
insurrections . . . consumed by revolutionary fever' (pp. 189–90).
Inspired by the Revolution, she takes up the cause of women:
'since men and women are alone they must help each other and
so break out of solitude' (p. 192). But her proto-feminism
inspires debate but not action:

So they considered and considered and considered and declared,
though a woman had a soul and intelligence which could be used

147

for the good of the state, they couldn't give her a vote. And these, friends, remember, were the best of times . . .

(p. 192)

And the worst of times are yet to come: after her unsuccessful campaign to get women enfranchised, she begins to incur the wrath of Robespierre and his 'harpies attacking anyone they thought was against their leader' (pp. 193–4). Her brother has her committed to the asylum 'to save [her] from Robespierre's wrath'. Fittingly, given that her story is an attempt to confirm her sense of self, to convince herself that she is not mad, it returns to the asylum, where she is 'walled up by the law and by language, walled up alive, a relic of the Revolution, mad in a world where the sane have learned to sneer at words like "brotherly love"' (p. 194). For Théroigne, the failure of the Revolution is the failure to achieve fraternity; all her exertions to have been thought of fraternally by those she perceives as equals. Her regret echoes Sauveur's – the two of them unwitting allies – and the structure of the play, their monologues the second and fourth respectively, draws attention both to the similarities between them and to the very different social and political circumstances in which they find themselves; each of them revelling in the personal journey they have made from egotistical amorality to social awareness; each of them profoundly affected by the possibilities of social change. As Théroigne expresses it:

In ordinary times we don't think the world can be any different from the way it is or ever will be world without end. But at certain moments in our lives when it falls to pieces . . .

(p. 190)

For Théroigne, 'The Revolution's crushed, trampled underfoot and the good seed lies buried with me' (p. 195). In spite of

148

this she remains positive, or, at least, she asserts an optimism that the situation seems not to justify: 'But one day green shoots will thrust to the sun'. This is double-edged, however. Her determination to assert her optimism ends with the chant 'Liberty, Equality, Fraternity! Liberty, Equality, Fraternity! Liberty, Equality, Fraternity! . . .' (p. 195). And the chanting of the slogan is exactly where we came in. Is she condemned to voice this as an endless loop, glimpsed only occasionally by 'flickering ghosts'? Has the slogan itself already been discredited by Palloy's opportunistic business enterprise? After all, Palloy's dream is to 'build a Monument to the Glory of Liberty' (p. 166) on the site of the Bastille: a monument which sounds more like an out-of-town shopping mall than a memorial to the spirit of the Revolution: 'There'll be . . . shops, gardens . . . fountains . . . The Street of Victory, the Street of Legality, the Streets of Equality, Abundance and Renewal' (p. 166). Notable for its absence in Palloy's *A to Z* of post-revolutionary Paris is the Street of Fraternity. The connections with Palloy are reinforced by Théroigne's description of herself as a 'relic of the Revolution' (p. 194); earlier Palloy has described himself as 'the exclusive purveyor of authentic souvenirs of the Revolution' (p. 159). For Palloy, the Revolution comprises nothing more than relics, souvenirs and slogans: commodities to be sold for individual profit. But if Théroigne is reduced to chanting the watchwords of the Revolution, whose meaning Palloy has so debased, she has an ally in Sauveur, who insists that the Revolution must 'honour its debts' to those who fought for it. Sauveur's Revolution, however, is in the 'Summer' of the Revolution, and it has not yet been sullied by infighting, by Robespierre's determination to destroy his 'internal' enemies, rather than 'the enemies outside' (p. 193).

These final moments of the play, however, refuse the resolution and closure that Robespierre's suppression of dissent might imply. If, in Palloy's terms, Théroigne and (by implication) Sauveur have become old stock, abandoned commodities past their sell-by date, it is important to recognise that Théroigne has the last words. She may be 'walled up by the law and by language' (and this act of the play makes it very clear that both law and language are inflexibly patriarchal), but she has survived, and her spirit of resistance remains indomitable. She is both constrained by language and empowered by it, for her repetition of her story is itself an act of defiance against patriarchy. 'We uttered one word and altered the rhythm of existence,' she proudly boasts. 'We gave [the word "Revolution"] new meaning, we gave everything new meaning' (p. 190). She may be limited by language, but she is also an agent of its change.

Barnes is sometimes accused of writing history plays because he is unwilling to tackle contemporary issues. *Revolutionary Witness* gives the lie to this. It may be nominally set in post-Revolutionary France, but, reading it in the early twenty-first century, it seems remarkably, and specifically, prescient. When Théroigne bemoans the scorn that is heaped upon the notion of 'brotherly love', one is put in mind of the way in which the term 'socialism' has been expunged (at least in the short term) from contemporary public debate since the collapse of the Soviet Union. And yet the play was written and produced before anyone had forecast the 'changes' in Eastern Europe. Although *Revolutionary Witness* has never been performed as a stage play, it cries out for an imaginatively staged theatrical production that would allow the four monologues to be read as acts of a single play. It is certainly one of Barnes' finest plays, and deserves to be seen in a production which would not only allow but also encourage an audience to read the complex interactions between the four monologues.

THE SPIRIT OF MAN

A Hand Witch of the Second Stage
'Tested and purged in the fires of faith'

Like *Revolutionary Witness*, *The Spirit of Man* comprises a group of short plays, in this instance a trilogy, which stand alone, but which accumulate meaning when read in active relationship to each other. The first of these, *A Hand Witch of the Second Stage*, returns to the torture chambers that we have seen in *The Bewitched* and *Laughter!*, but upends the logic of the witch-hunters by turning the irrational mystification of their oppression against themselves.

The play opens with Marie Blin, accused of witchcraft, '*spread-eagled on a raised rack*', Father Nerval trying to extract a confession from her, Claude Delmas giving evidence against her, while Henri Mondor, the executioner, impatiently waits to get on with the torture. But 'the witch' outwits her persecutors with her nimble improvisatory wit, speed of thought and agile cunning. Realising that if she were to deny being a witch, she would be 'sentenced and crisped in a day' (p. 139),[24] she tricks her persecutors into believing not only that she *is* a witch, but that she really does have satanic powers and that the only way for them to escape her vengeance is to free her. Marie Blin thus uses her persecutors' terrors and anxieties to give them exactly what they think they most want: her guilt. And she then uses that against them in order to gain her freedom. 'The fear that accused me, tried me, condemned me without hope of reprieve was the fear that freed me. So I say: to defeat Authority, use Authority's weapons' (p. 139). She terrorises her accusers by threatening them with an ideology to which they only partly subscribe. When she confesses, they are confused, shocked: 'Do you mean to hang there and tell me you flew on a broomstick . . . through the air . . .

at night? . . . If you were old and toothless, Mistress Blin, I'd say you were brain-blocked, moon-touched and babbling. However, you seem whole-brained and un-mooned' (pp. 129–130). The only weapons Marie Blin has at her disposal are her language and her wits; she can only use these successfully because she feeds her tormentors' bigotry, redirecting their prejudices against themselves, in much the way that a judo expert might throw an opponent by using body weight. The image of the judo exponent who uses their adversary's expectations against them is given more literal form in the television play *More Than a Touch of Zen*, discussed below. In *A Hand Witch of the Second Stage*, Marie Blin's persecutors simultaneously believe and do not believe. They do not understand the nature of their own faith. They tell stories of witches and satanic practices, but when Marie 'confesses', embraces their accusations – 'All real. All true.' (p. 129) – they are sceptical and a little disappointed: they are used to having to torture 'witches' to get confessions out of them. Witches may confess to having satanic powers, but evidently by the time they get into the hands of the witchfinders these powers have withered. Towards the end of the play, Marie sternly rebukes them:

> it's always safer to accuse innocent old crones, the poor, sick and defenceless, of Satanism and sorcery. Do not disturb true believers hidden like scorpions beneath the rocks . . . Take this advice on pain of soul's doom, do not meddle with the Prince, the Demon of Death . . . avoid . . . the Real Thing!
>
> (pp. 138–9)

And they flee in panic. Hitherto they have separated their mechanisms of torture and belief systems. Blin confronts them with the logical inconsistencies and absurdities of their creed by exposing the extent to which it is based on abuse and bullying.

But this is no more a play about medieval witchcraft than Barnes' large-scale theatrical history plays are documentaries. It feeds on an eclectic range of contemporary fiction (on *Witchfinder General*, for example, and on many far less 'respectable' horror films as well as *The Crucible*[25] and *The Devils of Loudon*) to generate its meanings as much as it draws on historical records and research. Marie plays with her tormentors' expectations, and the play toys with ours. As a modern, sophisticated audience, we too are uncertain of our ground when plays or films dramatise evil: we may be familiar with theories of mass hysteria and auto-suggestion, but it is clear from the success of numerous recent horror movies that contemporary audiences respond enthusiastically to the notion of demonic possession; and for the current president of the United States the concept of evil is as tangible as it is for Henri Mondor. Thus, when Marie Blin claims she is using the black arts to bring her one of Mondor's keys, when she squeezes his heart in her hand and he clutches his chest and falls to the floor, when she shows them her own hand covered in blood, we may not believe she is a witch, but I suggest that we are encouraged, however briefly, to believe that within this fictional world the witchfinders have met their match, that this time they have found themselves the real thing! The play twists again in the final moments after Mondor, Delmas and Father Nerval have fled: having invoked the 'Prince of Darkness' as the 'lawful Prince' of this world (p. 131), Marie Blin now offers thanks to 'the Father, Son and Holy Ghost'; and in a short speech, which concludes with a poem, she gives thanks to her Christian God for giving her 'the wit to help myself' (p. 19), and explains how she has used a 'cheap conjurer's trick' and acute powers of observation – 'I knew [Mondor] already had trouble breathing easy/Without my phantom squeezing' (p. 140) – to make them fearful. This speech may masquerade as a prayer of thanks, but it quickly metamorphoses into a direct address to the audience; and in one of Barnes' frequent allusions to Brecht, Marie Blin allies herself with Mother Courage in advising the audience:

> For those about to be broken under the wheel
> Wit, cunning and endurance are more important than heroism
> Though heroism, in small doses, helps too.

(p. 140)

This ending provides an unusual degree of resolution. It denies the openness and the productive ambiguities that characterise much of Barnes' more recent work, and confirms the play as ultimately materialist, perhaps even didactic. In his introduction to the play, Barnes wrote that he 'wanted *The Spirit of Man* to be about faith and language' (p. 122). Although *A Hand Witch of the Second Stage* locates this examination in a specific social context of oppression, the play's dramatic metaphors are more resonant than its conclusion might seem to allow. The witty debunking of the oppressors' catch-22 – where women are damned for being a witch, damned for claiming they're not – is itself all too familiar; but Barnes' treatment (despite the disappointingly determined resolution) can be read allegorically as an indictment of the bullying tactics of contemporary militant Puritanism, where biblical language is cynically manipulated to locate evil in a demonised 'other'. Marie Blin's triumph may not offer much hope to those who find themselves labelled as belonging within an 'axis of evil', but her wit and feisty resistance is celebrated wholeheartedly.

FROM SLEEP AND SHADOW
'The bright light of liberty and love'

From Sleep and Shadow, the second play in the trilogy, is also centrally concerned with relationships between faith and language, although they are examined from a rather different perspective. The play lies in territory that Barnes has made familiar, yet it confounds expectations. Another history play, it is set in 1656, in the last years of the English Commonwealth, the years when the glorious possibilities of the English Revolution are fading into memory, when people are already looking back nostalgically to the time when 'Englishmen turned all things topsy-turvy' and 'people dreamed of infinite liberty' (p. 156). There are clear echoes here of the final two monologues in *Revolutionary Witness*: momentous political events remembered from the point of view of those who seem to have made little impact on history; people whose brush with history seems tangential, yet whose personal stories, as revealed in the play, have been profoundly affected by the possibilities for change to which such times give rise.

As the play begins, Reverend Jonathan Guerdon is mourning the death of his young wife, Abegail, who *'lies on a funeral bier in a wedding dress and veil'*. He pleads to God for forgiveness, believing that her death is a punishment for his sins. The door flies open and Israel Yates enters.[26] Yates and Guerdon had once been 'comrades-in-arms in the glorious Army of the Saints' (p. 145). Now they have come to represent very different attitudes to religion: Guerdon has become 'a simple pastor . . . in Southwark' (p. 143), whereas Yates is now a Ranter,[27] refusing any kind of organised, institutionalised religion and embracing an anarchic, intensely personal relationship with God, 'everyone their own master, answering no authority except the God in their hearts' (p. 145). Guerdon begs Yates to help him heal Abegail, but Yates is a realist: 'I've seen the bright lights in Buckinghamshire[28] and Leicester but I've never seen a miracle' (p. 145); and later: 'Not even the faith that feeds us can raise the dead, if they are truly dead.' (p. 147) It transpires, however, that Abegail is not 'truly dead' but rather in some kind of cataleptic trance, 'Half-dead, in half-shadow' (p. 148). Together they 'pull her back' from her catalepsy. She sits up, only to speak '*in a strangely deep voice*', the voice of Sarah, Guerdon's first wife:

GUERDON   You've brought back the wrong one! . . .

ABEGAIL   Who disturbs my rest?

GUERDON   That's Sarah.

YATES   She has possession then.

GUERDON   Possession of who?

YATES   Sister Abegail.

GUERDON   Abegail is possessed by my first wife?

(pp. 149–50)

Although this exchange is comic, in that it creates an unexpected twist (there has hitherto been no mention of a first wife) that shifts the context, the generic expectations that this raises are themselves confounded. We might expect Guerdon, whose desire for Abegail has been so intense, to be horrified by the sudden reappearance of Sarah; we might expect Sarah to be shrewish. Barnes teases us, exploiting and subverting those expectations. After Abegail's revival, Guerdon and Yates talk with her and with Sarah (through Abegail). We find out that Sarah had welcomed Abegail into their 'home an orphan, raised her as our own daughter' (p. 151). It becomes evident that Abegail is consumed by her own guilt at taking Sarah's place; her possession by Sarah is a means of giving voice to this guilt, of making corporeal her own crisis of identity. As Yates' questioning evinces the true nature of this identity crisis, Abegail's own voice is heard: 'Sarah took me in as her child, gave me her home, made me her family. And I betrayed her love, broke my promise to her and God as Eve did in Eden. I am guilty' (p. 152).

Abegail sees herself as the daughter of Guerdon and Sarah, and simultaneously Guerdon's lover and wife. The second part of the play is surprising because it eschews the conventional comic structure that Sarah's 'appearance' seems to presage: Guerdon's first marriage was loving and mutually supportive, and Sarah was no shrew. Through a combination of reasoned argument and ranting, Yates (with Guerdon's help) convinces her that 'God is tired of guilt in every corner, punishment in every room' (p. 153). And finally, together, they succeed in shaking off her 'melancholy soul-dust' (p. 157). Yates uses the 'spell of quartz' (p. 150) to enable Guerdon to talk with 'Sarah', and the mechanisms of the play – Abegail caught between 'sleep and shadow', her possession by Sarah, Yates calling her back from the dead, Sarah's spirit which 'tore at Abegail's soul' (p. 152) – these are all of the time within which the play is set. Seen in the religious terms of the seventeenth century, Abegail may be 'possessed' by Sarah, but Yates eschews supernatural explanations for what has happened – and we are encouraged to do the same. His 'spell of quartz' is a swinging pendant; any modern audience will recognise this as a form of hypnosis. Guerdon and Abegail are ultimately both absolved of the guilt they feel in relation to Sarah. Yates' ranting is, however, more than a form of hypnotherapy. It is no coincidence that the young wife, Abegail, has a namesake in Arthur Miller's *The Crucible*, who also suffers from what Freud would have called hysteria. Although Barnes' play is a miniature, it too has a strong socio-political dimension. Yates' and Guerdon's attitudes and beliefs are both products of the social upheaval of the English Revolution (in some ways the play can be seen as a companion piece to *Revolutionary*

Witness), and Yates comments directly on the possibilities that the revolution has raised, and that now seem about to be given away:

> What days we have lived through . . . But they are already fading . . . People's great desire now is to say nothing. They see their new won freedom taken from them one by one . . . And we Ranters who cling to the bright light of liberty and love, are obsolete, and worse dangeorus, and must be pulled out by the roots.
>
> (p. 156)

Abegail's guilt is personal and sexual, but all the characters (including herself, and the persona of Sarah that she adopts) see her 'possession' as the product of a specific social context. Moreover, Abegail's possession by Sarah can be seen as a powerful metaphor for the political situation, with a population frightened by the freedom they have given themselves, haunted by the monarchy in exile, wanting to call back the prince who will become King Charles II. Abegail's guilt and her fear of freedom are directly confronted by Yates; but Yates is aware that he cannot confront the same fears in the general population: 'Those coming after us will wonder if it happened, that Englishmen turned all things topsy-turvy seeing no reason why some should have so much and others so little' (p. 156).

The danger of such a specific reading of the play is that it tends to constrain its meaning. There have been many fine plays that do function primarily as allegory – and, in spite of Arthur Miller's protestations to the contrary, *The Crucible* is one such – but while *From Sleep and Shadow* and *A Hand Witch of the Second Stage* both share parabolic qualities (most notably the rather didactic endings, which I have already remarked upon in connection with *A Hand Witch of the Second Stage*), they are more metaphorical than allegorical.

The Night of the Sinhat Torah
'The final end' or 'Carry on Regardless'

The final play in the trilogy, *The Night of the Sinhat Torah*,[29] is set in 1812 in Lublin, as three cynical, world-weary Polish rabbis ask God to show Himself and change the world for the better. They pray to God, and await His reply. They try words of praise; they try stories, but these, they judge, are 'too bitter, too sad or too funny' for God (p. 165). So they try songs and dancing – to no avail. They talk to each other of the different ways in which they might themselves be perceived as inadequate; maybe their failure to understand God's subtleties is why He is not answering them. But, eventually, they lose patience; and they decide to 'bring God Himself to Judgement' (p. 168), to charge God with the Talmud's thirteenth punishable offence, namely causing 'men and women to curse God Almighty' (p. 169). Each delivers a guilty verdict and they excommunicate Him: 'You are excluded from the community of Thy children till the end of time.' No sooner have they done so than there is '*a great sucking noise as a vast wind swirls through the room . . . and sweeps out into the dark*' (p. 169). God has taken His leave.

> **MAGGID**   We've driven God away. We tried to imagine the
> world without God, now we know. And the horror is, it's
> just the same . . .
> **SEER**   They did not believe us when we said He was here. So
> why should they believe us when we say He's gone?
> Nothing's changed.
> **MENDEL**   It's the final end.
> **MAGGID**   What do we do?
> **SEER**   Continue, of course.
>
> (p. 170)

The play is witty and complements the two which precede it, but it feels much more like a sketch than either of those. The conclusion has something of the homily about it, although it does beg questions about the notions of continuation and identity. Is the Seer's exhortation to 'continue' simply an appeal for perseverance, or are they to continue as priests? Are their identities so bound up in their actions that they must continue to pray and preach the word of a God who has abandoned them? The latter seems likely as the final line of the play is a stage direction: '*A Cantor chants Psalm XXII in Hebrew as the lights slowly fade out*' (p. 170). Although the ending of this final part of *The Spirit of Man* trilogy can be read as bleak, the play is surprisingly light-hearted in tone, and the sense of dogged survival is shared with many of Barnes' plays for radio and the theatre. And the ending could be read rather more optimistically: if these priests can find the strength to carry on, knowing that they have been abandoned by God, then action must be its own reward, and meaning must be found in actions, not sought in the approval of external agencies and higher authority.

NOBODY HERE BUT US CHICKENS

This theme of self-reliance is developed further in the trilogy of short television plays for Channel 4. The first of these short plays, *Nobody Here But Us Chickens*, is also the overall title of the trilogy, for which Barnes received the Royal Television Society Award for the Best Drama of 1989. The accolade must have been particularly pleasing, given that he directed the production himself. In his introduction to the plays,[30] Barnes wrote:

> These plays . . . deal with handicaps in the . . . sense of mental or
> physical disabilities such as blindness, deafness, palsy, mental

deficiencies; handicaps that are primarily motor, mental or sensory deprivations.

No special sympathy is shown for these disabilities . . . whereas the object is to emphasize the similarities. Acceptance is needed, not sympathy . . .

The disabled are not a different species but, like the rest of us, absurd and ridiculous; only they have it harder. They have so much more to overcome. Cripples are the rest of us, dramatized.

(p. 172)

This might give the impression that the plays are didactic: provocative and challenging, yes; but neither didactic as such nor patronising. For Barnes this is a most unusual introduction, in that it contains no jokes, no aphorisms, no irony. In writing it he was clearly concerned that the plays should be taken seriously. The use of the word 'cripples' is of particular interest here, for it confronts the issue of political correctness head-on. The plays are anything but worthy; they do not 'deal' with schizophrenia, spastic paralysis and blindness: those are not their subject matters. They do not assume some special knowledge of, or insight into, these 'conditions'; to do so would risk being patronising. The characters are not psychologically motivated; rather, the plays presents these handicaps and disabilities as obstacles to be overcome, as metaphors. In this respect they can be seen as parable plays, not teaching us lessons of right behaviour, but presenting us with potent metaphors.

Nobody Here But Us Chickens
'Act like a man'?

At the start of *Nobody Here But Us Chickens* we find ourselves in a '*totally white room with a heavy door*' in which 'GEORGE ALLSOP, *in his underpants, crows and talks urgently to himself as the light grows steadily brighter*' (p. 176). Allsop has an identity crisis. He thinks of himself as a chicken, a White Leghorn, although 'they' are convinced he is a man and 'against the evidence of their eyes' are trying to convince him of it. The key turns in the lock, the door opens and in strides Charles Hern.[31] Allsop assumes Hern has been sent to spy on him, and he is convinced that there is a trick when Hern '*clucks softly*' and '*makes tiny jumps at him like a fighting cock*' (p. 178). This turns into a full-blown cockfight, until they both collapse, exhausted. Gradually they grow to trust and confide in each other; the play ends with Hern persuading Allsop to go back into the human world as 'Feather Agent Four Five Eight . . . [to] keep watch on them and report to me . . . It's acting normal that counts with them. They're not interested in what you are inside' (pp. 186–7). As Allsop announces 'Open the cage and let us out . . . We know who we are!' (p. 188), we again hear the sound of a key turning in the lock and the door swings open. Allsop's resolute assertion that 'We know who we are!' may be an expression of staunch resistance against 'that evil strain called humanity' (p. 186); but the ending does not offer quite such simple narrative closure. There is some doubt as to whether Hern believes himself to be a chicken, although he claims he is 'the great Chanticleer' (p. 182). Allsop initially considers him an 'agent provocateur', though Hern convinces him that they need to 'adapt to survive . . . Remember, dressed like a man you'll still be a cockerel' (p. 183). It is, however, possible to read Hern's Chanticleer as a pretence, as the act of a man offering (rather eccentric) therapy for Allsop, recognising that while it may not be possible to change the 'inner' personality, behavioural modification can be achieved in a relatively short period. The play is concerned with issues of identity; it is a variation on the thematic interrogation of the relationships between 'truth' and 'reality', actions and acting, performance and behaviour that runs through much of Barnes' work. That there is some doubt about the status of Hern's 'performance' as a chicken not only creates a central narrative enigma, but also enlivens the debate – while not extending it. *Nobody Here But Us Chickens* is an amusing, engaging play, frequently very funny; however, it is limited in its scope, and only partially by its length (it runs at about twenty minutes). Allsop's (and possibly Hern's) schizophrenia has resulted in his incarceration, but there is only the vaguest, gener-alised indication of the human world which he rejects, and which is attempting to deny him his sense of his own identity. The play does not attempt a psychological examination of madness, nor does it try to invoke the social and political dimensions of *The Ruling Class* or *The Bewitched*, where madness, in both plays, is simultaneously individual and collective, and in which the individ-ual madness of Mariana and the Earl of Gurney is presented as an interaction with the political insanity of the worlds they inhabit.

More Than a Touch of Zen
'The universe in the movement of a hand'

Structurally, this trilogy echoes *The Spirit of Man* in that the most 'serious' of the three plays, *More Than a Touch of Zen*, is placed in the centre. Joseph Carver is a martial arts instructor, who has developed his own system of judo 'called Bujutsu-Carver. It's Judo sprinkled with T'ai Chi Ch'uan, a smidgeon of Shiatzu . . . and more than a touch of Zen . . . Bujutsu-Carver takes the best of the East for the West, *aya*!' (p. 190). He makes grandiose claims for his discipline, promising: 'Heaven's in a single breath, the uni-verse in the movement of a hand. And all for £8.50 a session, plus V.A.T.' (p. 191). There is certainly a strong satirical impulse here – Carver's catch-all appropriation and commodification of Eastern philosophies, movement systems, mysticism and martial arts for spiritual and material self-improvement are reminiscent of the tricksters' eclectic use of necromancy, alchemy and occult power in Jonson's *The Alchemist*.[32] But although this provides an important backdrop against which the action of the play takes place, the mechanisms of this play are quite different; the focus is not really Carver, but his new students, George Hills and Douglas Powell.[33] Having boasted that his 'Judo is available to all. There can be no barriers . . . either physical or mental' (p. 191), Carver finds that Hills and Powell suffer from spastic paralysis. They cannot conceal this, and have come to Carver's gymnasium in response to his sales pitch – which he now has to try to live up to. He attempts to get them to take up and hold specific starting positions, but their uncontrollable shaking and difficulties of balance make these impossible. He tries to convince them (and himself) of the power of 'mind over body', but to no avail. Close to despair, he reminds himself of his own promotional material – 'Bujutsu-Carver should be a system for all mankind . . . What good is it if some are left outside?' (p. 198) – and tries yet again to correct Hills' position: '*He moves forward and takes* HILLS*'s hand to direct his waving finger to the correct spot. As he does so* HILLS *judders convulsively sending* CARVER *crashing to the floor*' (p. 198).

Hills and Powell are embarrassed, but this is a turning point. Carver realises that he had been forgetting 'the great Zen principle of turning disadvantages to advantage . . . I made the mistake of trying to overcome [your shakes] instead of using 'em . . . you'll win not despite your handicaps but because of 'em – that's true Zen, gentlemen' (pp. 199–200). The invocation of Zen should not, however, be taken too literally; it is more useful to see it as a dramatic metaphor for dealing with misfortune and, as such, can be seen to inform much of Barnes' more optimistic work. Turn adversity and affliction to your advantage by refusing to see them in the way that others do. The play would have the feel of a parable, were the ending not so wryly ambiguous: an ambiguity that arises out of the connection with Jonson's *Alchemist*. While Carver is not a con man in the Jonsonian mould, he is an entrepreneur who feeds on his students' desire for self-improvement; it is very much in his interests, as he himself makes clear, to convince them that they can be winners. Thus the ending, in which '*all three are shaking and twitching furiously as the lights slowly fade out*' (p. 202) is more double-edged than it at first might seem, and can be read as either Carver making capital out of his students' afflictions, or a celebration of Zen philosophy, of turning apparent adversity to one's advantage. What gives the play its joyous quality, however, is that even if Carver is exploiting them, Hills and Powell benefit from this; they become winners where, in Hills's own words, they have 'always been LOSERS' (p. 200). Whereas in *The Alchemist* Jonson's gulls are humiliated by the tricksters because they arrive with no self-knowledge and want to change themselves at any price, Hills and Powell are disarmingly aware of their own limitations:

POWELL   Is it because you think we're cripples? . . . Handy handicappers . . . I'm an institute man born and bred . . .
HILLS   Now I'm in an Institute I h-h-have to lick my PLATE clean and p-p-praise the COOK.

(pp. 191–2)

And, in another break with *The Alchemist*, Carver's attitudes and perceptions change as much as the students'. Once he has got over his initial shock – 'Nobody told me about you. I could kill Bristow in Admin' (p. 192) – he tries to train them according to a standard set of exercises. It is only when Hills sends him crashing to the floor that he realises his teaching has to be interactive. His teaching thus becomes student-centred, as he understands that although he cannot change them, they can all, Hills, Powell and Carver, alter their perception of themselves, providing they work together collaboratively.

Not As Bad As They Seem
'Moles in a mist'

The last play in the trilogy is a bedroom farce, a genre which is conventionally driven by misunderstanding, misrepresentation and mistaken identities. In *Not As Bad As They Seem* it is the characters' own perceptions (and misperceptions) of themselves which become increasingly problematic as the play develops. Judith Sefton and Paul Berridge are lovers, disturbed by Judith's husband, Ernest Sefton, who breaks the routine of years by coming home in the middle of the day.[34] Sefton is professionally jealous of Berridge – the two men are both teachers, working in the same school. Sefton, Berridge's head of department, assumes that the younger man is trying to take his job, although he never suspects that he might be having an affair with his wife. Its acerbic view of love, marriage and pragmatic morality draws heavily on Feydeau (whom Barnes greatly admires).[35] What makes the play distinctive is that all the characters are physically blind. Sefton's unexpected homecoming is motivated by his desire to tell Judith that he thinks he is regaining his sight. His hope of seeing again, however, proves unfounded and self-deluding; Judith's affair with Berridge remains undiscovered – when Sefton realises his rival is in the house, Berridge claims he is there because he had heard that Sefton had been taken ill; Sefton ultimately accepts Berridge's presence as an act of friendship and resigns himself with good grace to the world 'going invisible' again. Sefton's announcement that he thinks he is regaining his sight functions as a dramatic device, raising the stakes for Berridge and Judith (and the audience), who imagine him able to see far more than he can; but it is also deeply poignant. Unlike Berridge, who had been born blind, Sefton was 'struck blind' eighteen years before, and so has known 'what light is', and is 'hoping against hope . . . to see a candle burning, girls bathing, *blue*. To see blue again' (p. 209).

As one might expect of a bedroom farce, there is much physical comedy – some of it slapstick, some of it consciously feeding the audience's sense of superiority, allowing us to see what the characters cannot. But this sense of superiority, in which the audience knows more than the characters (a common enough narrative strategy in all drama) is likely to be tempered by Sefton's misguided confidence in his own ability to 'read' others: 'blindness brings out the best in others . . . We blinders have ways of seeing the truth the rest're blind to' (p. 215). These stereotypical platitudes are likely to present a challenge to the audience, for the notion that the loss of one sense is somehow compensated by the enhancement of others is frequently voiced as patronising consolation to those who have lost their sight or hearing. Judith addresses this directly: 'I used to believe we had new ways of seeing too. I was sure . . . I had a sixth sense developed to the seventh degree. But now I wonder. Maybe we fool ourselves and we're as much in the dark as those who can see – only we're in a double darkness' (p. 215). Towards the end of the play, the light fades out, and the audience finds itself in the same position as the characters: it can see no more than the characters. The play ends in this shared darkness with Sefton seeking consolation in his new-found 'friendship' with Berridge: 'I don't think of the light I lost but the friends I've found, eh Paul . . . You see, things never are as bad as they seem' (pp. 216–17). In this instance, they are probably worse. But ignorance at least offers some consolation, if not bliss.

Each of the plays in the trilogy explores variations on this theme of self-delusion and self-perception, and the overall title can be seen as deeply ironic. But I would argue that, as in *The Spirit of Man* trilogy and the *Revolutionary Witness* quartet, the trilogy has meaning beyond the sum of the parts; there is a fruitful dialectic produced by the structural relationship of each play to the others. If Hern and Allsop are convinced that there is 'nobody here but us chickens', they are paralleled in their isolation by Sefton. *Not As Bad As They Seem* is richly comic, but Sefton's plight has something of the bitter loneliness that farce, as a theatrical form, often highlights. Contrasted with this, Hills, Powell and Carver create the most unlikely team – defiant and combative as they ready themselves to take on all comers.

HARD TIMES

The only major play of his own that Barnes has directed in the theatre is the revival of *Dreaming*, discussed in Chapter 5. He has, however, directed several of his adaptations of Jacobean plays, including *Bartholomew Fair* and *Antonio*; and, for television – in addition to *Nobody Here But Us Chickens* – he also directed *Bye Bye Columbus* (broadcast by BBC TV in February 1992), a large-cast drama mocking colonialism, commerce and imperialist exploitation through a self-referential and self-consciously anachronistic version of the Columbus story. In 1994 BBC TV broadcast his adaptation of Dickens' *Hard Times* (which he again directed himself) in episodic form for school television. The adaptation is a finely wrought Brechtian parable, shot on a tiny budget, with a superb cast.[36] In contrast with much period television drama (in which glossy production values tend to undermine any social critique), the very austerity of the production emphasises the radical politics of the novel. The BBC subsequently edited the episodes together and broadcast it as a single play during the 1994 Christmas period.

PART FOUR
Reflections

7

Traditions and Contexts

Barnes is a midnight raider. Each of his plays draws on numerous sources from both 'high' and popular culture. Shakespearean allusion alternates with songs plucked from Hollywood musicals (with their lyrics usually slightly adapted and their meaning mischievously subverted); meticulously researched historical detail is debunked and subverted by circus-like slapstick routines; a music-hall song and dance routine moves seamlessly into metaphysical reflection. His eclectic borrowings, quotations (and misquotations), parodies and playfulness would all seem to position Barnes as a postmodernist. But this is certainly not the way he sees himself. His work is deeply ironic, certainly, self-reflexive and frequently self-referential; but it is steeped in the modernist tradition, and makes use of formal experimentation to create meaning in its own right.

This chapter examines some of the various theatrical traditions within which Barnes' theatre can be shown to operate, starting by discussing the relationships between his own work and Early Modern English theatre[1] and then considering the affinities between Barnes' work and that of various theatre practitioners from the late nineteenth and early twentieth centuries.

While it is interesting to see how these different contexts and traditions inform Barnes' working methods, the danger of the notion of an 'informing context' is that it tends to lead to an approach which is biographical at best, anecdotal at worst. I argue here that 'tradition' and 'influence' are not static but dynamic forces, and that to explore how Barnes makes use of, challenges and subverts a range of theatrical traditions is to understand better how these plays make meaning, how they provoke a range of responses in their readers and audiences.

Problems of Influence and Tradition

Bernard Dukore asserts that Barnes' work is *'sui generis'*, that he is 'a true original' (1981, p. 145). 'Original', however, is one of those strange and problematic words that has reversed its meaning over the years. Paradoxically, even now it still contains vestiges of its early meaning: 'true to one's origins'. Dukore's implication is that Barnes' plays are unique; while I would certainly agree that his work is unfashionable, and that the dramatic forms that he has developed are unusual, they are rooted in theatrical traditions that are active, if occasionally neglected. This is not in any way to underestimate the extent to which Barnes is a theatrical innovator, nor to deny that his theatrical 'voice' is one of the most distinctive in modern drama, but rather to try to appraise his work in appropriate contexts.

Although I am reluctant to categorise Barnes, he is primarily a comic playwright, who has used comedy as a political tool. Here, and elsewhere in this chapter, I use the word 'political' in a broad sense. His theatre is essentially self-reflexive, in that it is conscious of its own artifice, using comedy not only as social and political satire, but also to examine the social and political functions of comedy itself. His explorations of the furthest reaches of comedy are not simply exercises in boundary-pushing, but attempts to understand the mechanisms of comedy and its uses and abuses *in extremis*: on the one hand as a means of social control, on the other as a means of healing. Although comedy and farce in the English theatre are sometimes associated with conservative impulses, there has also been a vibrant tradition of comedy as a politically radical form of theatre. Barnes' frequently stated enthusiasm for the work of Ben Jonson is rooted in his perception of Jonson's use of comedy as vibrant social and political satire. This use of comedy as a 'corrective' goes back at least as far as Aristophanes (Greek Old Comedy provided an important model for Jonson). The tradition of political-driven farce has probably been more active in Europe than in England; but plays such as Gogol's *The Government Inspector*, Kleist's *The Broken Jug*, Mayakovsky's *The Bedbug* and *The Bathhouse*, Schwartz's *The Dragon*, Erdmann's *The Suicide*, Goll's *Methusalem* and Brecht's *Arturo Ui* are all astringent political satires. That many of them are staples of the European repertoire perhaps gives some indication of why Barnes' work has been revived more frequently in Europe than it has in England. I do not think that Barnes has been directly influenced by these works, but he is aware of them, and greatly admires them. All of them are 'dark' plays, in which comedy is not offered as a respite from social and political injustice, but as a means of drawing attention to it.

A Neo-Jacobean?

In his introduction to *The Bewitched*, Ronald Bryden describes the play as

neo-Jacobean . . . [in that] it penetrates to the heart of the Jacobean melancholy which is also our own: the discovery that 'the new philosophy casts all in doubt', that the universe is absurd and all the comforting beliefs in which we were reared are frantic constructs to mask this intolerable truth.

(Barnes, 1989a, p. 187)

This 'neo-Jacobean' label is one which has frequently been attached to Barnes. His love of Jonson, Marston, Middleton and Webster, together with his extensive knowledge of Shakespeare, underpins and permeates all his work. Indeed, it is one of the qualities of his dramatic output that most clearly characterises it, and it is certainly the influence he most readily acknowledges. I want to consider what this term 'neo-Jacobean' might mean, and in what ways it might offer useful perspectives on Barnes' work. It is, however, worth laying down a caveat here: while Bryden clearly intended the term as an accolade, it could be seen as damning. Jacobean theatre is rich and diverse linguistically, for-mally and in its exploration of large issues; but it evolved in a very specific social, political and cultural context. The problem with a 'neo-Jacobean' theatre is that we live in a post-Jacobean (not to say postmodern) world, and such a theatre can all too easily fall into pastiche or parody for its own sake.

In his encyclopedic volume, *The Cambridge Illustrated History of British Theatre*, Simon Trussler briefly refers to Barnes' talents as 'richly Jonsonian' (1994, p. 353). While Barnes acknowledges Jonson as the most important single influence on his work,[2] the traffic is not all one way, in spite of the 350-year age gap between the two playwrights. Barnes has been a great champion of Jonson and has directed, edited and adapted several of his plays. His adaptation of *The Alchemist* opened (in Stuart Burge's Nottingham Playhouse production) at the Old Vic in 1970 and was subsequently used by Trevor Nunn in an acclaimed production for the Royal Shakespeare Company, which opened at The Other Place, Stratford-upon-Avon, in May 1977 before transferring to the Aldwych Theatre, London, in December of that year. He has also worked on *Volpone*, *The Devil Is an Ass*, *The Magnetic Lady*, *Bartholomew Fair*,[3] *Eastward Ho!* and *Epicœne, or The Silent Woman*. His enthusiasm for seventeenth-century theatre is, however, not limited to Jonson. He has also adapted Thomas Middleton's *A Chaste Maid in Cheapside*; *A Mad World, My Masters*; and *A Trick to Catch the Old One*; Thomas Otway's *The Soldier's Fortune* and *The Atheist*; John Marston's *The Dutch Courtesan*; and has used Marston's *Antonio and Mellida* and *Antonio's Revenge* as the basis for *Antonio*. In each case, these 'adaptations' make no attempt to update the plot or the characterisation; Barnes' stated intention was to edit and to modernise the language, where he viewed the allusions of the original as impenetrable to a modern audience. This project aroused considerable controversy in the late 1970s.

The most vocal critic of this method has been Bernard Levin, who has argued that while a full-blown adaptation (such as *Romeo and Juliet* into *West Side Story*) might have some merit, 'adapting' Jacobean plays by modernising the language is likely to result in 'mongrel work' and that the 'matter of integrity'[4] has to be considered alongside the issue of whether a play has the potential (in Barnes' words) to be 'theatrically alive' if it is performed in its 'original' form. This debate is discussed in some detail by Dukore, who comes down firmly on the side of Barnes,[5] concluding: 'If anyone believes that his adaptations desecrate the original plays . . . then he is free to produce the originals . . . The originals remain available for production' (1981, p. 93). The debate about whether an 'adaptation' of, for example, *The Devil Is an Ass* tells us whether Jonson's play retains theatrical relevance and vitality in the modern world is a complex one, but slightly tangential to the present argument. What is certain is that Barnes' version not only revived interest in that specific play (which had, hitherto, been unperformed for more than three hundred and fifty years) but also in Jonson's largely unperformed canon.[6] I would agree broadly with the position taken by Barnes (and endorsed by Dukore), but would add that the issues of integrity and originality are themselves far more contentious than Levin's position allows. Theatre is by its very nature a collaborative art; and, as Stephen Orgel has demonstrated,[7] even a text such as Jonson's *Sejanus* (which Jonson revised from an early theatrical version for publication) is a product of collective interaction, not only between Jonson and his much vaunted classical sources, but also between himself and theatrical institutions, audiences, actors, publishers and subsequent editors.

It is worth adding that one of the more pleasurable developments in British theatre over the past thirty years has been the way in which it has embraced theatrical excellence from other cultures. In the 1920s Brecht was very interested in Soviet art and theatre; in 1935 he met Meyerhold in Moscow.[8] The extent to which Meyerhold was a direct influence on Brecht is uncertain, but they certainly shared a fascination with oriental theatre and sought to create a non-illusionist drama in the service of a progressive social purpose.[9]

Many leading twentieth-century theatre practitioners have found inspiration in the plays of their colleagues working in other countries and other cultures. Fortunately it is no longer the preserve of a cultural elite to be able to see such work, and Britain regularly hosts directors and theatre companies from overseas. A high proportion of these productions are of plays by Shakespeare, performed in languages other than English. Thus British audiences can see Shakespeare played in, for example, Romanian, Japanese and Russian. Thus we have the strange phenomenon of Shakespeare translated into a foreign language and then played back to an English-speaking audience in a language other than English. This not only allows an audience to 'see' Shakespeare through strange eyes, to make Shakespeare strange (in the sense that Brecht and the Russian formalists proposed with their concepts of *Verfremdungseffekt* and *ostranenie*), but it also reminds us that translation involves a complex interaction with a text. Jeremy Sams (who has translated several plays for the National Theatre) observed that 'we are blessed and lucky in England to be able to update and make contemporary plays in foreign languages, just as the Germans are, in every generation, able to do a new version of Shakespeare'.[10] The corollary of this can be seen in the treatment of Chekhov. Chekhov's theatre has never been so popular in England as it has been for the past twenty years, and yet it seems that almost every major production of a Chekhov play demands a brand-new translation; however, these are rarely 'updated' versions or adaptations of the plays. Working with Shakespeare's or Jonson's texts in their 'original' is double-edged; and Barnes' adaptations need to be seen in this context.

Dukore has discussed in useful detail Barnes' working methods in his adaptations (of the Jacobeans, Brecht, Wedekind, Feydeau and others).[11] A complete list of these adaptations for the theatre and radio appears in the bibliography and filmography sections; I do not propose to attempt any further analysis of Barnes' editing and adaptations, as I have nothing to add to Dukore's work on them. It is evident, however, that Barnes' knowledge and understanding of the work of Jonson and his contemporaries is held in great respect by theatre practitioners; what is useful in the context of this book is to examine what precisely the term 'neo-Jacobean' might mean when applied to Barnes' work and, by extension, how the term might illuminate readings of the plays.

The most significant single debt that Barnes himself acknowledges is to Ben Jonson, whose plays he unashamedly prefers to Shakespeare's,[12] and he has specifically stated that what he admires in Jonson is the vitality and vulgarity of his comedy, its muscularity of language and its incisive social satire. So I want first to examine in some detail where specific 'traces' of Jonson's plays can be found in Barnes' work and, in doing so, to consider if, and how, these echoes move beyond mere pastiche or homage to create meaning through the relationship between the two. In recent times, one of Jonson's most frequently performed plays has been *The Alchemist*. It was also one of the most successful of Barnes' edited versions. The influence of *The Alchemist* can be seen in several of Barnes' original plays – for theatre and television. Jonson's play opens with a heated quarrel between the three tricksters, Subtle, Face and Dol. It is one of the finest examples available for anyone urging writers to throw their characters into the thick of things.

FACE   Believe't, I will.

SUBTLE   Thy worst. I fart at thee.

DOL   Ha' you your wits? Why, gentleman! For love –

(I.i.1–2)

This ferocious argument, always on the verge of turning into a physical fight, with Dol barely managing to keep the two men apart, does not simply serve to engage an audience with its ever present threat of violence, but it also presents us with a detailed 'back story' (to use Hollywood jargon) as they dispute their relative abilities, integrity and personal histories. As a dramatic strategy it is recommended in all the Hollywood screenwriting manuals, and given Barnes' experience as a screenwriter, his use of it in Scene 1 of *The Bewitched* is not surprising. The echo is, however, uncanny. Ana and Mariana trade insults and squabble furiously over who should be named in Carlos's will as his successor – while Ana's parrot makes a half-hearted attempt to keep them apart: '*Stop talking when I interrupt!*' (p. 200). As in *The Alchemist*, the scene engages us with its abundant theatrical energy, but it also provides us with essentials of both personal and political histories. On its own this has little more than anecdotal interest; what is significant, in terms of our reading of Barnes' play, is that the parallel draws attention to the roles of Ana and Mariana. They may be members of the royal family, but they too are tricksters, both of them trying to use the gullibility of those around them to manipulate the court to their own desires. And although neither of them ultimately succeeds – in the world of *The Bewitched* nobody can – each of them is far more canny than the male courtiers allow; and they both remain a significant driving force throughout the play. Where the tricksters in *The Alchemist* realise that, in spite of their differences, they have to work as a unit, as a 'venture tripartite', Ana and Mariana remain implacable enemies throughout.

More direct echoes of *The Alchemist* can be found in *A Hand Witch of the Second Stage*,[13] which distorts and wittily inverts the structures and gender balance of Jonson's play: Marie Blin has been accused of witchcraft. The play opens with her '*spreadeagled on a raised rack*' as her inquisitors try to extract a confession from her. Marie Blin adopts the kind of improvisatory wit, speed of thought and sleight of mind of which Dol Common would have been proud. She tricks her persecutors into believing not only that she is a witch, but also that she genuinely does have satanic powers and that the only way for them to escape her vengeance is to free her. Thus, in an elegant reversal of the psychological structure of *The Alchemist*, Marie Blin uses her persecutors' terrors and anxieties to give them exactly what they think they most want: her guilt. And she then uses that against them in the same way that Jonson's 'venture tripartite' uses the gulls' own desires to trick them. Where Jonson's satire exposes the gullibility and greed of those who seek to transform themselves and their lives without self-knowledge, Barnes' Marie Blin can turn her persecutors' fears and fantasies against them because she understands both the weakness of her own situation and the appalling logic of the Inquisition better than they do themselves. Dol Common may also be a distant ancestor of Grace in *The Ruling Class*. Grace's appearance as Marguerite Gautier, 'La Dame Aux Camelias', bears more than a passing resemblance to Dol's disguise as the 'poor baron's daughter' in *The Alchemist*; and the television play *More Than a Touch of Zen* also alludes indirectly to *The Alchemist*.[14]

Leonardo's Last Supper contains more overtly self-conscious Jonsonian references.[15] The three undertakers are clearly modelled on *The Alchemist*'s 'venture tripartite'. Lasca (whose name echoes Mosca in *Volpone*) and Maria are essentially tricksters in the mould of Jonson's; as in Jonson, their trickery is a means of examining the social and political frameworks within which it operates. In the eyes of Lasca and Maria, the medieval Guild of Apothecaries, which attempts to regulate and control their activities, is a corrupt and pernicious means of keeping them at the bottom of the social pile. They are tricksters because that is the only way they can survive. Allusions to *The Alchemist* permeate the play.

Jonson's *The Devil Is an Ass*, another favourite of Barnes, also provides several reference points, most notably the opening, where Fitzdottrel tries to summon up Satan to enter into a Faustus-like pact – only to be rewarded by the appearance of Pug, a very minor devil, totally out of his depth in corrupt seventeenth-century London. This is paralleled in the situation at the beginning of *The Night of the Sinhat Torah*, where the three Polish rabbis try to persuade their God to materialise; and in *From Sleep and Shadow*, where Ranter Israel Yates asks Jonathan Guerdon if he has the courage to plead with God that Abegail, Guerdon's young wife, might 'live again'. Jonson's play subverts the model of the Faustian pact, on which it draws; Barnes, in his turn, makes use of the pattern of the Jonsonian subversion, while not copying it. In every case a character, or characters, seeks assistance from the supernatural for material benefit, thus enabling each of the plays to develop a dialectic between the metaphysical and the materialist. Where Jonson differs from Marlowe, and provides a more appropriate reference point for Barnes, is that his construction of the supernatural is presented with irony and scepticism. Jonson and Barnes both present religion as the refuge of scoundrels; but although they may be far more sceptical about the supernatural than Shakespeare, that is not to say that they are any less interested in the metaphysical. Indeed, I would argue that one of the most significant 'neo-Jacobean' characteristics of Barnes' work is the way that he grounds his plays in solidly materialist fictional worlds, while exploring profoundly metaphysical questions around identity and existence, performance and appearance, illusion and reality. Barnes is by no means alone in the modern theatre in exploring the metaphysical; he is unusual in allowing the materialist and the metaphysical to coexist.

In addition to this reluctance to treat the materialist and the metaphysical as incompatible opposites, close consideration of the Jonsonian model draws attention to a number of specific characteristics that the two playwrights share: a facility with a wide variety of comic styles; a celebration of the grotesque and the carnivalesque; the use of comedy as a form of political satire; dramatic structures that are built on the principles of montage, while giving an impression of narrative linearity, and whose meanings derive as much from unexpected juxtapositions as they do from the unravelling of a finely wrought plot; and an approach to characterisation which constructs characters as types and in terms of social roles ('humours' to use the Jonsonian term) often resulting in vivid caricature. This observation about characterisation should, however, be qualified: Jonson's characters tend to seek to change themselves in material terms, but even when they succeed in hauling themselves up the social ladder, their innate character does not change. Thus, for example, Dauphine in *Epicœne, or The Silent Woman* and Compass in *The Magnetic Lady* do manage to improve their social standing, but they remain essentially opportunistic; their 'humour' may be reconciled to their social situation,[16] but their attitudes have not changed. While this holds true for many of Barnes' characters, there are some who do change – most notably Robert Sauveur, the Butcher, and Théroigne de Méricourt, the Amazon, in the television quartet *Revolutionary Witness*.[17] In these instances personal change becomes possible because of massive political upheaval; personal change and social change are seen as being interdependent.

A further useful point of comparison between Jonson and Barnes is their shared fascination with the processes and the workings of theatre, constructing theatre itself as a metaphor for mechanisms of illusion and self-delusion. I have noted above several allusions to Jonson's work, but these comprise only a small proportion of the eclectic borrowings, appropriations, and numerous quotations and misquotations that pervade his plays. This intertextuality is paradoxically one of the things that make his work distinctive. Barnes' use of intertextuality functions in various ways, one of which is to draw our attention as an audience to our own participation in the theatrical processes in which we assist and collaborate in the making of meaning. An example of this can be found in *Dreaming* (1999). Throughout the play Mallory and his band of war-weary mercenaries are tracked by Richard of Gloucester, a grotesque, pantomimic version of Shakespeare's Richard III, who, at his first appearance, announces: 'Now is the summer of my deep content . . . That has a good ring to it. People put words into my mouth, the wrong words usually' (1999, p. 7). The self-mocking Shakespearean misquotation undercuts the brutality of the short expressionist evocation of the Battle of Tewkesbury, which opens the play – thus signalling the tonal and stylistic instability of the subsequent scene and the whole play. It also hints playfully at an interest in preconceptions of character and assumed roles that the play goes on to develop into a central theme. Just as this Richard is trapped in audiences' perceptions of him as Shakespeare's King Richard, so Mallory is trapped in Richard's perception of him as a cold-hearted killer. This Richard of Gloucester is primarily a comic creation, who never breaks out of the role he appears initially to resent, essentially a caricature of the Shakespearean model; Mallory is a far more complex character, continually trying to break out of long-established patterns of ruthless brutality. For him, identity is troublingly uncertain; his determination to find 'home' is the embodiment of his dream of (re)discovering an alternative identity. Mallory and his band of refugee followers encounter numerous obstacles (human and geographical) as they attempt to cheat death, negotiating their way through the post-apocalyptic landscape; but whatever they do, they cannot for long keep out of Richard's clutches, and Richard's perception of Mallory is obdurate: 'You're a stone killer and a man of honour . . . You have no plans if they don't include Richard' (p. 28). The irony of this is that Mallory himself does something very similar to Percy Beaufort's widow, Susan, whom he insists is his own wife, Sarah, forcing her to (re)marry him. Each of the band of followers has to play a 'family' role, each pretending to be related to Susan in order to make the wedding seem more authentic.[18] Richard's 'plight', trapped with 'other people's' words in his mouth, becomes an extended comic turn, a running gag; we come to expect his appearances to be marked with Shakespearean misquotations: 'Prosper with me, friends, and rise with this sun of York . . . To horse, to horse! Why can I never find a horse?!' (pp. 29–30). As with all parody and pastiche, there is an element of mockery here: mockery of the nobility, of the very notion of kingship, of the Shakespeare industry, of the authorial voice in general, and of Shakespearean authority specifically. Within the action of the play, Richard is at once comic, pantomimic, menacing and merciless; sometimes genial, sometimes psychotic in his determination to annihilate the Beauforts. As an icon of repressive authority, the figure is drawn from the Early Modern theatre's archetype of the Machiavel. Characters such as Barabas in *The Jew of Malta*, Edmund in *King Lear* and Flamineo in *The White Devil* forge a charismatic relationship with the audience which simultaneously thrills, beguiles and horrifies with amoral charm. Barnes' Richard is less of a Machiavel than Shakespeare's Richard: *Dreaming* makes no attempt to dramatise his rise to power. What he shares with his Early Modern relatives, however, is a relationship with the audience that is as active as his relationship with Mallory and the other characters on stage. Barnes does not extend the figure – except in pantomimic terms. This makes the relationship between Richard and the audience highly unstable, making him at once more reassuring to an audience and more dangerous, because more unreliable. We do not know how to take him. As a pantomime villain we might expect him to get his comeuppance, to be punished for his villainy or allowed to find redemption. *Dreaming* alerts us at a very early stage that we are likely to be denied such easy reassurance. Barnes uses an audience's knowledge and experience of a wide range of theatrical traditions to stimulate a range of (often contradictory) responses.

Although Richard of Gloucester's appearance in *Dreaming* is essentially parodic, the dramatic function of the character is not restricted to that; and elsewhere in the Barnes canon, intertextual allusions to Shakespeare are by no means always rooted in parody. I have noted the similarities between Rafael in *The Bewitched* and Lear's Fool.[19] One does not need to know *King Lear* to understand Rafael's dangerous position in the court, but a familiarity with Shakespeare's play enriches a reading of *The Bewitched*. Lear's Fool, like Rafael, may amuse, but he is also an irritant, a reminder of the transience of earthly wealth and power. Rafael has to be more direct than the Fool; he cannot trip wittily through riddling abstractions, for he cannot appeal to the king's innate intelligence. Carlos has no wisdom, except when he is in the grip of epilepsy. Rafael's similarities with the Fool thus invoke Lear as an unseen point of comparison for Carlos. Indeed, close examination of the play reveals a surprising number of points of reference to and comparison with *King Lear*. Lear is losing his grip on authority and wants to hand over responsibility to others while retaining power; Carlos has virtually no responsibility, little real power and never any personal authority. In each case issues of disputed accession blight their respective kingdoms, resulting in catastrophic wars. The most useful points of comparison, however, are the key political differences between the plays. It would be pointlessly reductive to attempt a summary of the various political dimensions of *King Lear*; it is worth noting, however, that the play dramatises grave anxieties about chaos, civil war and anarchy that arise when the authority of the monarchy is weakened. The principle of divine right itself, however, is never questioned. *The Bewitched* presents us with a world in which the

Establishment's inflexible adherence to the doctrine is driving the whole society to war and madness. In his biography of Carlos, John Nada commented: 'Nobody can understand how powerful over the human mind the belief in the divinity of kings can be, unless he has watched its effects where the king has been an idiot' (1962, pp. 43–4). Lear's attempt to divide the kingdom between his daughters ultimately destroys his own sanity; his stubborn refusal to differentiate between private displays of emotion and rituals of state leads directly to his own madness and to civil war, his personal madness becoming both a cause of and a complex metaphor for a society that is tearing itself apart. Carlos is an imbecile, but he is not mad, although his epileptic seizures function in a similar way to Lear's madness, granting him the unexpected benefit of unwelcome insights into the nature of authority and the social hierarchy. Carlos is as pathetically ill-equipped to rule as he is to beget an heir. And yet the inverted parallels with *King Lear* are remarkably insistent. In Shakespeare's play the king's failure to ensure smooth succession is the catalyst for ensuing chaos. In *The Bewitched* the king's impotence is a symptom of a far-reaching social madness.

Tragedy has been theorised in many ways; the word has developed meanings which are historically and culturally contingent, and it is therefore impossible to offer a single useful definition – to attempt one is certainly beyond the scope of this volume. It is, however, worth noting that Early Modern tragedy tends to focus on the struggles and decisions of a central character against implacable external forces. Lear finds himself humiliated as much by the forces of nature and the absence of divine meaning as he is by his two eldest daughters. And, however one interprets *King Lear*, there is no disputing that the play is the tragedy of Lear. Even if *The Bewitched* were tragic, it could not claim to be the tragedy of Carlos. It is those who are bewitched whose fatal flaws precipitate the catastrophic events of the play. It is the tragedy of those who are bewitched by authority; those who unquestioningly accept the authority of rulers, of the Church; it is a tragedy driven by the grotesque superstition that God has invested His power in the monarchy with the same degree of gullibility as they have themselves. But *The Bewitched* is farce, not tragedy. Farce characteristically starts with an essentially absurd situation as a given, and then applies to it the most rigorous and unyielding logic. *The Bewitched* works on precisely this principle, using the principle of divine right and the unquestioning investment of authority in rulers as the twin basic premises for the farce, and then pursues the interaction between them to the most horrific conclusion.

It is worth briefly returning to Bryden's argument that *The Bewitched* is 'genuinely Jacobean in thought and texture' to consider further the term 'neo-Jacobean'. Bryden calls attention to 'the brilliant, thorny, fantastic speech of Carlos' courtiers, the two great verse tirades the stammering king speaks in the lucid aftermath of epilepsy', arguing that Barnes' use of language is both texturally and philosophically Jacobean in its resonance (p. 189). Central to his argument, however, is his assertion that the play uses the quality of its language and its scope to satirise contemporary Britain:

> The most striking difference between the British playwrights of the Sixties and their predecessors of the Osborne generation is that they, the neo-Elizabethans, saw themselves as forerunners of a meritocratic revolution . . . Peter Barnes and his contemporaries challenge that . . . satirising with grim Jacobean wit the society meritocracy has built. So that the title of *The Bewitched* spreads beyond the unfortunate Carlos . . . beyond the sleep-walking empire which collapsed about him, to the ghost-empire we in Britain inhabit now . . .[20]

While agreeing wholeheartedly with Bryden's contention that the power of *The Bewitched* lies in its contemporary relevance, I want to qualify further its relationship with Jacobean drama. Bryden clearly intended the term as a commendation, but until relatively recently it would not have been thought of as such. In 1920 William Archer,[21] regarded as the leading critic of his generation, who was seen as a progressive, and who had translated and championed the work of Ibsen, gave a series of lectures for the Education Authority of London County Council, entitled *Old Drama and the New*, in which he mounted a virulent attack on the work of Jonson, Chapman, Marston, Middleton and Massinger.[22] His censure of Jonson is particularly interesting. Discussing *Every Man in His Humour*, he damns the characters as 'all broad caricatures', arguing that their appeal is 'to audiences in a certain stage of culture – a stage of culture which is to this day largely represented in the lower-class theatres, the music-halls and the picture-palaces – [in which] character is unrecognisable unless it be violently overdrawn' (p. 80). We may read this as a curious kind of intellectual snobbery, but it is surprisingly useful in approaching Jonson – and, by association, Barnes. The implication is clearly that lower-class theatres, music halls and picture palaces are culturally inferior to the classical theatre; but perhaps the most significant characteristic of audiences at this 'certain stage of culture' is that they are *active*: and that sense of an active audience is indeed what both Jonson and Barnes thrive on – and demand. Archer then goes on to ask: 'Who ever could, or ever wanted to, recall the story of *Every Man in his Humour*?' and to claim:

> It would be difficult to find worse-constructed plays outside of Jonson's works: within the boards of his folio it is, unfortunately, only too easy. *Every Man out of His Humour* and *Cynthia's Revels*

are, I take it, the very worst plays ever produced by a man of talent. They are mere galleries of oddities and grotesques, with no more action than there is in Madame-Tussaud's or in a fashion plate.

(pp. 81–2)

These criticisms focus on characterisation and the plays' refusal of conventional narrative structure; but Archer seems to be trying to fit the plays into a preconceived notion of what a good play should be, following a prescription for dramatic shape that ignores the plays' highly crafted formal qualities. I would argue that there is no central character in either *Every Man in His Humour* or *Bartholomew Fair*; the plays do not have protagonists in the conventional sense. Discussing *Bartholomew Fair*, Barnes maintains: 'There are no leading characters. Or rather, there are thirty-two leading characters.'[23] It is a characteristic Jonsonian strategy to focus on the activities of social groups. That these groups are frequently socially incohesive and fragmented is an essential part of the Jonsonian dramatic project. While conventional dramatic protagonists drive most of Barnes' early work, *The Bewitched* marks a shift towards a more Jonsonian structural model,[24] with the court as a social group becoming the target of the satire.

Jonson was a restless experimenter with theatrical form, frequently interrogating his own practice, using the theatrical tradition(s) within which a particular play was conceived as a starting point and a framework from which (and within which) to challenge his own (and his audiences') assumptions about the forms and functions of theatre. Much Early Modern theatre displays a fascination with metatheatricality. It is manifest in numerous plays within plays (such as the bloody denouement of Kyd's *Spanish Tragedy*, the players' performance of *The Mousetrap* in

Hamlet, the puppet show in *Bartholomew Fair* and the masque in Middleton's *Women Beware Women*) where the responses of the on-stage audience become as important as the actions of the players within the play; in prologues, epilogues and speeches which ask an audience to reflect on the complex signification processes of theatre; and through devices built into the plays at a structural level (such as in *The Alchemist*, where Subtle, Face and Dol are not merely engaged in trickery on a grand scale, but are engaged in a prodigious display of improvisatory skill in performing for the on-stage gulls, paralleling their performance for the theatre audience). Metatheatricality in both Jonson and Barnes is used for a wide variety of purposes from provocative examinations of the relationships between socially negotiated identity and performance, to philosophical reflections on the nature of reality and humanity.

John Marston is another of Barnes' favourite playwrights from the Early Modern period. His work is less well known than Jonson's, and is characterised by even more radical tonal shifts: shifts which, by interrogating the stability of theatrical genres, thus become a metatheatrical device in their own right. In Marston's plays, violence, revenge and retribution lurk beneath the surface of even the most comic scenes; expressions of the darkest cruel intent and the most disturbing malignity are suddenly punctuated by comedy. Marston's use of language is riddled with puns, and thus the meaning of a character's speech becomes as elusive as the overall tone is unstable. Archer makes no mention of John Marston in his lectures. It is perhaps just as well, for one can only conjecture what he would have made of the structural qualities of plays such as *The Malcontent* and *Antonio's Revenge*. Marston's dedication of *The Malcontent* (to Jonson) refers to the play as a 'harsh comedy'.[25] It is as close as any Early Modern 'comedy' comes to tragedy. Similarly volatile tonal qualities can be found in much of Barnes' work, as can many of the metatheatrical devices discussed – the plays within plays, the use of direct address to the audience, the metaphysical musing. I suspect that had Barnes offered generic descriptions for any of his plays in their published versions, 'harsh comedy' would have been most apt. But Barnes does not simply try to emulate his Early Modern predecessors, although he frequently uses the metatheatrical to similar effect. He also brings to it a concern with the authority of the authorial voice that has become characteristic of the modern period. Where Jonson, in the Induction and Chorus to *The Magnetic Lady*, has Probee and Damplay discuss the merits of the play they are watching (with the latter, as might be expected, cynical about both the play and Jonson's merits as a playwright), Barnes subverts his own authorial voice by placing on stage a character named Author or Barnes.

Before moving on to consider how his work can be placed in the context of more recent theatrical traditions, it is worth briefly mentioning the sheer scale of Barnes' work. Like Shakespeare and Jonson, Marston and Middleton, he writes 'big plays': plays which require large casts – not for their own sake, but because they are concerned with the workings and interactions of groups; plays which tackle 'big' themes. Barnes has never written a tragedy as such, but although his work seems closer generically to Jacobean city comedy than to any other specific form of Early Modern drama, the themes and the scope of Jacobean tragedy can also be seen to inspire his work. The great tragedies of theodicy, such as *Doctor Faustus, Macbeth, Othello* and *The Duchess of Malfi*,[26] address themselves rigorously to the nature of evil, as do *Laughter!* and *The Bewitched*. Some might argue that their comic form, their jokiness, subverts their own serious intent, or that their use of comedy is so confrontational that audience members are likely to refuse to engage with the serious content which underpins the plays; some might disagree profoundly with the analysis that Barnes offers; but there is no denying that these plays are driven by an enquiry into the functioning of evil, and the mechanisms by which people become complicit with evil.

One of the strange contradictions that surround Barnes' work is that contemporary theatre critics frequently bemoan the absence of 'large-scale' new drama from the modern theatre – and yet that is precisely what we have in a plays such as *The Bewitched*, *Red Noses* and *Dreaming*. Perhaps the reason that Barnes' plays have been greeted with such a mixed reception is that it is so difficult to categorise his work. I have already noted the affinity between his work and Marston's in its tonal instability; few modern writers use comedy to explore such serious issues; few shift the ground from beneath the audience so regularly. He has undoubtedly developed a style which is at once immediately recognisable as his own, and yet draws heavily on a wide range of theatrical traditions. Indeed, this very eclecticism might itself be seen as a Jacobean quality.

Influence and Dialogue

Barnes is well aware of the wide range of theatrical influences on his work. His own contention that it is the Jacobeans whose influence has been strongest is certainly borne out by close analysis of the plays. But 'influence' is a problematic concept. And Barnes' own awareness of the complexity of the concept of authorship confirms the sense that his understanding and assimilation of Early Modern drama is at least partly mediated by the many theatrical practitioners and theorists who, throughout the twentieth century, have revisited and revived Early Modern

English theatre in a variety of contexts. The influence of the Jacobeans on twentieth-century theatre may have been enormous, but the explorations and experiments, the revivals and the academic essays have been as revealing of twentieth-century concerns as they have of Early Modern theatrical practices. Thus it is not possible to quantify the extent to which Barnes has been 'influenced' by, for example, William Poel,[27] Edward Gordon Craig or, more latterly, Peter Brook's experimental work on Shakespeare. The work of these practitioners has become so culturally embedded that virtually all theatrical productions of Early Modern plays owe a debt to them – either directly or indirectly. Given that Barnes works as a director as well as a playwright, and that his stage plays (even in written form) demonstrate an acute awareness of modern scenography, it is reasonable to assert at least a strong relationship between his work and the staging of Early Modern theatre in the twentieth century. Peter Brook's productions for the RSC of *King Lear* (1962) and *A Midsummer Night's Dream* (1970) are often seen as landmarks, as is his book *The Empty Space* (1968). But it is more appropriate to think of Brook as establishing and developing a dialogue with certain key figures, rather than owing them a debt. Brook's reading of Antonin Artaud, Bertolt Brecht and Vsevolod Meyerhold and Jan Kott undoubtedly informed his own thinking, but his practice, in its turn, shed new light on their work.[28] Of all these, however, it is Brecht whose practice and theory Barnes perceives as the most pervasive and most direct influence on late twentieth-century drama. I shall conclude this chapter by examining the conceptual dialogue that Barnes has established with specific late nineteenth- and early twentieth-century practitioners.

Georges Feydeau and Frank Wedekind

I want first to discuss two playwrights whose work Barnes has adapted, and of whom he speaks with great admiration: Georges Feydeau (1862–1921) and Frank Wedekind (1864–1918). Although they are not usually spoken of in the same breath, each shares with Barnes a desire to push the boundaries of what is possible in comic forms. In 1976 Barnes' adaptations of *The Purging* by Feydeau and *The Singer* by Wedekind were staged as *The Frontiers of Farce* at the Old Vic Theatre, London.[29] The title of the double bill gives a clear indication of the reason for his interest in the material. In 1970 *Lulu*, his adaptation and condensation of two Wedekind plays, *Earth Spirit* and *Pandora's Box*, had been staged at the Nottingham Playhouse.[30] And in 1986 the RSC staged *Scenes From a Marriage* (adapted from three one-act Feydeau plays)[31] at the Aldwych Theatre, London. Barnes considers Feydeau to be lamentably underrated as an incisive social critic illuminating the darker areas of human experience; but although Barnes' admiration for Feydeau's craftsmanship has undoubtedly had an impact on his own work, Feydeau's particular kind of domestic, sexually driven farce finds few direct echoes in the theatre of Barnes. *Not As Bad As They Seem*, one of the short plays that makes up the trilogy *Nobody Here But Us Chickens*, can be seen as a tribute to Feydeau – although, perhaps uncharacteristically for Barnes, it is nowhere near as dark or as acerbic as *Scenes From a Marriage*, on which it is very loosely modelled. The remarkable bedroom scene in *The Bewitched* also clearly draws on Feydeau.[32] But although it is difficult to trace a direct line from Feydeau's claustrophobic domestic farces to Barnes' public manipulations of history, the impulses of Feydeau's theatre to push the use of humour to its limits, to portray physical and mental aberrations as metonymic of wider social dysfunction, to realise theatrically a nightmare vision of moral anarchy: these impulses are all shared by Barnes.

Although Feydeau and Wedekind were writing for theatre in the same period, their plays bear little superficial resemblance. Feydeau was writing for a popular audience, and many (though by no means all) of his plays were hugely successful commercially; Wedekind's plays were banned and widely condemned.[33] They have subsequently found an audience, but it took more than half a century for them to do so. Feydeau's work, however, is more experimental than it might at first seem. Certainly, Wedekind is a more political writer, and his experimentation with theatrical forms is more radical, but both writers submit their characters to the most relentless and excruciating physical and emotional agonies arising directly out of the hypocrisies of the value systems in which they are enmeshed. Both Feydeau and Wedekind created a theatre of madness in which dominant values are turned upside down; a theatre in which the characters' struggle with the contradictions of bourgeois morality results directly, or indirectly, in varying degrees of catastrophe.

I suspect that what attracts Barnes to Wedekind is at least partly his ability to ruffle feathers, his iconoclastic desire to offend bourgeois sensibilities. His plays depict a society in which the self-appointed moral guardians are driven by their fear of sexuality; a fear which they dress up in clothes of sanctimonious moral rectitude and which exhibits itself in repression.

Wedekind is sometimes thought of as a forerunner of the expressionists, but although his work shares some of the qualities of expressionism (the exaggeration, the use of caricature, the attempt to find a concrete theatrical form to represent on stage the tormented internal state of mind of deeply disturbed characters), it refuses the singularity of expressionism, seeking instead to represent multiple perspectives, to dramatise the repressions and the cruelty of a social world, rather than one individual's response to it. In *Spring Awakening*, for example, there is a scene in a school staffroom where the teachers have gathered to condemn Melchior, a student who has written what the head teacher refers to as a 'document . . . entitled *On Copulation*, profusely illustrated with life-sized indecencies, and packed with the most shameless obscenities to meet the demands of the most degenerate reader' (Wedekind, 1969, pp. 56–7). The teachers – Breakneck, Tonguetwister, Strychnine and Rector Corona Radiata[34] – are determined to exact 'retribution for the disastrous effect he has exerted on his fellow pupil'; but they do not allow Melchior to speak, and instead of discussing his 'document' they call on the most abstruse and absurd combination of pseudo-philosophy, false logic, counterfeit morality and inflated rhetoric to argue whether or not to open one of the windows. Throughout the play, Wedekind's sympathies lie clearly with the students – the victims of their elders' fears and denials of sexuality. The scene in the staffroom dramatises the students' perceptions of their teachers as hideous, intimidating grotesques, whose 'learning' and erudition is a mask that barely conceals a terrifying retreat into infantilism. The distortions of the scene are at once comic and deeply shocking. The claim that it is Melchior's influence that has driven his friend, Moritz, to suicide (the 'disastrous effect' that they refer to with such characteristic euphemism) is a self-serving reversal of the truth: it is the repression and deceit that he encounters that drive Moritz to suicide, not Melchior's rather crude attempts to understand his sexuality. I have discussed this scene in some detail because it illuminates Barnes' dramatic method. While Barnes' theatre is not driven directly by sex, there are strong thematic links between the two playwrights. The concern with the effects of the convoluted logic by which those in power retain that power and exercise their authority is clearly echoed in the theatre of Peter Barnes, as is Wedekind's eclectic and grotesque appropriation of popular forms such as cabaret and circus. The links between Wedekind and Barnes are thus not only thematic, but also structural and formal.

Even recent critics have accused Wedekind of amorality.[35] The tone of much journalistic criticism of Barnes' work adopts a similar stance of disapproval,[36] assuming, for example, that Barnes' exploration of the 'frontiers' of humour in *Laughter!* and *The Bewitched* indicates an amoral insensitivity to the subject matter. For both Barnes and Wedekind their ultimate theatrical weapon may be distortion, but their theatre demonstrates a shared belief that it is immoral not to address taboos directly. For Wedekind these taboos relate to the repression of sexuality; for Barnes, compliance with forces of repression. Indeed, I would go so far as to argue that the two playwrights with whom Barnes has the greatest affinity are Ben Jonson and Frank Wedekind, and to draw attention to the unlikely similarities in their work at least offers an indicator as to how Barnes' tonal shifts and formal strategies can be read.

I have noted above that Wedekind is sometimes thought of as a kind of proto-expressionist. Although this is misleading, for it ignores the traditions of the grotesque that pervade much popular culture, he broke new ground in his integration of popular forms in what is effectively an avant-garde theatre with radical subject matter. The resulting exaggerated, gestural performance style that Wedekind's plays demand opened up new possibilities which the expressionists found very attractive. But if the early expressionists championed Wedekind, not least for his representations of highly problematic relationships between the individual and society, they also tended to ignore the critiques of Romantic individualism that his work embodies.

Bertolt Brecht

Brecht's first play, *Baal*, which he acknowledged as directly influenced by Wedekind, presents us with one of the great dramatic anti-heroes. The play opens with an energetic satirical onslaught on the bourgeoisie, who both individually and collectively are excited by the presence of Baal, a hedonist bohemian poet, thinking they can bathe in the reflected glory of his fame – until such time as he attacks their values. As the play develops, however, Baal becomes ever more egotistical, ever more excessive in seeking new sensations. The play is highly critical of bourgeois hypocrisy, but it is also deeply ambivalent in its critiques of individualism and the Romantic view of the artist.

Barnes' work contains several direct references to Brecht's plays. Charlie Ketchum, the central character in the early play *Clap Hands Here Comes Charlie*, is a dissolute tramp and anarchist, and an outrageous egotist who bears more than a passing resemblance to Baal. Barnes' play is similarly ambivalent about its anti-hero. Both Baal and Charlie are antisocial characters in antisocial societies.[37] The *Mother Courage* motif that runs through *Dreaming* presents those who know Brecht's play with complex counterpoints both in specific moments, such as the scene involving Pedlar Cobett and his two teenaged children,[38] and in the comparisons between the two plays' treatment of heroism. But it is the theoretical underpinning that links Barnes most closely to Brecht.

Barnes has contended (perhaps somewhat mischievously) that what he really likes about Brecht is his use of popular song.[39] There is more to Barnes' ironic self-deprecation than meets the ear, for one of the strongest connections between Barnes, Brecht and Wedekind is their use of popular culture: their enthusiasm for cabaret and circus, for those cultural forms which William Archer referred to as 'largely represented in the lower-class theatres, the music-halls and the picture-palaces' (1923, p. 80). The key to Brechtian theory is his focus on the audience, his concern to develop in the audience an active intellectual engagement, an audience that would be conscious of its own participation in the theatrical event, and would learn from it. For Brecht the use of popular forms is integral to his intention to reach and attract new audiences; but this use is also an important aspect of 'epic' theatre, for the forms simultaneously engage an audience with the theatrical event, and distance it from the kind of uncritical involvement that Brecht sought actively to discourage. I do not propose here to summarise Brechtian theory, beyond noting the ways that Barnes, consciously or unconsciously, incorporates particular strategies that are often associated with Brecht to similar, but not the same, purpose. Barnes is highly critical of hegemonic social structures – even his monologues for radio and television dramatise a social context rather than individual psychology – but although his satire is frequently informed by socialist perspectives, he does not write from a socialist agenda. *Silver Bridges*,[40] one of the duologues in the *Barnes' People II* series of radio plays, is an interesting example of this in practice: Vanderbilt, director of the New York Central Railroad, says: 'My idea of competition is to lower the fares to smash all rivals, then double 'em when you're the only robber left' (p. 21). Gould, his arch rival, director of the Erie Railroad, echoes this: 'Legal? . . . In business, "legal" is what you can get away with' (p. 18). The two railroad barons are as crooked as Brecht's Arturo Ui, and they resort to similar chicanery to achieve what they want – total domination. *Silver Bridges* is unusual, however, in that its only characters are railroad tycoons, men at the top. Elsewhere in Barnes' work such 'top-heaviness' is rare. And it is, perhaps, revealing that the play began life as 'an idea . . . for a comedy about that perfect symbol of red-meat capitalism, the blood-stained, clapped-out Erie Railroad and the monsters who manipulated it' (Barnes, 1984, p. v).

Writing about Brecht's influence on late twentieth-century theatrical productions of Shakespeare's plays, Margot Heinemann wrote: 'The acid test, probably, for a production that has assimilated the most important elements of Brecht's thinking is how it deals with the crowd, servants and lower orders generally' (Dollimore and Sinfeld, 1985, p. 248). Her argument is essentially that a Brechtian production shifts perspectives, encourages its audience to see the events of the play through the eyes of the 'lower orders', those who are usually deemed unimportant. One of the finest examples of this in practice can be seen in Grigori Kozintsev's film of *King Lear*, which opens with an extended sequence showing numerous peasants struggling through a hostile landscape to witness Lear's division of the kingdom. While Lear remains the central character, the film shows us a 'pyramid of suffering', the effect of civil war on those who live in Lear's benighted kingdom. This shift of social emphasis, which relates to Brecht's *Verfremdungseffekt* discussed below, is echoed in Barnes' theatre. It is perhaps most evident in *Dreaming*, where Shakespeare's Richard of Gloucester appears as a minor character, harassing the ragged band of mercenaries and oddballs that gather around Mallory. But the strategy is one which informs much of his later work. In his introduction to the quartet of monologues for television, *Revolutionary Witness*, Barnes wrote:

> Most of history is still written from the view from the top. This [*Revolutionary Witness*] is history from below. These four, obscure characters are always in the background – one of the crowd, part of the mob. But they speak more directly to us than

King Louis, Robespierre or Danton ever could. It is always difficult to feel any human kinship with leaders or politicians, past
and present.

(1989, p. ii)

The claim is specific to the monologues that make up
Revolutionary Witness, but it can be seen to relate to much of
Barnes' later work. Even the most notable apparent exceptions,
The Ruling Class and *The Bewitched,* are interested in mechanisms by which 'ordinary people' become enmeshed in compliance with repressive social and political structures which work
against their own interests. Barnes has argued that he does 'not
write about ordinary men and women. The variety and enormity
of the world and its people and their infinite possibilities make
belief in the ordinariness of ordinary people a blasphemy' (1986,
p. ix).[41] And this statement seems in itself to represent an
endorsement of Brechtian practice, in as much that it asserts an
attempt to make the ordinary seem extraordinary, the familiar
seem strange. Brecht first coined the term *Verfremdungseffekt* in
1935. It has sometimes been translated as the 'alienation effect',
but this is misleading. A literal translation, the 'making strange
effect' might seem clumsy, but it is more useful. In Brecht's own
words, the term means 'stripping events of [their] self-evident,
familiar, obvious quality and creating a sense of astonishment
and curiosity about them'.[42] The *Verfremdungseffekt* exposes the
ways in which the 'natural' is socially and politically contingent.
'What is "natural" must have the force of what is startling. This
is the only way to expose the laws of cause and effect. People's
activity must simultaneously be so and be capable of being different' (Brecht, 1964, p. 71). Brecht developed a number of theatrical devices and strategies – including gestural acting styles,
the use of song, the projection of written texts and documentary

information – all intended to disturb spectators' relationships with characters in a play, to encourage them to engage with the situations intellectually, but not to sympathise emotionally, to be alert to suppressed or unconsidered alternatives. This notion of 'alternatives' is highly significant in Brechtian theatre, and refers as much to characters as to situations. Although Brecht is often characterised as reacting against naturalism, he regarded naturalism as only one manifestation of what he termed 'dramatic theatre', a theatre in which the events represented on stage are seen as inevitable and inescapable. He argued that audiences' responses to such a theatre may be emphatic, they recognise 'truthfulness' in the 'tragic', but that their responses are essentially passive: 'The dramatic theatre's spectator says . . . Yes, I have felt like that too . . . it'll never change . . . the sufferings of this man appal me, because they are inescapable' (1964, p. 71). He appropriated the term 'epic' to describe the kind of theatre that he wished to see, a theatre in which the spectator sees that the behaviour of characters as much as the situations in which they find themselves could be otherwise than as presented. One of the key distinctions that he makes between dramatic theatre and epic theatre relates to the function of humour in the theatre: in the dramatic theatre 'I [a spectator] weep when they [the characters on the stage] weep, I laugh when they laugh'; whereas in the epic theatre 'I laugh when they weep, I weep when they laugh' (Brecht, 1964, p. 71). This is particularly pertinent when considering the relationship between Barnes' plays and Brechtian theory. In a programme note for *Red Noses*, Barnes wrote:

> The aim is to create, by means of soliloquy, rhetoric, formalised ritual, slapstick, songs, and dances, a comic theatre of contrasting moods and opposites, where everything is simultaneously tragic and ridiculous.

As has often been observed, many of the strategies which Brecht developed in order to achieve the *Verfremdungseffekt* have become commonplace in Western theatre; they have been separated from their original radical social and political purpose. But although devices such as the use of the Brechtian half-curtain, the open stage with visible light sources and the use of placards and projections have almost become theatrical clichés, the radical effects that Brecht sought to achieve by using them can still be achieved. To do so demands seeking new means, not mannerist reproductions of Brechtian 'technique'. Brecht himself acknowledged that theatre, by its very nature, needs to constantly reinvent itself, not through innovation for its own sake, but by considered reflection on its relationship with the changing cultural contexts in which its meanings are made – by theatre practitioners and by spectators.[43] New means would have to be sought to ensure that spectators are drawn to the theatre and challenged by it.

While I would not argue that Barnes wears Brecht's mantle, there are many aspects of his theatrical practice whose functions are similar to those sought by Brecht in his use of the *Verfremdungseffekt*. Perhaps the most significant 'strangeness' in Barnes' work is his radical use of humour. Certainly this owes as much to Jonson, Marston, Feydeau and Wedekind as it does to Brecht; nevertheless, Brecht acknowledged the profound influence of Early Modern theatre on his own work. The tonal shifts, which are such a marked characteristic of the humour in plays of the Early Modern period, create effects which range from unsettling, through disorienting, to deeply disturbing. Some of the many effects of the shifts of tone in Barnes' theatre are: to draw attention to the theatrical artifice; to engage an audience in the humour, while simultaneously disengaging it from an empathetic relationship with characters, thereby creating a self-reflexive and active audience; and to break up narrative flow in order to deny the inevitability of any given narrative and create a sense of alternatives. Chapter 9 examines in detail, and through reference to specific moments in the plays, how Barnes' use of humour aims to achieve these effects.

I hope to have shown that in examining the way that Barnes' theatre draws on Brecht, it has been more useful to consider his own strategies for making the world seem 'strange' than noting those theatrical devices that directly echo Brecht's. As I have already argued, Barnes does not bring a clear political agenda to his theatre. Taken with his desire to represent 'ordinary' people as unique, this might lead one to think of Barnes as a liberal humanist; but, although he offers no easy prescriptions, his plays cry out for social and political change. His own claim that his 'Writing . . . has a moral purpose in the service of politics; not politics as propaganda but, rather, teaching by example'[44] may seem rather generalised, but it confirms the affiliation with playwrights such as Jonson, Marston and Brecht, all of whose work can be thought of as 'educative' in the broadest sense of that word. In the same 'Notes', Barnes discusses his aim to create a

> drama of extremes, trying to illuminate the truth as contradictory. Instead of eliminating those contradictions as untrue, they are emphasised; melancholy and joy, tragedy and comedy, the bathetic and the sublime are placed side by side. The similarity of such opposites is shown by such juxtapositions. What we call tragic or comic are, in fact, their opposites, for it is a principle of dialectical logic that what seems on the surface one thing, is essentially its opposite. So incompatible and widely 'contradictory' elements are superimposed on each other until they are transformed into reality, which is itself made up of similar contradictory elements also existing side by side with each other.
>
> (1986, p. 113)

Barnes' use of contradictions thus echoes Brecht's while not replicating it. His is a theatre in which characters are constructed so as to embody contradictions. In *Dreaming*, for example, Mallory is at once a hero and a liability: an egotistical visionary whose friends and followers look to him for guidance, a paternal figure who seeks to extricate them from the brutality of war, who leads these same people to their death. These contradictions are foregrounded rather than smoothed over and psychologised as they would be in naturalism; as in Brecht, the contradictions are presented to us in order to interrogate the social context which gives rise to them. In relation to the 'Notes' referred to above, it is also worth adding that towards the end of Brecht's life, he began to find the term 'epic theatre' inadequate as a term for the kind of theatre that he wanted to make. As yet, 'the actual phrase "dialectical theatre" was still to be held in reserve' (Willett in Brecht, 1964, p. 282), but that is undoubtedly what he sought. I would not argue that Barnes has achieved such a theatre, but merely note that this notion of a 'dialectical theatre' is what he has striven to create.

Episodic Montage

Brecht's 'epic theatre' is essentially episodic in structure, each episode contributing meaning to the whole while developing alternative perspectives on the central theme. The episodes in Mother Courage's journeys through Poland and Germany during the Thirty Years War are linked by the contradictory desires of 'the merchant-mother' to safeguard her family and to profit from the war. Every scene offers a different perspective on this, but this is far more ideologically significant than the variations on a theme that one might encounter in a picaresque novel: these different, alternative perspectives, which Brecht in a slightly different context referred to as 'complex seeing', are as important as the overriding narrative drive. Barnes' theatre too is episodic, not only eschewing naturalism, but also creating an episodic montage which seeks to develop multiple perspectives, and consciously points up its own artifice through a range of metatheatrical devices such as the Author (or a character named Barnes) who appears in the prologues to *Clap Hands Here Comes Charlie*, *Laughter!* and *Jubilee*: characters who are aware of their status as characters in a play (such as in *Dreaming* or *Red Noses*). One of the functions of the metatheatricality in Barnes' plays is to encourage audiences to be reflexive, to think critically about what they are watching, and about their own responses to it. Barnes does not want his audiences to forget that they are in a theatre; although his formal strategies do not replicate Brecht's, his use of montage structure also encourages 'complex seeing', demanding that we see things both as they are and, at the same time, as alterable, as other than they are.

I began this chapter by considering how Barnes might be thought of as a neo-Jacobean, a question to which I would like now to return. One of the most important formal characteristics of Early Modern theatre is its use of what might now be termed 'montage'. The structure of many plays of that period is often thought of in terms of plot and sub-plot; but, as I argue in the next chapter, 'A Montage of Attractions', while the division might be useful for a play such as *The Taming of the Shrew*, such a hierarchical division of function is both reductive and misleading when applied to plays such as *Bartholomew Fair*, *The Changeling* or even *King Lear*. Division into plot and sub-plot implies that the latter merely echoes or supports the former, perhaps offering variations on a theme. I shall argue, however, that meaning is generated in the montage of differing narrative strands, the juxtaposition of different episodes. In developing his own thoughts about epic theatre, Brecht drew heavily on Early Modern theatrical practice.[45] Brecht was, however, by no means the only practitioner in the first half of the twentieth century who was profoundly influenced by the Early Modern theatre. In Russia, Vsevolod Meyerhold, whom Brecht greatly admired, was developing new theatrical forms and seeking new audiences. The next chapter focuses on the theatre of Meyerhold and that of his one-time student, Sergei Eisenstein, examining how their theories of montage might illuminate the theatre of Peter Barnes.

8

A Montage of Attractions

Forget urgent narrative – this is a series of gorgeously observed moments . . .

(From a review of Dreaming)[1]

I look for the similarity in opposites, the swirls of smoke over Battersea Power Station and the whirls of a ballerina's skirt, the eddies of an estuary and the vectors of an iris.

Peter Barnes[2]

Peter Barnes has written numerous film scripts. He has often claimed that his work as a screenwriter is not to be taken seriously – in the sense that he sees his other work (for the stage, the radio and British TV) as more personal and richer in meaning.[3] As noted in my introduction, he refers to his screenplays as 'assignment work, craft work',[4] the implication being that this craft brings in enough money to enable him to write plays on his own terms. Indeed, he has spoken of his beloved Ben Jonson's work on the masques for the Stuart court in much the same terms. He believes that the fees Jonson received for work on the masques enabled him to write those plays that Barnes perceives as radical and subversive.[5] Furthermore, recent scholarship has explored how Jonson's late plays seem to have been influenced by his work on the masques,[6] not least by the experience of working with women playing female roles, with the result that the later plays – from *The Devil Is an Ass* onward – are far more sympathetic towards women than the early and middle period comedies. 'Influence' is a more problematic concept than the simple notion of a one-way transference of ideas allows; in the case of both Jonson and Barnes the influence of one form on another seems far more of an interactive process than is immediately evident. In Chapter 7 I examine some of the relationships between Barnes' theatre and Jacobean theatre; in this chapter I want to narrow my focus to a consideration of how one of the key structural elements of the theatre of Jonson and his contemporaries, episodic juxta-position, relates to the concept of 'montage', a term which is more frequently associated with film-making than with theatre, but which, I shall argue, is of great importance in reading the drama of Peter Barnes off the page, and in realising it theatrically.

Given Barnes' wide knowledge of cinema history and his depth of understanding of cinematic practice and theory, it is hardly surprising that his stage plays resonate with cinematic allusions. The purpose of this chapter, however, is not to explore these reference points, but to consider how montage theories, a key development in the cinema, inform the formal, structural qualities of Barnes' plays; and to examine how, in turn, these montage-like structures might affect both the performance style and the possible meanings of the plays.

One of the key differences between illusionist and non-illusionist theatre practice is in the latter's use of episodic structure, rather than a straightforward linear narrative flow. The structural components of illusionist theatre are deliberately concealed, making the artifice invisible; whereas in much non-illusionist theatre, the basic dramatic unit is the episode, and the artifice of dramatic construction is not only revealed, but frequently drawn attention to. Brecht referred to such theatre practice as 'epic', contrasting it with the 'dramatic'. As I have argued in the previous chapter, there are certainly links between Barnes' theatre and Brechtian theory and practice; but in relation to Barnes' theatre, I think it more useful to invoke the theories and practices of Russian directors Vsevolod Meyerhold[7] and Sergei Eisenstein, who worked with Meyerhold as a student and then as a theatre director, before shifting his attention to the cinema, where he became a highly influential and radical director.

'I should call cinema the "art of juxtapositions",' wrote Eisenstein, and he provided a simple illustrative example: the first set of shots depicts a woman in poverty with her undernourished child with an empty bowl; cut to the second set of shots depicting an overweight man with a golden watch and chain stretched over his fat belly; he is seated at a table groaning with food. The juxtaposition of these two sets of images causes a 'collision' that in turn 'creates a third set of images (construed in the spectator's mind): that of the oppression of the proletariat by the bourgeoisie'.[8] In Eisenstein's theory, a sequence of images 'in conflict' provokes a creative reaction within the spectator who produces for him/herself a third meaning, and thus the spectator becomes 'responsible' for creatively reading what he or she sees. As David Mamet puts it in a *Guardian* article:

> Eisenstein's theory of montage comes down to this: the juxtaposition of shot A, followed by shot B, should create in the viewer the idea C. The viewer should not be told the idea, but should come to it himself.

(2003, p. 5)

While Eisenstein's montage theories are usually thought of primarily as a practical tool, whose main use is for film-makers, applying them to Barnes' theatre offers valuable insights both into the formal systems that he employs and the ways that his plays generate meaning. The concept of 'collision montage' grew out of a term that Eisenstein and Vsevolod Meyerhold each used in connection with their theatrical productions: 'the montage of attractions'.[9] Although it is not certain which of them first coined this phrase, Eisenstein acknowledged a substantial debt to Meyerhold; the two worked together extensively in the theatre before Eisenstein turned to the cinema. Indeed, for about a year, in 1921 to 1922, he had formally become a pupil of the GVYTM (State Higher Theatre Workshop). While there, under Meyerhold's direct supervision, he had designed stage sets for a production of Ben Jonson's *Bartholomew Fair*. The play had a considerable impact on Eisenstein; in Jonson he recognised both a precedent and an inspiration for his own work:

> I think that an unsurpassed example of the contrapuntal montage of fragmentary scenes, in which several plot-lines are pursued simultaneously and whose totality adds up to a marvellous generalised image – an image of the dizzy whirl of a fairground – is Ben Jonson's structuring of *Bartholomew Fair*.
>
> (Eisenstein, 1991, p. 186)

While it is important not to confuse and conflate the work of Eisenstein and Meyerhold, Meyerhold himself maintained that 'All Eisenstein's work has its origins in the laboratory where we worked together as teacher and pupil. But our relationship was not so much the relationship of teacher and pupil as of two artists in revolt.' (Braun, 1969, p. 311). In 1936 the cinema director Kozintsev wrote: 'It seems to me that the Soviet cinema has learned more from the brilliance of Meyerhold's work than the Soviet theatre' (Leach, 1989, p. 170). And it is precisely because of the light that Eisenstein's work sheds on theatrical practice that I want to dwell a little longer on the project that he set himself, before turning to its particular relevance to the theatre of Peter Barnes.

As far as narration goes, given Eisenstein's revolutionary task (to present the proletarian story), it is unsurprising that his editing style indicated a privileging of the image over narrative and characterisation (that is, there is no single hero, only the proletariat as hero). While Barnes' theatre is not driven by the same political urges, it is essentially social rather than individual drama. Even *The Ruling Class* is more concerned with the social and political systems that invest such power in the Gurney family than in Jack Gurney's personal psychosis, which is presented more as a product of an insane society than a dysfunctional family. Eisenstein further developed his ideas about the workings of montage in an essay written in 1929, 'Beyond the Shot', arguing that Japanese script, with its use of ideograms (or hieroglyphs as he mistakenly called them)[10] had important lessons for cinema:

> The point is that . . . the combination . . . of two hieroglyphs of the simplest series is regarded not as their sum total but as their product, i.e. as a value of another dimension, another degree: each taken separately corresponds to an object but their combination corresponds to a *concept*. The combination of two 'representable' objects achieves the representation of something that cannot be graphically represented.

In Eisenstein's view,

> *montage is not an idea composed of successive shots stuck together but an idea that* DERIVES *from the collision between two shots that are independent of one another.* As in Japanese hieroglyphics

in which two independent ideographic characters ('shots') are juxtaposed and *explode* into a concept. THUS:

Eye + Water	=	Crying
Door + Ear	=	Eavesdropping
Child + Mouth	=	Screaming
Mouth + Dog	=	Barking
Mouth + Bird	=	Singing
Knife + Heart	=	Anxiety etc.

(Taylor, 1998, pp. 95–6)

Whereas Eisenstein evidently sought to control the spectators' response, Meyerhold spoke of his desire to create juxtapositions which play on the spectators' need to make connections, provoking 'a whole chorus of associations . . . You can no longer distinguish between what the director is responsible for and what is inspired by the associations which have invaded your imagination.'[11] There are elements of both these urges in Barnes' plays: the desire to guide an audience, to produce specific effects; and the desire to create self-consciously open texts, in which readers make their own meanings. It is an unresolved tension.

In developing their respective theories of epic theatre and of collision montage, both Brecht and Eisenstein drew heavily on their knowledge of and admiration for English theatre of the Early Modern period. Thus, although the term 'montage' was not coined until the early twentieth century,[12] Early Modern theatre is frequently structured in such a way that the juxtaposition of episodes itself creates meanings beyond those contained within the separate episodes. The episodes themselves might be relatively self-contained and as such they have meanings in themselves; but these meanings are modified, subverted, enhanced, and mediated by the episodes with which they are juxtaposed. In *King Lear*, for example, Lear's division of his kingdom, if taken

214

on its own, can be read as a miscalculated act of political ruthlessness, a means of ensuring that the wealthiest part of his kingdom goes to his favoured, youngest daughter and that his two other daughters are given 'equal' but less significant shares to ensure their relative political impotence. This is not, however, the first episode in the play. It is preceded by Kent's exchange with Gloucester, which not only introduces the 'division of the kingdom' (I.i.4) but also the issue of Edmund's bastardy. If one reads this in thematic terms, as linear readings of narrative tend to, then this short exchange can be seen as alerting an audience to the likely significance of Edmund in the plot and to the importance that the play places on patrilineal lines of descent. As montage, however, meaning is created not only by the episodes themselves, but also by the juxtaposition of the two episodes, and by the rhythmic relationship between them. The shortness of an episode may even add to its weight. In this instance, Gloucester's account of Edmund's birth 'rhymes' with Lear's peremptory treatment of Cordelia. For all the brevity of the exchange between Gloucester and Kent, the rhythmic juxtaposition of the treatment of Edmund and Cordelia draws attention to similarities and differences between them.

Grigori Kozintsev's magnificent film of *King Lear* offers a more graphic example of the way in which the meanings of this specific episode can be specifically mediated by the effects of montage. The film opens with what in narrative terms might be seen as a prologue: a lengthy sequence without dialogue in which we follow a ragged mass of peasants as they journey through barren wasteland towards what will shortly be revealed as Lear's castle. As Sergei Yutkevitch observed: 'the whole film begins remarkably, not as an incident within the walls of the castle, but as an event with repercussions far beyond. It is not only the characters of the drama who are involved but an important new hero:

the people' (1971, p. 194). There is no direct narrative link between this sequence and the exchange between Gloucester and Kent and the division of the kingdom which follows it. The meanings it generates arise out of juxtapositions. The sumptuous, though cold, interior of the castle contrasts with the wilderness outside, and generates meaning in much the same way as Eisenstein's famous example of the 'collision' between the undernourished child and the overweight man. The opening sequence remains in the mind's eye, reminding us that 'the people' are those who will suffer most from their ruler's irresponsible inability to distinguish between public office and private whim.

MONTAGE STRUCTURE IN THE PLAYS AND FILMS OF PETER BARNES

But how does all this relate to the theatre of Peter Barnes? Barnes' plays are self-consciously theatrical. This does, however, raise the problem of finding an appropriate means of discussing them in theatrical, rather than literary, terms. Focusing on theatrical 'attractions' and their function within the plays is a means of doing this. Although Barnes does not acknowledge a direct line of influence between his own plays and the work of Meyerhold and Eisenstein,[13] their practice and theoretical reflections on montage, rhythm and dramatic structure are potentially richly illuminating in considering Barnes' work both in terms of the production of meaning and in seeking appropriate playing styles for his theatre.

There is no doubt that Barnes' immersion in cinema, both as a screenwriter and as a cinephile, has had a profound effect on his theatre. It is therefore a little ironic that, with one notable exception, his screenplays are far less daring in their use of montage structure than his stage plays. His screenplay for *Enchanted*

April, for example (for which he received an Oscar nomination),
is more linear in its narrative structure than almost all of his
major plays. The notable exception amongst his screenplays is
the miniseries *Arabian Nights*,[14] which creates a rich montage of
dramatisations of the different stories told by Scheherazade, each
punctuated by and juxtaposed with events in Sharyar's palace, as
the shah's young bride spins out her elegant stories in her
attempt to beguile her husband and avoid the executioner. Not
surprisingly, given its subject matter, *Arabian Nights*, in Barnes'
version, becomes a disquisition about the need for narrative, an
examination of the ways that identity is closely interwoven with
identification, of the reader's active participation in making
meaning. The same actors appear in several different stories;
although each of the 'episodes' is self-contained, its contribution
to the text as a whole is a function both of its immediate effect
on the shah and its rhythmical relationships with the stories that
surround it; there are numerous visual rhymes and motifs that
echo back and forth through the different stories. The subject
matter of *Arabian Nights* undoubtedly encourages this approach,
but it nevertheless allows Barnes to bring to the screenplay his
remarkable talents as montageur. The structural technique of
Arabian Nights draws attention to a peculiar characteristic of his
work for theatre and gives a significant indicator of what it is that
differentiates the majority of his work as a screenwriter from his
work as a playwright, for it demonstrates that, although Barnes,
like Jonson before him, is renowned for his verbal dexterity and
his celebratory use of language, it is the abrupt juxtapositions –
between the comic and the philosophical, the metaphysical and
the materialist, the abject and the sublime – and the resulting
densely rhythmical quality that most clearly characterise Barnes'
best work for the theatre.

Barnes has often been criticised on the grounds that his work contains such shifts of tone, such contradictions of form and style, as to make it incoherent.[15] As I hope I have shown in the chapters on specific plays, it is these shifts and contradictions as much as the narrative, the exuberant imagery and the characterisation, which make Barnes' theatre so distinctive. Such abrupt contrasts and juxtapositions make for a very unstable theatre, in which it is difficult for audiences to find points of security, which forces individual members of an audience to exercise their own judgement in matters of taste; but instability is far from incoherence.

As Edward Braun has observed of Meyerhold, he 'sought to reveal the ruling idea of a play by creating a series of "attractions", constructed according to musical principles, not with the conventional aim of advancing the narrative' (1969, p. 318). Robert Leach makes a similar point:

> There is . . . a plainly dialectic relationship between the montage of fragmented episodes . . . and the [overall] rhythmic and musical conception. The final strength of Meyerhold's mature work lay in large measure in the tension which precisely this contradiction created.
>
> (1989, p. 125)

But it is Meyerhold himself whose thoughts about tragedy and comedy come closest to touching what might be termed the spirit of Barnes' theatre work:

> A director who claims he can only stage tragedies, and doesn't know how to stage comedies or vaudevilles, is certain to fail because in genuine art the high and the low, the bitter and the funny, the light and the dark stand side by side.
>
> (Gladkov, 1997, p. 128)

A brief consideration of the series of four short television plays that make up *Revolutionary Witness* demonstrates the value of approaching Barnes' work in these terms. Each of the plays that comprise the series lasts about twenty minutes, and is a monologue, allowing a character who has been profoundly affected by the French Revolution to tell his or her story. The plays are related in terms of form and subject matter; superficially this is the only connection between them. None of the four characters are named in each other's stories, and there is no direct narrative link between them. On television the plays were screened over four consecutive nights; thus they would have appeared as thematically connected but self-contained – in much the same way that an episode, or an 'attraction' in a montage, creates meaning in its own right and, simultaneously, evokes meaning through its relations to other 'attractions' with which it has a temporal, a spatial or a rhythmic relationship. When the four plays of *Revolutionary Witness* are juxtaposed, however, as the plays might be in a theatrical production, the meaning of the work as a whole is potentially greatly enriched. A detailed analysis of the way the play works as montage can be found in Chapter 6. Here I will briefly note that it is one of the rhythmic effects of montage, not narrative, that relates Théroigne de Méricourt's restless chanting of the revolutionary anthem 'Liberty, Equality, Fraternity' (which opens and closes the fourth play, *The Amazon*) to Palloy's cynical exploitation of revolutionary 'relics'; and it is thus the effect of montage that creates such rich ambiguities and provocations when the play is seen as an integrated whole.

It should, however, be noted that the linear and the lateral are not mutually exclusive. Eisenstein's *Battleship Potemkin* tells a story, but rather than one person's story, it is 'the people's' story; and its meanings are far richer than a straightforwardly linear reading would allow. My argument about montage structure in

Barnes' work is not that his plays are exclusively lateral in structure, nor that approaching them as montage denies the pleasures of their linear narratives (like Ben Jonson, he is a master of plotting), but that considering their structure in terms of a 'montage of attractions' enriches a reading of the plays; and is particularly useful when considering *Red Noses, Dreaming* and *The Bewitched*, the last being the play I shall focus on for the final part of this chapter.

Before looking at *The Bewitched*, I want briefly to consider the difference between the concept of an 'attraction' and that of a 'unit'. It is common theatrical practice to break up acts and scenes into smaller components. Stanislavski coined the term 'units' to describe this. If a scene were to be divided up into units would the result be much the same as breaking it down into its constituent attractions? The unit of action is psychologically driven; it is a unit of meaning for the actor(s). In Stanislavski's terms, if the actors find the 'truth' of the scene, the audience will understand it. This has narrative implications: it implies a linear narrative, one which reveals cause and effect. But Chekhov's naturalism is already very different from Ibsen's. Whereas the Ibsenite model is essentially linear, employing gaps in the flow of narrative information (or narrative enigmas – *why* does Nora fear Krogstadt; what are Dr Rank and Oswald suffering from?) not only to retain our interest in the drama but also to reinforce the model of human behaviour as determinist, Chekhov's later drama is more lateral in construction. Interestingly, the Ibsenite structural model is the one wholeheartedly adopted by Hollywood, in spite of some significant early experimenting by D. W. Griffith. And although early naturalists conceived of their work as radical and critical of the hegemony, the problem with naturalism's determinist foundations is that it can lead to a sense that any given social situation is inevitably thus. This is what

Brecht and Meyerhold before him rejected in the naturalist project: the idea of socially contingent human behaviour being seen as 'natural'. Breaking a scene into attractions is not concerned with inner psychological truths, but with audience perceptions. If a unit is conceived of as a means by which the actor can find psychological truth, the attraction is conceived of in terms of audience and audience response. It is as likely to be something strange, inexplicable, perhaps surrealist, as it is to be a circus trick or a Commedia style *lazzi*.

I have sketched out below a summary of the Prologue to *The Bewitched*, noting some of the theatrical attractions that it contains, to demonstrate firstly the diversity of what might be considered an attraction, and then to consider how the montage of these attractions might create meaning.

Prologue
- In darkness, Pontocarrero's prayer.
- The spectacle of Philip's bedchamber.
- Appearance of Sebastien de Morra, the court jester to Philip.
- Ritual undressing of Philip.
- Spectacle of the pomp and formality of the court.
- The sexual inadequacy of Philip.
- Philip undertaking 'sheet duty' with Beatriz and then Mariana.
- The grotesque spectacle of the birth of Carlos.

Some of these attractions function as part of the linear narrative. Pontocarrero's prayer, for example, sets up expectations which are then met and challenged. It dwells on death and decay; it is steeped in Old Testament imagery: 'Egypt's eight plagues maketh not such sorrow' (p. 192). We are immersed in a world which is dominated by Pontocarrero's vision of a vengeful God who puts believers to trial through suffering. The collision montage, however, develops meanings in the space between the attractions, in the parallels and contrasts, in the logical gaps and lateral jumps. Pontocarrero's belief in a punitive deity is not the cause of Philip's sexual dysfunction, but an audience is made aware that this is a world in which such hideous associations are made all too readily. Sebastien de Morra is '*dressed exactly like the grandees*' complete with goatee beard (p. 193); the jester's pompous self-importance is absurd, but no more so than the highest officials of state. The lavishly opulent setting is the scene for the most abject baseness; the most material of human actions, sexual congress, birth and death, dressing and undressing, become the subject of grand rituals – but the spectacle, while an attraction in itself, ridicules the attempt to deny the stench of putrefaction that pervades the court.

On a larger scale, the montage of attractions works between scenes as well as within them. The three scenes which immediately follow the Prologue contain the following attractions, amongst many others:

Act One, Scene 1
- Ana and Mariana squabble, trading insults.
- Their squabble outlines the grounds for the War of Succession.
- Sexual repression and violent self-harm as Ana, Mariana and Carlos all fall into epileptic fits.
- The increasingly bitter confrontation between Ana and Mariana punctuated by Carlos babbling and Ana's parrot screeching and passing disrespectful comments.

In Meyerhold's sense of the term, the quarrel is an attraction, as are the fits. These may not be 'attractive' in the sense of being

aesthetically pleasing, but they attract an audience, in the way
that such events in the street might. As an audience, we may be
horrified by Ana's '*body jerk[ing] up and down as she tears her
dress and hits her crotch in excitement*' (p. 202), we may even
want to look away, but the fit functions as a grotesque turn,
which simultaneously develops the narrative and stands independently of it. If the rhythmic patterns of the scene do not exactly
equate Carlos with the parrot, they draw attention to Carlos
being as politically impotent, but even less articulate. '*Kill for
Lent! Kill for Lent!*' screeches the parrot; and if this is the darkest of humour, it makes us laugh because of its horrific anticipation of the impending auto-da-fé.

Act One, Scene 2
- The duelling dwarfs – Sebastien and Rafael de Morra, father
  and son – with Rafael blindfold.
- Father teaching son to survive as court jester.
- Discourse on the function of fools.
- A brief patter of jokes.

The duelling with tiny rapiers is itself an attraction, conceived
of as a circus turn, with Rafael blindfold. And so too is the teaching, the philosophising on fooling and the jokes themselves.
Again, the constituent elements of the scene contribute to the
narrative indirectly, but they also function independently of it.
The telling of jokes in vaudevillian style is related to the duel and
to survival at court, both logically and rhythmically – 'I'll defend
my honour and the King's and cling t' "Mother Bunch's Joke-
book" as 't were my Bible,' says Rafael (p. 203). For Sebastien,
an understanding of the patterning of jokes is as important as the
protocol of the court and the formality of the duel.

Act One, Scene 3

- The Council Chamber. Spectacle.
- Contrast between the power of the assembly and the absurdity of its proceedings – presented in vaudevillian style.
- Discussion of whether or not the king is conscious, and how it may be possible to tell.
- The queen mother contracts cancer (an Old Man appears from the shadows and squeezes her breast).
- Argument between the grandees about privilege, wealth and status.

When Sebastien tells of the importance of honouring the king, it is immediately after we have seen the king mocked by a parrot. In Scene 3 the appearance of death in the shape of the Old Man is also a kind of levelling. Playing the scene for its attractions is likely to produce a style of theatre which resembles vaudeville, which seeks out and celebrates the contradictions and instability of the play, which forces the audience to make its own meanings. But the rhythmical structure of these three scenes produces meanings over which Barnes has undoubtedly attempted to exert a degree of control. Each of the scenes opens with a ferocious argument. Just as the internal logic of Scene 3 mocks the grandees' determination to conflate privileges conferred by the state with personal worth and merit, so the structural relationship between the scenes ensures that the circus-like routine of the duelling dwarfs (in which the world-weary elder Morra gives sound advice to his son) offers a benchmark against which to measure the crabbed personal wrangling between queen and queen mother and the vainglory of the council. Focusing on the attractions in these scenes highlights the rhythmical relationships between them.

Further on in the act, the destabilising effect of the montage becomes even more unsettling as the juxtapositions of suffering and comedy become increasingly extreme. Scenes 11 to 14 include the following:

Act One, Scene 11
- Bedroom farce.
- The scene concludes with Carlos having a fit, after which he becomes lucid, and rants against God.

Act One, Scene 12
- Carlos is still lucid, but chanting, almost as a mantra, 'WWWWWhy do I suffer?'
- Motilla glories in the pain of the human predicament, making a speech about God making men suffer, using man's suffering as a way of punishing him for his sins.

This scene is as 'serious' as the previous is farcical.

Act One, Scene 13
- The throne room. Carlos is slumped.
- While the central arguments take place about 'what's to be done', torture instruments are displayed in the background.
- Guilt, superstition and fear – all manipulated relentlessly by those in power.

Act One, Scene 14
- The confession of Duro (the Jew).

The confession is simultaneously comic and horrific, as he resists torture, then confesses, only for Valladares to insist that Duro 'Recant your new found faith' because it would be more convenient to the Inquisition to burn a live Jew than a dead

Christian (p. 261). Valladares' hideous distorted logic is itself an attraction, contributing to the montage effect within and between these scenes: a montage which tramples the barriers between the comic and the horrific. As we become increasingly uncertain of our responses to the comic, the equations between healing and pain, punishment and salvation, suffering and redemption become ever more absurd; and Carlos's declaration of war against God Himself becomes a moment of sanity.

I would like now to analyse in greater detail an extended sequence from *The Bewitched*: Scenes 6, 7 and 8 of Act Two (pp. 293–303). In Scene 6 Motilla is praying in the darkness, 'abject in despair' (p. 293). He imagines a time when God will come to him, at which point a messenger arrives. Motilla asks: 'out o' Zion wi' a message from the Blessed Saviour?' 'No,' replies the messenger, 'out o' Madrid wi' a message from the Blessed Cardinal-Archbishop o' Toledo.' Motilla is briefly elated – and then has his throat slit. A second messenger appears, announcing that he is from the Cardinal-Archbishop. 'Live and let live,' he proclaims – and then kills the first (p. 294). This develops into a repeating routine: messengers killing messengers in an endless loop. There is no way out of the cycle of assassination. The scene, as so often in *The Bewitched*, is simultaneously horrific and comic, with the comedy arising from the juxtaposition of Motilla's spiritual aspirations and the ghastly reality of his dispatch at the hands of the messenger. The meaning of the scene also derives from the repetition of the cycle, the relentless accumulation of corpses, itself a product of the montage structure.

The action of Scene 7 comprises the build-up to, and action of, a duel between Almirante and Rafael. The scene seems relatively self-contained, in that it could be performed as an independent turn; it is as elegantly structured as a Commedia routine. In terms of plot, and sub-plot, it contributes little to the overall play: Rafael is resented by the court, loathed by Ana, but the outcome of the duel does not hasten his demise. It simplifies the action to get rid of Almirante at this point (Ana is more isolated within the court), but even that is not essential. The meanings of the scene arise out of its juxtaposition with what precedes and follows. The move between Scene 6 and Scene 7 feels like a cinematic cross-cut. Scene 6 ends as *'we hear diminishing snatches of conversation as the cycle of assassination continues in the darkness'* (p. 295). The *'cycle of assassination'* itself echoes the Prologue in which the monarchical succession is presented as an unbreakable cycle of madness.

Scene 7 opens with *'Birdsong. Dawn lights up on a woodland clearing.'* (p. 295). This may create a pastoral atmosphere but, at least for some members of the audience, the sound of birdsong is also likely to create a tinge of apprehension – given the association between birdsong and the carnage of First World War battlefields.[16] Following examples set by Eisenstein and Meyerhold,[17] I shall consider Scene 7, and the first moment of Scene 8, as a sequence of attractions to demonstrate further the inclusiveness of the term, and to indicate how the scene might work theatrically when approached in this way.

Act Two, Scene 7

• Almirante, Alba and Torres (grandees and courtiers) discuss the concept of honour and bemoan Pontocarrero's power. Nostalgia for the days when duels were fought to decide issues of honour. The attraction lies in the comic mockery of honour (echoing back to Act One, Scene 2, where Rafael insists that he will defend the king's honour), in the verbal humour of catch-22 logic: 'Challenged the first f' looking at me sideways, the second f' staring straight at me, the third f' not looking at me at all!' (p. 296).

- We learn that Almirante has been challenged to a duel by Rafael. He removes his cloak in preparation, and registers his serious intent: 'Our midget Zany must be taught a lasting lesson' (p. 296). The 'attraction' of the ritual preparation for the duel, the expectation aroused that the pompous, self-important Almirante will be taught a lesson.
- Rafael and Morra (his father) arrive. Morra has a hangover – allowing, and indeed demanding, some character-based stage business.
- Verbal confrontation between Almirante and Morra. Almirante seeks an apology; Morra a fight. The mismatch, together with the reversal of expected roles, is a potential source of humour.
- Rafael makes a self-mocking joke that seemingly reveals his cowardice and reluctance to fight – 'puff pastry at eighty [paces]' (p. 297). Rafael appears to have been bullied into the duel by his aggressive and domineering father. Further business between father and son.
- The formal set-up for the duel – visual incongruity. Rafael's tiny paces contrasted with Almirante's.
- Almirante fires water over Rafael. Visual humour, and a further reversal of expectations.
- Morra is '*white-faced with rage*' (p. 297). Caricature of a father's indignation that his son has not been taken seriously.
- Rafael shoots Almirante with a 'real' bullet. Almirante '*spins slowly round, drops his weapon and puts his hand to his forehead; it is covered with blood*' (p. 297). Parody of the noble death for honour.
- Circus clowns rush in, dressed in '*huge shoes, baggy pants, red noses and yellow wigs*' to drag Almirante off. It is Almirante (with his absurd notions of honour) whom the play ultimately treats as a clown.

Act Two, Scene 8

- '*Canons thunder a salute out of the darkness. Lights up on the Royal Reception Room and the whole Court . . . Amid triumphant fanfares the Court advances ceremoniously Down Stage and lines up, waving regally to the audience.*'
  A reminder that we are *not* in a circus, but a repressive state in which personal notions of honour are revealed as absurd, in which personal value is conflated with privilege, in which those in high office assume great dignity but behave with peevish petulance; and in which the on-stage audience for the antics of the court becomes metonymically associated with the theatre audience.

Christine Kiebuzinska has observed that

> Meyerhold's theatre was . . . intent on selecting dynamic moments, episodes, fragments, or 'attractions' and presenting them without seemingly paying attention to connecting meaning to the preceding or subsequent scene. The disjointedness of action was thus a way of underscoring its relativistic nature. Fragmentation then marked a new, fundamentally important aesthetic approach by Meyerhold's theatre to deny 'the flow of life,' and break down illusion. To achieve these ends, Meyerhold diminished the individual psychological development of characters and concentrated on the principle of 'social mask' . . .
>
> (1988, pp. 55–6)

The concept of the 'social mask' is particularly appropriate to Barnes' theatre. In the extract considered above it is not the psychology of the characters that is significant, but their social function or, rather, the social function to which they aspire. *The Bewitched* interrogates the 'social mask' that is assumed by each of the characters. In each of the sequences discussed above, the characters vigorously assert their social role; the juxtapositions, the parallels and contrasts to which the rhythmical structures of the play draw attention destabilise these roles, revealing them as postures and masks. When the corpse of Almirante de Castilla, formerly a member of the highest council of state, is carted off as part of a circus clown routine, it is one of the clearest examples of this in action; this methodology pervades *The Bewitched* and much of Barnes' mature theatre work.

Many of the techniques of episodic montage developed by radical practitioners such as Eisenstein and Meyerhold in the early part of the twentieth century have been appropriated by advertising agencies and bombard us nightly on our television screens, inverting and subverting the political impetus that drove the work of the early Soviet pioneers. This appropriation of the montage form attempts to present itself as apolitical, while vigorously endorsing late capitalism, a commodified culture in which political discourse is masked, in which montage itself becomes a potent weapon in the service of 'hidden persuaders'. For Eisenstein and Meyerhold the concept of the 'montage of attractions' was developed as an agent of social awareness; it was conceived of as a means of activating audiences, not concealing a political agenda. It is in this spirit that Barnes' use of the technique should be seen. His 'bayonet attacks on naturalism'[18] demand an audience as alert to its own responses as it is to the startling shifts of tone and genre that go to make up the plays' montage structures.

'My credo is a simple and laconic theatre language leading to complex associations,' observed Meyerhold in conversation with Aleksandr Gladkov.[19] I suspect one of the reasons that Barnes' theatre has not been more widely valued is that it has been taken far too literally; that his own 'simple and laconic theatre language' has been mediated by journalists who are so immersed in the iconic systems of naturalism that they refuse to accept the rich structural montage of Barnes' best work as anything other than linear narrative. This is nowhere more evident than in his use of comedy or, rather, his interrogation of the functions of humour and laughter. And that is the subject of the next chapter.

9

Laugh, I Could Have Died

Though I am a comic writer I have always been uneasy about the comic muse. The easy generalisations about comedy being life-giving, and good for what ails the world, are just that, easy generalisations. Perhaps comedy is another drug to make us bear those injustices we should eliminate and not bear.

Peter Barnes[1]

In the periods when theater is most vital, comedy and tragedy are not stable dramatic forms, but horizons of possibility which may be played off against each other.

William Gruber[2]

In her review of *Dreaming* at the Royal Exchange Theatre in Manchester, Lyn Gardner wrote: 'I'm sure Barnes has a copy of One Thousand And One Jokes That Are As Old As The Hills. But he is a sly old devil and a brilliant craftsman.' Whether conscious or not, the reference to a joke book echoes Morra's exhortation to Rafael in *The Bewitched* to 'never be wi'out "Mother Bunch's Joke-Book"' (p. 203). Barnes' plays are, indeed, full of quick jokes: some good, some weak; some visual, many verbal. But the use of humour is not limited to jokes. There are running gags; puns; double entendres; slapstick

233

routines – which range from the relatively innocuous (such as the washerwoman episode in *The Bewitched*) to the hideous cruelty of Ivan spearing Shibanov through the foot in *Laughter!*; situational comedy; a spectrum of incongruities from the mild to the wild; character-based comedy; and, running throughout the work, tensions between the characters' aspirations and the actuality of their situations. Audience expectations are continually undermined. Gardner's comment reveals a certain surprise that a play full of 'old jokes' can be brilliantly crafted; and, indeed, her review proposes that the overall 'effect is of a Howard Barker play done over by Morecambe and Wise', drawing attention to incongruities of tone and style.[3] Barnes' theatre is inherently unstable, and the use of humour in the plays is central to this instability.

In his introduction to *Leonardo's Last Supper*, Peter Barnes wrote that his aim was to create 'a comic theatre of contrasting moods and opposites, where everything is simultaneously tragic and ridiculous'.[4] While the contrasting moods and unstable tone are undoubtedly characteristic of all his work for the theatre, to describe the corpus as 'comic theatre' is rather more problematic. Not one of the plays is described as a comedy in their published versions. Indeed, this stated aim is very revealing – in that it is not primarily to inspire laughter. Laughter may, or may not, be a by-product of this comic theatre. There are several concerns that run throughout Barnes' work. The most evident of these is his insistent interrogation of the nature of authority and our responses to it, of the means by which people attempt to resist authority or comply and collude with it. One of the functions of comedy in these plays is to examine the mechanisms of complicity, denial and resistance. Comedy thus becomes a formal strategy that is used to investigate its own social functions – in short, what we have here is metacomedy;[5] theatre that is centrally concerned with the means by which we use comedy to shape our responses to our social environment and to negotiate our social identities.

Theories of Humour

I emphasise the social because Barnes's is not a psychological theatre. There have been many theories of comedy. Freud's, developed in *Jokes and Their Relation to the Unconscious*, focuses on the teller of jokes, the author of the comedy.[6] While there may be some who would want to scrutinise Barnes' comedy as a means of examining the working of his unconscious mind, that is beyond the scope of this book. My concern is with the way that an audience reads humour, the way that humour demands active engagement in the meaning-making process and, in the case of Barnes' theatre, the self-reflexive consciousness of that engagement. Theories of comedy can be thought of as falling into two distinct groups or traditions: theories, such as that propounded by Aristotle, which argue that laughter arises in response to whatever has inherently laughable qualities, that the comedian, the joke-teller and the playwright merely point to what is inherently comic; and, on the other hand, theories which allow for comedy to be far more dangerous, in which the 'artist actively distorts reality in such a way as to evoke laughter' (Schaeffer, 1981, p. 4). Although it could be maintained that at the heart of Barnes' theatre is an assumption that authority by its very nature is essentially laughable, and that Barnes sees his job as a moral playwright to point this out to us, such an argument is limited and does little to illuminate the various ways in which Barnes uses comedy. In this context, the second of these groups of theories is more useful critically. The groups can be subdivided into two broad categories: superiority theories and incongruity theories. The former category proposes that humour is used as a means of asserting superiority: superiority over others, superiority over situations. Incongruity theories propose that all humour arises from unexpected juxtapositions.[7] Many proponents of theories of comedy seek an equivalent of the physicists' unifying theory, a theoretical approach to humour, comedy and laughter which is all-embracing and exclusive. To take such an approach to Barnes is self-defeating. Because his theatre interrogates the diverse functions of humour and laughter, it necessarily places before us examples which operate in many different ways. I would, however, argue that even where characters use humour in an attempt to assert superiority, it is the incongruity of their position that potentially gives rise to laughter and demands an active response from the audience. I emphasise the word 'potentially' because laughter is never a guaranteed response. Even when one finds something very funny, the social context in which one 'receives' the comedy is deeply affecting.

In the theatre, comedy has the potential to be both celebratory of community and deeply divisive. In all theories of comedy there is an assumption that most people will find a good joke funny; but comedy is both a unifying and a divisive force. To sit silently in an audience that seems predominantly to be enjoying itself is to feel very isolated. Comedy draws attention to audience response, makes it audible, visible and highly significant to the meanings of the theatrical event. Even in plays which aim primarily to make audiences laugh, audience responses are volatile. When actors talk of good audiences, they mean a responsive audience: for tragedy one that sits rapt, silent and attentive; for comedy one in which the audience 'gets' the jokes, in which laughter becomes 'infectious', in which, as an individual audience member, one feels not only the individual joys of laughter, but also a celebratory sense of community, of having much in common with a disparate group of strangers. It can, however, be remarkably dispiriting to find a comedy unfunny, especially when all around seem to be enjoying themselves. This is one of the risks of any comic theatre. Seeing a 'serious' play as a member of a small audience can be a richly rewarding experience. Seeing a comedy in such circumstances can force one to imagine what it might have been like in other circumstances. A 'serious' play might produce an equally wide range of responses in each member of the audience, but they would be far less visible. Comedy not only draws attention to the social environment of its reception, but it also foregrounds the complex relationships that exist between actor, character and audience in any theatrical event. In his book *Comic Theaters*, William Gruber argues that 'the varying dialectics which develop from the confrontation of performer and beholder are the wellsprings of power and meaning in the theater' (1986, p. 167). In any theatrical event, even in naturalism, an audience is constantly reading both the character and the actor playing the character. Naturalist theatre forms may ask us to try to forget that we are watching actors, but the attraction of well-known actors in naturalist plays gives the lie to the notion that in such theatre the actor becomes a kind of invisible presence behind the role that they are playing. It is not that we temporarily forget that we are watching an actor so consummate in her craft that we only see Nora in *A Doll's House* or Blanche in *A Streetcar Named Desire*, but that our previous knowledge of the actor, our appreciation of her skill and our awareness of her performance are integrated with our reading of the character. In a naturalist play our reading of character is perhaps dominant, but even in naturalism the relationship between these different ways of perceiving the theatrical event is more fluid than is often acknowledged. When, for example, in *The Cherry Orchard*

Madame Ranyevskaya berates Lopakhin for watching plays,[8] the balance between these different perceptions shifts, perhaps only briefly, and we may smile, or even laugh, as we are made aware of our own position as an audience, and our own relationship with an actor interpreting what has become a canonical role. Henri Bergson might explain this as resulting from the 'reciprocal interference of series'. An audience, according to Bergson, would in this instance 'waver between the possible meaning and the real' (the real in this instance being the actor's performance, not the illusion that her performance creates). 'And it is this see-saw between two contrary interpretations which is . . . apparent in the enjoyment we derive from an equivocal situation' (Bergson in Sypher, 1900/1956, p. 123).

Chekhov called *The Cherry Orchard* a comedy, 'even a farce'. There have been numerous debates as to what he meant by this; but, whatever weight we might give to the comic elements of the play, it regularly invites what Bergson describes as 'contrary interpretations' of the same moment. The more overtly comic moments place us in more direct relationships with the actors. The 'equivocal situation' in the moment discussed above arises from being reminded that we are watching a performance. In his examination of the nature of humour, Arthur Koestler coins the term 'bisociative' to describe how we are thinking at such moments. In his analysis, all creative thinking is rooted in what he terms 'bisociation', arguing that the 'logical pattern of the creative process . . . consists in the discovery of hidden similarities' (1964, p. 29). Koestler's theory of humour, which he develops as an introduction to his more general theory of creativity, is an 'incongruity' theory. He argues that laughter is produced by 'behaviour that is both unexpected and perfectly logical – but not of a logic usually applied to this type of situation . . . It is the clash of the two mutually incompatible codes, or associative contexts, which explodes the tension' (p. 35). And this 'explosion' results in laughter. Thus humour draws on and induces 'bisociative' thinking, bringing together two normally incompatible but logical worlds.

Koestler's theory is particularly useful in relation to Barnes' theatre: while it does specifically attempt to examine the mechanisms of humour, it also relates humour to its various contexts, and with the numerous other ways in which 'bisociative thinking' enables us to see the world afresh; it focuses on the active role of an audience, arguing that to laugh is to interpret, to make meaning; it draws attention to the performative elements of the work; and it allows for the notion of metacomedy. I have frequently referred to the metatheatrical qualities of Barnes' theatre in this book, and I have noted on several occasions that his plays are remarkably attractive to actors. One of the attractions is clearly that he writes in a style which encourages actors to adopt some of the qualities of more gestural performance that characterise pantomime and vaudeville – forms which allow actors more direct relationships with audiences than is possible in more naturalistic theatre. Perhaps it is this very visibility that makes Barnes' plays so popular with actors. Barnes' characters rarely settle into the illusion that they exist independently of the actor playing them. The plays – be they for the stage, the radio or television – all foreground performance, with the actor and the actor's performance figuring strongly in the plays' production of meaning. I would argue further that one of the most distinctive and integral characteristics of Barnes' work is its pervasive use of bisociation – in its approach to characterisation, its shifting tonal quality and its formal structures: actor and role, the 'comic' and the 'serious' inseparable; the past seen through the lens of contemporary popular culture and the present seen in terms of cruel histories; and a montage of attractions juxtaposing philosophical discourse against slapstick brutality. Whether this always 'works' in practice is a different matter. But if the primary aim is not necessarily to produce laughter, but to interrogate how comedy contributes to our negotiation of our social identities, then what 'works' as comedy cannot be measured solely in terms of audience pleasure.

The Christmas Concert

The Epilogue of *Laughter!* is notoriously uncomfortable. In a different context, some of the jokes told by the '*hollow-eyed comics*, BIMKO *and* BIEBERSTEIN' might raise laughter. That they are more likely to produce shock and revulsion is partly because the play has just had Gottleb and the Sanitation Men confront Cranach and his bureaucratic cronies (and us, the theatre audience) with the most monstrous images of the gas chambers in action. These images are so strong, the horror so great, that we are being defied to laugh. And, as Koestler argues, for a joke to make us laugh, we need enough time to register the incongruity of the bisociation, but not so much time that we can analyse it. We need to have dropped our guard, to be caught unawares for humour to shock us. In order for us to laugh at a joke, we must have the cultural knowledge that enables us to understand its bisociated frames of reference, but to be caught out by the connections that are being made.[9] If, for example, we do not know that 'dying' is a theatrical idiom for failing to engage an audience, then some of the puns in this routine cannot work; but if we know too far in advance what frames of reference the bisociation will draw upon, the incongruity does not take us by surprise. The introduction to the Epilogue to *Laughter!* alerts us to what is coming. 'Stop. Don't leave. The best is yet to come. Our final number,' proclaims the Announcer's Voice over what should sound like the Auschwitz tannoy, '. . . the climax of this Extermination Camp Christmas Concert, the farewell appearance of the Boffo Boys of Birkenau' (Barnes, 1989, p. 410). Far from dropping our guard, we are more than likely to be anxious and determined not to laugh at what follows. The play bisociates numerous pairs of ideas here: the end of term Christmas concert with its implications of a holiday to come, which not only bisociates but contrasts shockingly with the 'reality' of extermination; the idea of a 'final number' as a climactic attraction on a vaudeville bill with the literal finality of the final solution – as an audience at this point in the play we also bring to the phrase 'the final number', the frame of reference established by Cranach's bureaucrats, who see the inmates of Auschwitz as 'units', and Gottleb, who has earlier argued that 'Future cases of death must be given consecutive Roman numbers' (p. 402). Many of the jokes in this Epilogue hinge on just such puns between literal and metaphorical meanings. The most disturbing of them are the puns around death and dying. In the final moments of the play, Bieberstein says: 'I could be wrong but I think this act is dying.' And Bimko's last words are 'Hymie, you were right, this act's dead on its feet' (p. 411). On each occasion the pun brings together 'two strings of thought, tied together by an acoustic knot' (Koestler, 1964, p. 65): the frame of reference which relates the word to a failing performance and the frame of the fiction of the play. This bisociation is, however, doubly complex, for the 'act' is by now, indeed, likely to be 'dead on its feet' – in that nobody is likely to be laughing at it – and the 'fiction of the play' is for many so imprinted into the collective consciousness and guilt that it cannot be read as fiction in the way that the horrors of *Tsar*, the first part of the play, can. Furthermore, in the 1978 Royal Court production of the play, the normal bisociation of actor and role was made even more complex by the deliberate doubling of Timothy West (who played Ivan, Gottleb and Bieberstein) and Derek Francis (Samael, the Angel of Death, Cranach and Bimko). If comedy draws attention to the performance of the actor, we can be left in no doubt here that Bimko and Bieberstein are presented as impersonations of extermination camp victims.

For those subscribing to superiority theories of humour, who argue that all humour, even the most innocent, is an attempt to position oneself as a superior either to others or to misfortune,[10] it might be appealing to interpret the 'Christmas Concert' routine as an example of the ways in which people attempt to use humour in even the most desperate of situations to assert a kind of resistance – to death, to the camp, and to the Nazi regime. And there is no doubt that this possibility is part of the dialectic that Barnes sets up. But the audience experiences the comic routine in a range of contexts: the shock of having seen, only minutes before, the work of the Sanitation Men in which we and the bureaucrats are forced to witness the effects of the gas chambers in action; the foregrounded double-casting; and the persistent use by Cranach's bureaucrats of euphemism to describe what is happening in the camps. All of these make it difficult to read the routine as an act of resistance. But the most immediate context is that provided by the Announcer, who frames the entire routine. This is a 'Christmas Concert', a Christian festival at which Jewish comedians are performing the 'final number'. This joking is not only licensed by authority, it is commissioned by authority. The performers are parodying Jewish comedians' tendency to tell self-deprecating jokes. Koestler argues that 'Parody is the most aggressive form of impersonation . . . The parodists' favourite points of attack are all situated on the line of intersection between two planes: the Exalted and the Trivial'

(1964, p. 69). In this instance the exalted plane is that from which the joker might mock death and ridicule his oppressors for assuming they can humiliate him; the alternative reading locates Bimko and Bieberstein as trivialising the horror of their wretched plight for the pleasure of their guards or, worse still, as oppressors mocking their victims by imitating them.[11] This examination of the way that context radically alters the functions and indeed the potential of humour becomes a central theme in *Red Noses*, where humour is presented as a force that celebrates and unifies community, while subverting the political authority of the Church – until the moment that the Church licenses the Noses, only for Flote to reject this, knowing that such a licence will render their humour impotent.

This analysis of the Epilogue to *Laughter!* gives a sense of the tensions and dialectics at work within this short scene. I have attempted to show how the metacomedy interrogates the functioning of the comedy itself; to examine the demands it makes of its audience; and to demonstrate why *Laughter!* is likely to be such an uncomfortable experience in the theatre. There are two further points I want to make in connection with the scene. The first returns to the issue of the casting. I have suggested elsewhere in this volume that one of the characteristics of Barnes' drama is its theatricality. The point has been made by Dukore, amongst others, but often without more detailed consideration of what is meant by 'theatricality'. At its simplest, in reading a 'theatrical' play, one has to take into account those decisions that have to be made when realising it in the theatre. The end of *Laughter!* is a metonymic example of how Barnes' plays are far more open to interpretation than is often allowed – and that interpretation is crucially affected by issues of performance. The decision to double-cast Timothy West and Derek Francis may have been pragmatic[12] (doubling Ivan/Cranach/Bieberstein and Samael/Gottleb/Bimko is not specified by Barnes), but it crucially affects an audience's reading of the Epilogue. How is an audience to read the double-casting? I have argued that comedy draws attention to the performance of the actor and, indeed, to the persona of the actor; and that this is likely to accent the issue of impersonation. But there is another way of reading the doubling: that Ivan and Samael, Cranach and Gottleb, Bieberstein and Bimko, all are accidental tourists. That any one of us has it in us to become the tyrant, the brutal oppressor, the officious, self-deluding bureaucrat, or the victim of a holocaust. It may be possible to inflect a performance towards one or other of these readings, but Barnes' theatre is built upon the notion of bisociation: any given moment leads simultaneously to different meanings. As an active audience, we are asked to experience any given attraction from at least two viewpoints at the same time.

The problem for Barnes with this method is that critics have tended to read the plays at only one level. Thus Michael Billington entitled his review of *Laughter!* for the *Guardian* with what was clearly read (if not intended) as a damning observation: 'It's Not Funny'. And that leads me to the final point I wish to make in connection with the Epilogue to *Laughter!* The jokes in Barnes' theatre are not always funny; nor, in an intelligent theatrical production, should they be. I have assumed throughout this discussion of the Epilogue to *Laughter!* that, while it is constructed as a 'comedy routine', it is unlikely to make people laugh in the theatre. I have to admit, however, and with a certain reluctance, that I do find some of the jokes funny. The reluctance arises from the interaction of the different frames of reference already discussed – likely to be a powerful factor in the theatre. And that leads to a curious paradox. If the 'house' roars its approval at these jokes, if the comic routine does not 'die on its feet', then *Laughter!* the play would indeed have failed. The risk that Barnes takes is that if nobody laughs during this sequence, if the 'act' 'dies' and the auditorium is silent, then it is Barnes who stands accused of insensitivity, tastelessness, crassness. But what if some members of the audience cannot help themselves? What if their nervousness (for the play does indeed provoke considerable anxiety, even when read from the page) causes them to laugh when all around them are angrily hushed? I suspect that many would resist the question 'Why do we laugh?', for the play offers no answers, but that is the question that is being posed – and a divided audience actively participates in asking it.

Good Jokes and Bad Jokes

The use of humour in *Dreaming* is rich and heterogeneous. Every character's dialogue is sprinkled with jokes or humorous observations that are directed simultaneously to the theatre audience and to other characters. Humour is woven into the structural fabric of the play but, as in *Laughter!*, this is a risky strategy: for it can either engage or alienate – depending largely on one's response to the joke or routine. I want to consider one specific moment from the play to explore how an audience's response to 'good' and 'bad' jokes are integral to the play's examination of complicity.

Jokes and humour can be used to subvert the hegemonic structures of authority or to reinforce them. Comedy is often used to support the status quo. Comedians of the political right tend to use their act to assert their own affiliation with those who deplore difference of any kind as evidence of weakness and inferiority. The telling of jokes thus becomes a means of locating oneself (and those in the audience who share the joke) within a particular social grouping. If we laugh at a joke we become complicit with the joke-teller. A prime example of this comes in

Act Two, Scene 5 (the scene is also discussed in the essay on *Dreaming* in Chapter 5), where Mallory (re)marries Susan, insisting that she is Sarah, and Christ tells Susan a series of jokes, the last of which provokes her to laughter. Christ goes through a stand-up comic routine to which Susan and the audience are party, but which is not attended to by the other characters. Audience responses to this routine are crucial in reading the scene as a whole. I saw Barnes' own production of the play three times.[13] On each occasion there was no doubt that some audience members were deeply offended by the blasphemy of a scene in which Christ is presented as a self-deprecating Jewish stand-up comedian, complaining about his father as a parent who never listens and who hasn't created enough money to go round; and which concludes with a joke about Jewish mothers as martyrs. If one is immediately offended by this, it would be difficult to read the scene as anything other than trivialising the marriage ceremony and the Christian religion. But Christ's jokes are varied: they range from the crude, through a philosophical conundrum about the existence of God, to the Jewish joke already noted. They are all, however, in some way religious. The constant shift of tone even within the routine itself makes this both challenging and uneasily provocative.

Susan Purdie observes that 'All habitual joking – recurrent patterns of who makes jokes and who is joked about – will both reflect and create patterns of power' (1993, p. 6). Presenting Christ as a comedian seems initially to disrupt and subvert hegemonic structures of Judaeo-Christian power (hence some of the offence); the routine ends when Susan, who has hitherto not found any of Christ's jokes funny, '*bursts out laughing at* CHRIST'*s joke*' (p. 39). And her laughter not only marks her acceptance of her new identity as Sarah and as Mallory's wife but also, by implication, her complicity with the patriarchal systems that the Jewish mother joke implies. Her reaction to the earlier jokes indicates not only that she thinks of them as 'bad' jokes, but also that she would like to resist the patterns of power that Christ's discourse implies. As an audience, we simultaneously observe and participate in this discourse; we are being asked to monitor and reflect on our own responses. If, as is likely, we laugh at some parts of the routine and grimace elsewhere, that only serves to focus on the ways that the play examines and differentiates between the various levels of complicity in different forms of metanarrative: the refugees who struggle with and against the roles they find themselves in as a result of war; the men and women who construct their narratives of marriage or comply with them for amusement or convenience. To argue, as some newspaper critics did, that *Dreaming* has more than its fair share of 'bad jokes',[14] and is evidence that the playwright is losing his touch,[15] is to ignore or refuse the terms of the play. The unevenness of Christ's comic routine is thus crucial to the meta-comedy.

This is not to argue that all the jokes that permeate Barnes' plays are successfully integrated into a broader structural pattern, nor that bad jokes always serve a higher purpose. If one criterion for a joke to be bad is that the bisociations of the twin frames of reference are too obvious, they do not take us by surprise, that does not necessarily make the joke unproductive in the context in which Barnes is operating. There are occasions, as I have shown above, when a negative reaction to a joke is a significant staging post on our journey through a scene. But there are examples, in even his finest work, where the jokes occasionally seem to detract from the central discourse rather than contribute to it. Act One, Scene 14 of *The Bewitched* is a case in point. It is set in the torture chambers of the Inquisition and, given Barnes' dramatic method, we might expect juxtapositions of the horrific and the comic, of philosophical debate and Grand Guignol imagery. For the most part, these juxtapositions are disturbing and profoundly unsettling. In picking out an example of an unproductive joke, I do not mean to reproach Barnes, but to use an exception to prove the generality, if not the rule:

> DURO   'Tis a trick t' test my faith. Testing, one-two-three-I-believe-in-God-the-Father-Almighty-and-in-Jesus-Christ-His-Only-Son-born . . .
>
> (p. 261)

It might be argued that the bisociation here is contained in the anachronistic use of the phrase 'Testing, one-two-three'; the anachronism reminds us that although *The Bewitched* is set in the seventeenth century, it is about today, in the same way that Brecht frequently used history in his plays as a distantiation device. The problem here is that the anachronism is generalised and unfocused, not socially specific, and it therefore distracts from the central focus of the scene, which is the horrific contradiction metonymically embodied in the plight of Duro. Elsewhere in the scene, the juxtapositions of comedy and cruelty expose this contradiction. Duro has converted from Judaism to Christianity after five years of torture. Unfortunately for him, this is not convenient for the state:

> MOTILLA   If Duro's truly converted, he's earned God's mercy and must be garrotted at the stake afore the fires are lit, like the rest o' 'em. All penitents reconciled t' Christ must be strangled afore burning. Wi'out Duro we've no-one t' burn *alive*.
>
> VALLADARES   . . . I was relying on Duro t' stand firm in his accursed heresy.
>
> (p. 260)

In order to perpetuate its own reign of terror, the state needs enemies, and it requires that those accused are found guilty. It exercises control through a combination of brutal oppression and licensed entertainment. It needs its citizens to feel beleaguered and, at the same time, for those not currently accused of a crime to be entertained by the suffering of the 'guilty'. The scene concludes with everybody, torturers and tortured alike, breaking into song, in which words such as these are sung to the tune of 'That's Entertainment': ' "Great names who go right up in flames/Or the Jew who is put t' the screw./He's a wreck but he'll never confess./That's entertainment" ' (p. 266).

The auto-da-fé is presented as entertainment. The questions that Barnes poses about the nature of popular entertainment become all the more difficult and uncomfortable if we have laughed at least at some point during the scene. There is something hideously incongruous about Alcala, the chief torturer, talking about the craft of torture with all the pride, attention to detail and love of his work that one might expect of a master carpenter (pp. 263–4). It may not actually make us laugh, but it is certainly humorous, and this moment of comedy (unlike Duro's anachronistic testing of a microphone) is rooted in an examination of complicity, one of the central concerns of the play; it is a grotesque caricature of those who uphold staunch values of assiduousness in their work, but who separate their work from all wider moral contexts.

In *The Ghost in the Machine* (1967), Koestler discusses what he has termed the two inherent tendencies that drive all human beings as social animals: the self-assertive and the self-integrative. He observes that it has usually been assumed that it is when the self-assertive tendency dominates that crimes are committed, violent aggression being an extreme form of self-assertion. His argument, however, is that all the most appalling acts in human history are carried out by groups; that it is when the self-integrative tendency gets out of balance that human beings are at their most dangerous; that this tendency manifests itself in extreme antisocial behaviour such as, for example, hooliganism, religious extremism, ethnic cleansing, the persecution of minority groups; and that collective, socialised brutality is always more hideous and more destructive in its effects than individual aggression. His argument is long and complex – the entire book is devoted to it – as he argues that this imbalance between the self-assertive and the self-integrative tendencies is the 'Ghost in the Machine' to which human beings have to be alert, and that it is this imbalance, not rampant self-assertive aggression, that threatens our self-destruction. Koestler's argument offers valuable insights into one of Barnes' central concerns and to a recurrent motif that runs through his use of comedy. Alcala's devotion to his work is similar to Cranach's in *Laughter!* For both of them, succeeding at their work raises their self-esteem because 'success' in these contexts is easily defined. Their attitudes can be seen as a grotesque comic distortion of the self-integrative tendency. To question hegemonic values is to assert the self over the larger group. Frequently in Barnes' theatre this balance between self-assertive and self-integrative tendencies is explored in relation to discourses of authority and power. The social sickness that results in catastrophic social self-destruction in *The Bewitched* is depicted as arising out of the failure of individuals to interrogate the ridiculous contradictions that underpin this society at every level. Barnes' use of comedy to alert us to this failure may be shocking, but it is entirely fitting to his purposes, for, as Koestler argues in *The Act of Creation*, satirical comedy 'focuses attention on abuses and deformities in society of which, blunted by habit' (and, I would argue, by ideological pressures) 'we were no longer aware'. By projecting these customs 'onto a different background . . . we are made suddenly conscious of conventions and prejudices which we have unquestioningly accepted . . . The bisociative shock shatters the frame of complacent habits of thinking' (1964, p. 73).

'Sick' Humour and Absurdism: To Luna Park and Beyond

The Bewitched, Laughter! and *Dreaming* may well have been controversial, but the kinds of humour they contain are by no means new. As David Barrett comments in his essay 'Aristophanes, Comedian and Poet':

> Whatever else has changed over the centuries, the deeper springs of laughter have not. 'How modern it all seems!' is a comment frequently overheard after an Aristophanes performance. 'How ancient all our jokes are!' would be a better way of putting it.[16]

There is, indeed, nothing new about Barnes' jokes. It is the purposes to which he puts them that is distinctive. It has been argued that Barnes is an absurdist, in the sense that, for all the humour in his plays, his vision of the world is ultimately bleak, and that his humour points to the absurdity of the human condition. There are, indeed, similarities between Barnes' theatre and that of some of the absurdist dramatists, in particular Beckett's (the fascination with music-hall routines, the interest in surrealism, the self-reflexive humour).[17] But the absurdists are essentially apolitical; where there is humour, it bisociates frames of reference in ways which ultimately lead to a sense that human aspirations to rationality are always constrained by and contrasted with the irrationality of the world we inhabit.[18] Barnes' humour may frequently point up the schism between his characters' aspirations and the realities of their situations, but he is ultimately a deeply moral dramatist. And if the fictional worlds of the large-scale stage plays are irrational and absurd, they are so because human agencies have made them thus. In *The Bewitched*, Carlos cannot conceive an heir because he is the product of superstitious credulity and incestuous inbreeding, not because of the random mutations of the natural world. In the same play, Sister Inez, one of the nuns of Cangas, may chant 'Chaos's my true Lord! Blind chance rules the world!' (p. 304). But the play clearly identifies the chaos that rules in Spain as originating in the superstitious nonsense that masquerades as religion in this society. And in *Red Noses*, where the Black Death is wreaking such havoc, it is not the natural disaster that renders life meaningless, but the Church's draconian reimposition of its authority when the plague is over. The fictional world in Barnes' major stage plays is bleak and harsh, brutal and cruel; but although the rejection of authority frequently leads to a flirtation with anarchy, and individual characters (such as Skelton in *Dreaming* and Scarron in *Red Noses*) seem to embrace a kind of nihilism, this should be seen as contributing to a developing dialectic, not as an authorial position. Ultimately, even *Laughter!*, the darkest of all Barnes' plays, rejects nihilism as wholeheartedly as it refuses optimism.

It could be argued that the closest Barnes' theatre comes to absurdism is the experimental play that he wrote for the National Theatre Studio, *Luna Park Eclipses*.[19] It was staged in August 1995 in a closed production that he directed himself. He wrote of it, in an essay for *New Theatre Quarterly* (1996), that his intention was:

> not to depict plot or character but show directly the contrast between what viewers apprehend and what they provide for

themselves as in an abstract painting or collage. The audience is faced with the same dilemma the author faced when writing the play – it must make choices . . . The play's audience is made up of . . . individuals who are not coerced by the authority of an omnipotent author and therefore can enter new fields of self-expression.

(1996, p. 203)

In the play, Barnes attempts to avoid any kind of linear narrative, exploring the ways in which audiences seek out meaning and causality in apparently random dialogue and between seemingly unconnected characters. On the surface this seems to be a radically new development in Barnes' work, but the desire to entangle the roles of author and audience in the meaning-making process can be seen as a development of continuing interests in the dynamic and ever changing relationship between the two. Although his large-scale works for the theatre are carefully plotted and their narrative is essentially linear, they are more open as texts than might at first be evident and, as argued in Chapter 8, they are frequently structured around principles of montage. One of these principles is that seemingly incongruous attractions are juxtaposed in such a way as to create new meanings over and beyond those contained within the attractions themselves. This principle can also be seen to underpin the use of humour throughout Barnes' work.

Although not primarily a comedy, *Luna Park Eclipses* is occasionally humorous, and is certainly funny in the sense of being very strange. In a Brechtian manner, however, this very strangeness casts valuable light on Barnes' theatrical methods. It is made up of six short playlets: *Sleeping on a Razor, A Mirror in Oyster Bay, Cast Up on the Coast of Japan, If You Don't Want the Peaches Stop Shaking my Tree, So's Your Old Man* and *The Head Invents,*

The Heart Discovers. One of the six, *Cast Up on the Coast of Japan*, is a three-hander; all the others are two-handers. Each playlet lasts between ten and fifteen minutes. Whether or not Barnes intended the playlets to be thought of as 'eclipses', it is an indicative title. In describing some of the radio plays I have used the phrase 'intersecting monologues'. That does not apply here, however, for, even if interrupted, a monologue implies coherence, or at least some kind of connection between one utterance and the next. These characters, however, eclipse each other; if there are connections to be made, it is for the audience to make them meaningful. But I use the term 'character' hesitantly, for the play eschews conventional notions of characterisation. If we, as an audience or as readers, attribute character to the voices, that too is our choice.

Consider, for example, the following – the opening of *Cast Up on the Coast of Japan*:

GREEN, **BROCK** *and* **BARBARA** *sit in battered armchairs.*

BARBARA   My breath still whitens the air.

BROCK   I told them to pepper my ragout.

GREEN   For no good reason I started to run in circles like an idiot.

BARBARA   I have a large Adam's apple and a large expanse between my thumb and forefinger.

GREEN   Don't know where to go, sitting down, standing up, moving forward, moving backward, hitch up the wagons and move out. Eating breakfast with a wooden spoon.

BROCK   I said Alexander the Great was a hero, but why destroy the furniture.

Any connection between utterances has to be forged by the reader. The *Eclipses* can be read as a montage of very short stories, odd jokes and occasional aphorisms. The play is not a rejection of meaning, but a dramatisation of the search for it. The audience is placed in a situation which echoes that of the characters, grasping at connections, seeking narratives that will make sense of what they are experiencing. One of the ways in which the characters themselves find fleeting security is in their use of aphorisms. The use of aphorisms in fiction sometimes appears to point us in the direction of an author's meaning, but it is always a mistake to ignore context. This is even more problematic than usual in Barnes' work, because of the ways that his metatheatricality and metacomedy foreground the actor's role in creating the performance text. As 'received wisdom', an aphorism implies a higher authority that knows better (be it a political authority, or the ideological authority of 'common sense'). Here, aphorisms are used parodically: 'It's dangerous for the body to dream too much,' says Brock in *Cast Up on the Coast of Japan*. To which Green says: 'It's the same with stones.' If there is a connection between these strange statements, it is not immediately evident. Reading these *Eclipses* (either from the page or in performance)[20] is like trying to 'see' a joke. The reader has to make out what seems to be implied – even though the author has denied all intentions to imply anything. The reader has to solve what seems to be a riddle. As Koestler argued:

> Seeing a joke . . . comprises the transformation of metaphorical into literal statements, or verbal hints into visual terms . . . To make a joke 'unfold', the listener must fill in the gaps, complete the hints, trace the hidden analogies. Every good joke contains an element of a riddle . . . which the listener must solve. By doing so, he is forced out of his passive role and forced to co-operate.
>
> (1964, p. 85)

Luna Park Eclipses may be an experimental piece, but its bid to make an audience aware of the extent to which it is an active participant in the meaning-making process is closely akin to the way that comedy and metacomedy function in Barnes' theatre. And, for all its apparently baffling incoherence, *Luna Park Eclipses* is, in its conclusion at least, optimistic. The final eclipse, *The Head Invents, The Heart Discovers*, ends thus:

JACK   We were on a beach, counting our heartbeats, counting the grains of sand.

ALICE   I knew then, one day when we were old trees, near death, we'd sit here on an empty bench, looking up at the sky.

There is the gentle sound of the sea lapping the shore.

JACK   I remember you said then, 'When we're old trees and near death, we won't really be on that empty beach, looking up at the sky, but here, on this beach, young, counting our heartbeats, counting the grains of sand.'

ALICE   It's a comfort.

JACK   Oh, yes, it's a comfort.

The sun rises filling the sky with light.

However brief and however enigmatic the occasional contact between characters, it offers both comfort and consolation, if not redemption. And this is the ultimate contradiction in Barnes' theatre. In spite of its frequent bleakness, its terrifying juxtapositions of comedy and cruelty, its unstable tonal qualities, as a body of work it seeks to remind us that it is up to us to make meaning in our lives; and that to make meaning we have to assume both individual and collective responsibility for the social world we live in.

Earlier in this final *Eclipse*, the following exchange takes place:

JACK   If there's no judge or judgement, life is without meaning or hope . . .

ALICE   What does it matter to you if there's no judge or judgement . . . ?

JACK   What else should matter to me?

ALICE   If it matters that much, then there *is* meaning and hope!

EPILOGUE

While researching this book, I had several very enjoyable conversations with Peter Barnes, in which we discussed, amongst other things, theatre and cinema, radio and television – and his own work for those media. On one occasion I asked him if he had ever been interested in writing a novel. I wondered if he might find it easier to get a publisher for a novel than to find theatre companies willing to invest the considerable sums involved in producing his stage plays. It seemed a reasonable thing to do for a writer who is so fascinated by individuals' stories, by story-telling, and whose most recent plays frequently feature competing monologues. He was adamant that he would not. Although still extraordinarily active – he regularly writes screenplays to commission and, even now, with three major plays as yet unperformed, he continues to work on new full-length plays for the theatre – he has no desire to write for the solitary reader. This is perhaps puzzling, given his mastery of the monologue and the remarkable qualities of his radio plays, many of which brilliantly dramatise the pain of isolation. He insisted, however, that writing novels would entail learning a new craft. This is less a case of an old dog being reluctant to learn new tricks than a recognition that he is essentially a man of the theatre, someone who cares passionately about theatre, who believes in the potential that theatre has as a moral force, and who sees his work for television and radio as a way of capitalising on the skills he has honed as a dramatist.

But which kind of theatre is he writing for? Although he has had considerable success in the mainstream – almost all his plays are in print, and his work has been performed at the RSC, the Royal Court, the Manchester Royal Exchange, the West Yorkshire Playhouse, and even (just occasionally) in commercial theatres – he refuses to write on its terms or to follow theatrical fashions. This is a particular problem for Barnes, many of whose plays demand large casts which cannot be afforded by smaller theatre companies. I suspect, however, that it is not primarily the physical scale of the plays that makes them difficult to stage, but rather the theatrical forms that he has adopted and developed for them. It is difficult to describe these forms without being reductive, but the following definition of the grotesque offers a remarkably accurate account of the formal qualities of Barnes' theatre:

> A perpetual play of contrasts following each other. Sublimity and triviality, beauty and ugliness, joy and sorrow, courage and cowardice, are all interwoven in a fantastic pattern as were the flowers and human figures on the walls of Roman grottoes.[1]

While the word 'grotesque' can be misleading because it is now often used pejoratively, Bakshy's interpretation reminds us of the original sense of the word, and that Barnes' use of the grotesque arises out of rich traditions. The 'play of contrasts' is a key characteristic of Barnes' theatre. Indeed, it is partly this which gives his plays such rich metaphorical resonance; but it is also a quality which defies easy responses.

There is something constantly challenging, even defiant about Barnes – not only in his public proclamations about his theatre, but also in the plays themselves. They defy critical assumptions about comedy, they defy straightforward readings, and they defy generic categorisation. They are inherently unstable and some- times contradictory in the meanings that they produce, and this is frequently uncomfortable and even alarming for audiences and critics – both academics and journalists. The plays demand that we make unexpected connections; they demand that as audience members we participate actively in the meaning-making process; they demand that we read them metaphorically. Barnes has claimed that he is attacking naturalism, but it is literalism that is the real enemy of his theatre. Constantly, the plays defy literal- ism, and yet that is the way they are frequently read. Nowhere has this been more apparent than in *Laughter!*. by far the most controversial of all Barnes' plays. In 1977, Charles Marowitz (who had directed Barnes' *Leonardo's Last Supper* and *Noonday Demons* in the Open Space, a small studio theatre on what was then termed the London Fringe) wrote a letter to Trevor Nunn, then Artistic Director of the RSC, in a spirited attempt to per- suade him to change his mind about staging *Laughter!* I quote at length from Marowitz's letter because it remains as relevant now as when it was written:

Dear Trevor,

Briefly – and directly – it's Peter Barnes' play *Laughter!* . . . This is the best play Peter has written. It is more than that . . . Its theatrical virtues aside, it is a play about something, and some- thing that ought to be aired in the theatre today. It's about . . . the totalitarian use of language in order for government to retain greater control over our lives for purposes which, were we allowed to know them, would be abhorrent to us. It's about the innate savagery inside every power structure and the way it works to assert its will – first subtly, then overtly, then with tanks, ultimately with missiles and nuclear warheads. It's about everything that is going on inside the insidious corridors-of-power, where the most daemonic plans are hatched and how these plans are camouflaged under the guise of technological advancement and 'progress' . . . It's about the language of the White House and the oppressions it attempts to conceal. It's about the way we use amusement (laughter) to conceal or obscure the unbearable truths we know, but which become too distressing personally to combat, so we allow them to be dealt with by others (politicians usually) in whom we have no faith but who are our surrogate finks, the embodiment of our abdication of responsibility . . . I beg you to consider them for the Aldwych . . . A premier production in Dusseldorf is now gestating; I can probably organise one in Munich, but it would be outrageous for this first-rate play by a leading British playwright to have a first production in Germany. Why, people would ask, are they not on at the RSC, at the National, in the country which spawned them and where they belong?[2]

Some might take issue with Marowitz's political position, though others might feel that his analysis is as acute now as it was when written. And some might argue that *Laughter!* is too openly confrontational to have the political effect that Marowitz claims for it, though I have attempted to refute that in my own analysis of the play earlier in this volume. What is indisputable, however, is that Marowitz's reading of the play is richly metaphoric, and that is what Barnes' theatre demands: an audience that is as responsive to its own shifting reactions as it is to the multiple layers of meaning inherent in the plays themselves.

NOTES

PROLOGUE

1. Hobson, in *Barnes Plays: 1* (1989, pp. 2–4).
2. Bryden in *Barnes Plays: 1* (1989, pp. 185–9).
3. *The Bewitched* was first produced by the Royal Shakespeare Company at the Aldwych Theatre, London, in May 1974.
4. In spite of Barnes' relative unpopularity in England, his plays have frequently been revived outside the UK. Performing rights contracts have been taken out to perform various of Barnes' plays in Austria, Belgium, Czechoslovakia (and subsequently the Czech Republic), Denmark, France, Germany, Greece, Holland, Hungary, Israel, Italy, Yugoslavia, Poland, Portugal and the USA. Outside of the UK, *Red Noses* is probably the most popular of Barnes' plays. It has been revived several times in America – the most recent production in 2003 at the Theatre Banshee in Los Angeles, where it won several awards, including the Back Stage Critics' Best Production of 2003 and a Maddy Award for Best Production. In Poland it ran in repertoire at the Teatr Nowy in Poznan from 1993 to 2002, during which time it received 190 performances and played to more than 59,000 people; and at the Teatr Ludowy in Krakow from 1994 to 1996. Of Barnes' other plays, *The Ruling Class* has been produced in Germany and Greece; *Laughter!* in Denmark and the USA; *Leonardo's Last Supper* in Vienna (in 1979 and 1995); *The Bewitched* in Vienna in 1995; and *Noonday Demons* in Berlin and the USA.
5. *Laughter!* was first produced at the Royal Court Theatre, London, on 25 January 1978 under the direction of Charles Marowitz.
6. Bernard F. Dukore offers a detailed account of this hostility in *Barnestorm* (1995, pp. 6 and 178).
7. Wardle, 'Laughter!', *The Times*, 25 January 1978.
8. He has described his own theatre writing as 'repeated bayonet attacks on naturalism' (1989, p. ix).

9. An extract from *Luna Park Eclipses* was, however, published in *New Theatre Quarterly*, 47, August 1996, p. 203 et seq.

AN INTRODUCTION

1. 'Peter Barnes', *Contemporary Authors Autobiography Series*, Vol. 12, ed. Joyce Nakamura (New York, London, 1990); p. 4.
2. *Contemporary Authors Autobiography Series*, Vol. 12, ed. Joyce Nakamura. (New York, London, 1990), p. 4.
3. In an interview given to Brian Woolland in July 1999.
4. Beatrice Lillie (1894–1989) started working as a music hall entertainer in 1914. She became very popular in the 1920s, not least for her renditions of Noel Coward's 'Mad Dogs and Englishmen' and 'There Are Fairies at The Bottom of Our Garden'; and made her Broadway debut in 1924. See autobiography, *Every Other Inch a Lady*, Beatrice Lillie, W. H. Allen, 1973; and Bruce Laffey's biography, *Beatrice Lillie: The Funniest Woman in the World*, Baker Book House, 1989.
5. Cited in Dukore, (1995, p. 12).
6. The play is published in *Peter Barnes Plays: 3* (Methuen, 1996).
7. *The Ruling Class* is discussed in detail in Chapter 1.
8. In the theatrical production of the play, Tucker was played by Dudley Jones. Arthur Lowe took the role in the film version. His performance is one of the film's great delights.
9. See n. 5 , p. 264.
10 & 11. I have not discussed *Heavens Blessing* or *Eggs in Gravy* in this volume. As I noted in the *Prologue*, this volume is not intended as a comprehensive overview of Barnes' work. I have deliberately focused on those plays that I regard as landmarks in the development of his theatre. A detailed account of *Heavens Blessing* and *Eggs in Gravy* can, however, be found in Bernard Dukore's book, *Barnestorm* (1995, pp. 64–74 and 74–83).
12. *Jubilee* opened at the Swan Theatre, Stratford-upon-Avon in an RSC production in July 2001.
13. Since completing *The Butterfly Effect*, Barnes has written two more full-length plays and, at the time of this book going to press, is working on another. It is clear that he has no intention of giving up writing just because theatre managements do not choose to produce his work, although given that *The Butterfly Effect* was written for a cast of three men and two women, and would be reasonably inexpensive to produce, there is perhaps a good chance that it will enjoy a theatrical production in the reasonably near future.
14. He has described his own theatre-writing as 'repeated bayonet attacks on naturalism'. Introduction to *Peter Barnes Plays: 1*, (1989, p. ix).

15. The quotations from all plays are taken from the currently available edition; in this instance, *Peter Barnes Plays: 1* (Methuen, 1989).
16. He has also adapted plays by Thomas Middleton, Thomas Otway and John Marston from the early modern period and by Feydeau, Wedekind and Brecht, amongst others, from the modern period. This volume does not examine any of these numerous adaptations, although the relationship between them and his own work (and an indication of the critical debate around them) is considered in Chapter 7, pp. 174–7. See also n. 5, p. 272. See the bibliography, pp. 282–3, for a complete list of the adaptations he has undertaken.
17. Barnes himself coined the term 'Barnesonian' in his Introduction to *Leonardo's Last Supper* (1989, p. 123) when discussing appropriate acting styles for his plays. The implication is that his theatre, like Jonson's, is a theatre which foregrounds the skills of the actor, and is in many ways about the business of acting, of role-play; about negotiating and adopting social roles and identities.
18. Interview with Bernard Dukore, 4 October 1978, cited in Dukore (1995) p. 114.
19. Strehler's theory, and this quotation, first appeared in *Corriere della Sera*, 14 May 1974. The theory is discussed at length in David L. Hirst's *Giorgio Strehler*, which appears in the Cambridge University Press *Directors in Perspective* Series (Hirst, 1993), pp. 28–9.
20. In 1861, Tsar Alexander II passed an act freeing Russia's twenty two and a half million peasants from serfdom. Tucker, in *The Ruling Class*, may delude himself into thinking that he is a closet revolutionary, but one senses that he, like Firs, would rather know his place than struggle in a 'free' world.
21. Charles Marowitz, who directed the first productions of both *Laughter!* and the double bill of *Leonardo's Last Supper* and *Noonday Demons*, had collaborated with Peter Brook on his 'Theatre of Cruelty' Season. See Chapter 3, pp. 82–3.
22. Editorial comment in *The Twentieth Century Performance Reader*, ed. Huxley, M. and Witts, N., 2nd edition (2002), p. 36.
23. Artaud, Antonin, 'Theatre and Cruelty', *The Theatre and Its Double*, trans. Victor Corti (1970), p. 64.
24. Taken from the unpublished lecture given by Peter Barnes at the conference *Ben Jonson and the Theatre* held at the University of Reading, 1996.
25. Bernard Dukore's *Barnestorm* (1995) is a reworking and updating of his earlier *The Theatre of Peter Barnes* (1981).

CHAPTER 1

1. Hobson, *Sunday Times*, 2 March 1969.
2. 'Before the curtain rose on *The Ruling Class* no one appeared to have heard of its author, Peter Barnes. Nobody in the theatre appeared to know whether he had been to university, had written any other plays, was a stripling in his last year at school, or an old gentleman of ninety.' Hobson, Introduction to *The Ruling Class*, in *Barnes Play: 1* (1989, pp. 2–3).
3. There have recently been several proposals to stage the play, but at the time of writing none have been realised. The play is discussed briefly in my introduction.
4. Bryden, *Observer*, 2 March 1969.
5. On 9 November 1965 the Murder (Abolition of Death Penalty) Act suspended the death penalty for murder in the United Kingdom for a period of five years. On 16 December 1969 the House of Commons reaffirmed its decision that capital punishment for murder should be permanently abolished. *The Ruling Class* was given its first production in the period during which the death penalty had been suspended, but not yet permanently abolished; and it can thus be read as a political intervention in the public debate about the abolition of capital punishment.
6. All quotations from the play are taken from the currently available edition *Barnes Plays: 1* (1989). All subsequent page references refer to this edition.
7. The extract that Bishop Lampton reads is from 60:7.
8. The film of *The Ruling Class* retains much of the stage play's dialogue, and uses this hymn at the fourteenth earl's funeral. It does *not*, however, include the two lines quoted here, and so rather misses the point.
9. Prior to 1861, when Tsar Alexander II passed an act 'freeing' Russia's 22.5 million peasants from serfdom, serfs had been controlled by landowners, unable to move freely, unable even to marry, without their 'owner's' permission.
10. These comments are taken from the sleeve notes to the Criterion Collection DVD of the film of *The Ruling Class*. To be fair to Ian Christie, he refutes this assertion, and is very enthusiastic about both the film and the play, which he considers to be a 'great, disturbing black comedy'.
11. This is perhaps not surprising, given that Barnes was a great admirer of Spike Milligan – he wrote a witty and deeply affectionate obituary of Milligan for *New Theatre Quarterly* (2002a). Although Barnes acknowledges that he admires *An Inspector Calls* for its ingenuity, he is not aware that Priestley has had any influence on his work. The reference here is perhaps more generic – to the country house murder mystery.
12. One of the most disappointing features of the film of *The Ruling Class* is its slack rhythmical structure.

13. Whether Dennis Potter was consciously influenced by Barnes, I do not know (Potter does not acknowledge Barnes' work in any of his own writing about drama); but Potter's famous use of popular song in *Pennies from Heaven* and *The Singing Detective* bears remarkable similarities to Barnes' use of song in *The Ruling Class* and *The Bewitched*. *The Ruling Class* was first produced in 1968; Potter began work on *Pennies from Heaven* in 1977 and it was first broadcast in 1978. The choreography in Potter's famous sequence using 'Dem bones, dem bones, dem dry bones' in *The Singing Detective* (first broadcast in 1986) may owe nothing to Barnes, but the appropriation of the song in *The Ruling Class* certainly pre-empts Potter's use of it.

14. These 'Notes' can be found at the end of *The Real Long John Silver and Other Plays (Barnes' People III)* (1986, p. 113).

CHAPTER 2

1. This figure of thirty-four does not include the numerous attendants, monks, priests, prisoners, peasants, mourners, ladies-in-waiting, guards and messengers that the play demands. The 1974 RSC production had a cast of thirty-two. Although some doubling would be possible, and the play could certainly be cut for performance, it would be difficult to realise theatrically without at least some of the major spectacle.

2. All quotations from the play are taken from the currently available edition *Barnes Plays: 1*, (1989a). All subsequent page references refer to this edition.

3. The concept of abjection is discussed in detail by Julia Kristeva in her book *Powers of Horror* (1982). See also Barbara Creed's *The Monstrous-Feminine* (1993).

4. *The Alchemist*, one of Barnes' favourite plays, opens with a ferocious argument between the three tricksters, Subtle, Face and Dol. It uses their hurling of insults to reveal to the audience the back story. Books on screenwriting for Hollywood recommend the method as an economic way of introducing a back story, but the opening of *The Alchemist*, which starts in mid-sentence, has never been bettered. The parallels between this scene and *The Alchemist* are considered further in Chapter 7.

5. Historically, Carlos was the last Hapsburg king of Spain, and his failure to beget an heir resulted in the War of Spanish Succession (1701–13). See John Nada's biography *Carlos the Bewitched* (1962).

6. The period between 1966 and 1976 saw, for example, *Belcher's Luck*, *Morgan: A Suitable Case for Treatment*, *In Two Minds* and *One Flew Over the Cuckoo's Nest*, among others.

7. Shakespeare, *Macbeth*, I.vii.1.

8. For further discussion of farce in these terms, see Susan Purdie (1993, p. 114).
9. To call this tradition 'Shakespearean' could be slightly misleading, for it goes back very much further. See Howard Jacobson (1997). But although Barnes is well aware of earlier manifestations, he draws directly on the Shakespearean associations, and in particular on the Fool in *King Lear*, with which an audience is likely to be familiar. The similarities between Rafael and Lear's Fool are discussed further in Chapter 8.
10. This scene (Act Two, Scene 7) is discussed in detail in Chapter 8, where it is considered as a metonymic example of Barnes' use of dramatic structure.

CHAPTER 3

1. Fromm (1981, p. 21).
2. Jonson, *Sejanus*, Act Three, lines 732–5. The edition referred to is edited by Philip J. Ayers (1990).
3. Charles Marowitz was an expatriate American who had also worked with Peter Brook on his famous RSC production of *King Lear*, and on the 'Theatre of Cruelty' season at the LAMDA Theatre. Marowitz's direction of *Laughter!* is discussed in the final paragraphs of this chapter.
4. All quotations from the play are taken from the currently available edition *Barnes Plays 1* (1989).
5. The ending of *Laughter!* echoes the final act of Trevor Griffiths' *Comedians* (first performed in Nottingham, 1975) in which Eddie Waters, a retired comedian teaching a night class for would-be stand-up comics, tells his students that he stopped performing after hearing a fellow comedian telling jokes about Buchenwald. He argues that 'the death camp was the logic of our world . . . extended . . . There were no jokes left . . . Every joke was a little pellet, a final solution. We're the only animal that laughs' Griffiths (1976, p. 55).
6. See Dukore for a full discussion of this (1995, pp. 6 and 178).
7. Wardle, 'Laughter!', *The Times*, 25 January 1978.
8. The Epilogue to *Laughter!* is discussed at length in Chapter 9, pp. 239–44.
9. Although Barnes does not make any stipulations about double-casting in the published text of the play, in the 1978 Royal Court production, Samael and Cranach were played by the same actor, Derek Francis. The implications of this double-casting are discussed further in Chapter 9, pp. 242–3.
10. In his profound and far-reaching book *Explaining Hitler*, Ron Rosenbaum (1998) examines various 'explanations' of Hitler and Hitler's rise to

power. There is not space here to do justice to Rosenbaum's book, but it is worth noting that he contextualises the arguments for and against the notion of absolute evil with great clarity.

11. The play has, however, been revived in Denmark (where it ran in repertory between June 1994 and June 1996 at the Mammutteatret in Copenhagen) and twice (in 1982 and 1995) at Temple University Philadelphia, USA.

12. Billington, 'Laughter', *Guardian*, 25 January 1978.

13. Artaud never suggested that the director should become dominant,but argued, rather, that 'the old duality between author and producer will disappear, to be replaced by a kind of single Creator . . . responsible for both play and action' (Artaud, *Collected Works*, p. 72). One of the effects of Brook's work was to foreground the role of the director. This apparent contradiction is explored in David Selbourne's accounts of Brook's production of *A Midsummer Night's Dream* (Selbourne, 1982).

CHAPTER 4

1. His introduction was written for the first published edition of the play, by Faber and Faber in 1985. It is reproduced in *Barnes Plays: 2*, 1993).

2. It is worth noting here that Terry Hands' production of the play at the Barbican swamped the play in theatrical wizardry, including such a storm of dry ice that one actor lost his way on the stage and fell from it, breaking his leg.

3. Billington, 'Red Noses', *Guardian*, 2 July 1985.

4. All quotations from the play are taken from the currently available edition *Barnes Plays: 2*, (1993). All subsequent page references refer to this edition.

5. Barnes' childhood experiences in Clacton-on-Sea are discussed in Part 1, 'An Introduction', pp. 3–4.

6. This recollection of Mamoulian's direction appears in David Thomson's *Beneath Mulholland*, where he discusses Garbo's screen persona (1998, p. 39).

7. In *The Empty Space*, Brook's chapter entitled 'The Rough Theatre' begins: 'It is always popular theatre that saves the day. Through the ages it has taken many forms, and there is only one factor that they all have in common – a roughness . . . The theatre that's not in a theatre, the theatre on carts, on wagons, on trestles, audiences standing, drinking . . . joining in, answering back' (1968, p. 73).

8. I am grateful to Elaine Turner for this observation, and for her infectious enthusiasm for *Red Noses*, which she regards as Barnes' masterpiece. She has also written an excellent distance-learning module on

Red Noses for Rose Bruford College, in which she briefly raises the question of whether the play can be seen as a 'critical parable of the 1960s where the political consciousness to put ideals into structural practice came too late'.

9. In America I am thinking in particular of such groups as *The Living Theater*, *The San Francisco Mime Troupe*, and the *Bread and Puppet Theater*; in Europe companies such as *Le Grand Théâtre de Panique*; and in England *The People Show* and *Welfare State*. Although some of these groups have been disbanded, others have mutated and survived.

CHAPTER 5

1. *Le Morte D'Arthur*, Book xvii, Chapter 22. (See also note below).
2. *Sunsets and Glories* is discussed briefly in Part 1, 'An Introduction', p. 15.
3. For the revival at the Queen's Theatre, Barnes slightly revised the play. Several scenes were cut, and it played in two acts – with the interval between what is designated Act Two, Scenes 7 and 8 in the published edition. In this essay I refer to the production at the Queen's, but use the annotation of scenes from the published edition of the play for ease of reference.
4. All quotations from the play are taken from the single edition published by Methuen (1999).
5. These 'Notes' appear as an afterword to the collection of short plays in *The Real Long John Silver and Other Plays* (1986).
6. The influence of Brecht on Barnes' work is discussed in Chapter 7.
7. Brecht, *The Life of Galileo*, Scene 13, 1938, (first performed in 1943); translated by John Willett (1980).
8. For further discussion of Meyerhold's interest in surrealism see Leach (1989), pp. 120–2.
9. In *My Last Breath*, Buñuel wrote: 'Even now, when I ask myself what surrealism really was, I still answer that it was a revolutionary, poetic and moral movement' (1984, p. 109).
10. Brecht's *Verfremdungseffekt* relates closely to the Russian formalist concept of *ostranenie*. For a more detailed discussion, see Leach (1989) pp. 170–2; and, in relation to Barnes, pp. 201–3 of this work.
11. In the written text (prepared for publication before Barnes' own Queen's Theatre revival of the play) the crows do not appear until Scene 1: '*two men in black cloaks and bird-masks enter stage right with iron hooks to pull off the corpses*' (Barnes, 1999, p. 4). Theatrically, the decision to have them prowling the battlefield *before* Bess and Davy have arrived is visually striking and deeply ominous.
12. Scene 4 (in the published edition), a scene set in a tavern, was cut from the Queen's Theatre revival.

13. This is the final scene of Act One in the published version of the play. In the Queen's Theatre production, the play was performed in two acts, not three, with an interval taken between Scenes 7 and 8 of Act Two of the published text.
14. For the revival at the Queen's Theatre in London, Alan Miller Bunford's design was based on Stephen Brimson Lewis's for the Royal Exchange in Manchester. At the Queen's, Bunford used the same basic idea of a glass floor with corpses and skeletons beneath that Lewis had designed for the Manchester production. As the audience in the stalls would not see what was beneath the glass floor, an enormous round mirror hung at an angle upstage of the main action. Depending on the way the floor was lit, the 'pit of Hell' appeared and disappeared.
15. Gardner, *Guardian*, 31 March 1999.
16. His entrance line – 'Now is the summer of my deep content' – sets the tone, linking him clearly with Shakespeare's Richard III.
17. They may have come to the mountain top to escape Richard, but it leaves them nowhere to go – except to dreams. I am put in mind of another Mallory: it was the mountaineer, George Leigh Mallory, who, when asked on his American lecture tour of 1923: 'Why do you want to climb Mount Everest?', responded: 'Because it's there.' Mallory has another namesake lurking in the background of the play: Sir Thomas Malory, who wrote *Le Morte D'Arthur* and who died in 1471, the year in which *Dreaming* is set. While *Dreaming* can be seen as a romance in the Arthurian tradition, I have not pursued that line of argument in this essay because the play itself never foregrounds the allusion. The name Skelton also conjures up associations: skeleton, of course, but also the medieval poet, John Skelton, and, perhaps most significantly, the lugubrious American comedian, Red Skelton.

CHAPTER 6

1. The quotation is taken from an interview with Brian Woolland on 19 March 2003.
2. It was not until 1985 that the Royal Shakespeare Company finally produced the play – seven years after Barnes had finished writing it.
3. In his introduction to *Barnes' People II: Seven Duologues* (1984).
4. The first series of Alan Bennett's *Talking Heads* was broadcast in 1987; the second series went out in 1998.
5. Barnes notes that this monologue, *The End of the World – And After*, is based on a true story, as is *Glory*.
6. In the 1981 radio production Miller and Anna were played by Leo McKern and Peggy Ashcroft respectively.

7. Betty and Carol were played by Barbara Leigh-Hunt and Eileen Atkins respectively in the 1984 radio production.
8. Peter Barnes, or a character named as Author, appears in several of his plays. Perhaps the most notable of these appearances is in *Laughter!*, where the author's authority is thoroughly debunked. In the RSC production of *Jubilee*, the character named Barnes was played as an impersonation. Where the character appears elsewhere – as in *Clap Hands Here Comes Charlie*, *Three Visions* and *Laughter!* – impersonation would be inappropriate.
9. The 55-year-old Peter Barnes was played by Robert Stephens, the Young Barnes by Anton Lesser, the Old Barnes by Lionel Jeffries. Barnes had initially hoped to have the play cast using three playwright–actors in the roles: Harold Pinter was to play the 55-year-old, and John Osborne the Old Barnes. The problem was in finding a young man who was both sufficiently well known and accomplished as an actor and a playwright.
10. Harry, Tom and Max were played in the 1986 radio production by Sean Connery, Donald Pleasance and John Hurt respectively.
11. Here I am thinking not only of *The Ruling Class*, *The Bewitched* and *Laughter!*, but also *Time of the Barracudas*, *Sclerosis* and *Leonardo's Last Supper* (see pp. 5–6, 12–13 of Part One, 'An Introduction' for a discussion of these plays).
12. *Silver Bridges* is one of the duologues in *Barnes' People II*. In the 1984 radio production Vanderbilt was played by Peter Ustinov and Gould by Alec McCowen.
13. In the 1984 radio production Mary was played by Joan Plowright, the Priest by Paul Scofield.
14. The Priest in Barnes' play is referring accurately to the case of Domenico Scandella (generally known as Menocchio), a miller born in 1532 in Friuli (in what is now northern Italy). He was burnt at the stake by order of the Holy Office for his heretical propositions. Carlo Ginzburg's brilliant book *The Cheese and the Worms* (1980) gives a detailed account of the development of the heresy and of the fate of Menocchio. The book may well be the source for Barnes' play.
15. In the 1984 radio production Joseph was played by Harry Andrews, John by Trevor Howard.
16. It is worth noting here that the monologues in the *Barnes' People* series are also experimental in that, while the majority of monologues are in some way retrospective, dramatising characters' memories, Barnes was attempting to use the monologue form to look forward.
17. In particular I am thinking of Peter Cook's E. L. Wisty, a tramp-like character who propounded ever more bizarre theories and philosophies, while not for a moment entertaining even the slightest doubts about his eccentric world views.

18. In particular, see Chapter 9.
19. *Luna Park Eclipses* is discussed in detail on pp. 250–56.
20. *Revolutionary Witness* was first published in 1989 by Methuen in a compilation of television plays – *Revolutionary Witness* and the three plays that were broadcast by Channel 4 in the same year under the overall heading *Nobody Here But Us Chickens*. It was subsequently republished as part of Methuen's collected works: *Barnes Plays: 3* (1996a). Because the 1989 volume is now out of print, page numbering in this essay refers to the later edition.
21. *The Spirit of Man* was first published in 1990 in an edition that also included the seven monologues *More Barnes' People*, first broadcast on BBC Radio 3 in 1989 and 1990. It was subsequently republished in *Barnes Plays: 2* (1993).
22. Barnes' author's note to *Revolutionary Witness* appears only in the 1989 edition of the play; it is not reproduced in the 1996 edition.
23. In particular there seems to be an allusion to *The Cherry Orchard*, in which each of the four acts is set in a different season. Although in *The Cherry Orchard* most of the characters may resist change, the play is underpinned by a growing sense of impending social upheaval. Barnes does not acknowledge this as a conscious influence on the play, though (as noted in Chapter 7) the issue of influence is a complex one.
24. Although *The Spirit of Man* was first published in 1990 – see note 2 above – the page numbering here and elsewhere in this essay refers to the later edition: *Barnes Plays: 2* (1993), which is more readily available.
25. Indeed, Barnes intended it as a wryly comic riposte to *The Crucible*.
26. In the 1989 BBC TV production of the play, Guerdon was played by Nigel Hawthorne, Yates by Alan Rickman and Abegail by Eleanor David.
27 The ideas of the Ranters, one of the more extreme radical sects that emerged in the 1640s and '50s in the aftermath of the English Revolution, are discussed with great clarity by Christopher Hill in his book *The World Turned Upside Down* (1972).
28. The phrase 'light shining in Buckinghamshire' (to which 'bright lights in Buckinghamshire' alludes) originates in a pamphlet produced by the Diggers in 1649. The Diggers were one of the radical political groups that emerged in the mid-seventeenth century. They argued that property and land should be redistributed amongst the people and, in the words of their leader, Gerrard Winstanley: 'There can be no universal liberty till this universal community be established.'
29. Like much of Barnes' drama, the play has its origins in a historically documented incident. In the 1989 BBC TV production of the play, the three rabbis were played by Ian Cuthbertson, Harold Innocent and Peter Jeffrey.
30. The trilogy was first published in a single volume with *Revolutionary Witness* (1989b). It can also be found with the same introduction in the

second volume of collected plays: *Barnes Plays: 2* (1993). Page numbers in this chapter refer to the more readily available collected works.

31. In the 1989 Channel 4 production Allsop was played by Jack Shepherd, Hern by Daniel Massey.

32. Alchemists sought to transmute base metals into gold, a metaphor which informs Jonson's play as much as it does Barnes' miniature.

33. In the 1989 Channel 4 production Carver was played by David Suchet, Hills and Powell by Nicholas Farrell and Michael Maloney respectively.

34. In the 1989 Channel 4 production Berridge was played by Stephen Rea, Judith by Janet Suzman and Sefton by Norman Rodway.

35. See Chapter 7, pp. 194–5.

36. The cast for *Hard Times* included Bob Peck (Gradgrind), Alan Bates (Bounderby), Richard E. Grant, Alex Jennings, Harriet Walter, Bill Paterson and several of those actors who have appeared regularly in Peter Barnes' plays: Dilys Laye, Diana Fairfax, Peter Bayliss and Timothy Bateson.

CHAPTER 7

1. I use the term Early Modern here to indicate that I am referring back to the theatre of the late sixteenth century as well as to Jacobean theatre as such. Throughout this essay, except where quoting or paraphrasing from other critics, I use the term Early Modern in preference to Elizabethan, Jacobean or Caroline to refer to theatre of the late sixteenth and early seventeenth centuries. My reluctance to identify theatre by reference to reigning monarchs is now academically widespread, but is particularly appropriate in connection with the work of a playwright who proclaims himself a Republican.

2. Elsewhere, I have looked at the ways in which considering Barnes' work as Jonsonian illuminates its dramatic strategies. See my essay, 'Peter Barnes – His very own Ben Jonson', in Woolland (ed.) (2003, pp. 30–43).

3. Barnes has directed two productions of *Bartholomew Fair*: the first at the Round House (1978); the second at the Regent's Park Open Air Theatre (1983).

4. Bernard Levin, 'The Ungentle Art of Doctoring Jonson,' *Sunday Times*, 8 May 1977, p. 37.

5. Bernard Dukore offers a detailed and useful account of Barnes's method in adapting these plays, and of the debate referred to here, in *Barnestorm* (1995, pp. 205–8).

6. Prior to this production of *The Devil Is an Ass*, the only Jonson plays produced in the theatre with any regularity were *Volpone*, *The Alchemist* and

Bartholomew Fair. Epicœne or The Silent Woman had enjoyed professional revivals in Birmingham (1947) and Bristol (1959), and *Every Man in His Humour* had been revived in 1903, 1937 (in Stratford-upon-Avon) and 1960 at Joan Littlewood's Theatre Royal, Stratford East. But the majority of Jonson's plays had not been performed since the seventeenth century. Barnes' adaptations did not, of course, single-handedly change attitudes to Jonson, but they certainly contributed to a growing interest in his work in the late twentieth century.

7. Orgel, Stephen (1981), 'What is a Text?', *Research Opportunities in Renaissance Drama*, 26, pp. 3–6. Orgel's essay argues that even where a playwright has tried to exorcise the spirit of his collaborators, as Jonson did in his published version of *Sejanus*, the written text that we unproblematically receive as authored 'by Ben Jonson' is the product of collective work.

8. In 1930 Brecht saw *Roar, China!*, performed by the Meyerhold State Theatre in Berlin.

9. For more details of Brecht's meeting with Meyerhold, see Leach (1989, pp. 171–2).

10 Jeremy Sams' comments appear in a booklet produced by the Publications Department of the Royal National Theatre entitled *Translation* (1992, p. 21). It was the first of a series of *Platform Papers* sold only at the National Theatre's bookshop. It was not published nationally, and does not carry an ISBN number. I have therefore not included it in the bibliography.

11. Chapter 6 (pp. 205–87) of *Barnestorm* (1995) is entitled 'Editings and Adaptations'.

12. In an unpublished lecture given by Peter Barnes at the conference *Ben Jonson and the Theatre* held at the University of Reading in 1996, Barnes asserted: 'Jonson is subversive. Shakespeare, on the other hand, retired to the Jacobean equivalent of Eastbourne to end his days, thankful no doubt to be finally finished with the sordid business of earning a living. No wonder Shakespeare is beloved of the English Establishment'. For a detailed account of the conference see R. Cave et al. (1999).

13. More detailed discussion of the play can be found in Chapter 6. The play was broadcast by BBC TV in August 1989, as the first part of *The Spirit of Man* trilogy; it was published by Methuen in 1990.

14. Discussed in Chapter 6, pp. 163–6.

15. The play is discussed in greater detail in my introduction. It was first produced at the Open Space Theatre, London, in November 1969, and was directed by Charles Marowitz. Published in *Barnes Plays: 1*, (1989, p. 126).

16. The subtitle of Jonson's *The Magnetic Lady* is *Humours Reconciled*.

17. *Revolutionary Witness* is discussed in detail in Chapter 6. pp. 141–50.

18. The wedding scene in *Dreaming* is discussed is greater detail in Chapter 5, pp. 116–18.
19. In Chapter 2, p. 58.
20. Bryden, cited in *Barnes Plays: 1* (1989a, p. 189).
21. Archer (1856–1924) also championed the work of Shaw and Galsworthy. In 1904, with Granville-Barker, he had published an elaborate *Scheme and Estimates for a National Theatre*.
22. The lectures were published in 1923 under the title *Old Drama and the New*. The attack on these playwrights, whom he lumps together in Lecture IV as 'Five Elizabethan Masters', can be found on pp. 78–109. Of the five, he values Massinger far higher than any of his peers: 'Massinger was, in a sane and sober way, one of the best writers of the period' (p. 101).
23. This quotation is from an essay entitled '*Bartholomew Fair*: All the Fun of the Fair', in B. Woolland (ed.) (2004, p. 40).
24. It could certainly be argued that Flote and Mallory are the protagonists of *Red Noses* and *Dreaming* respectively, but both plays are as interested in the impact of leadership on the social group as they are in their 'heroes'.
25. Modernising the spelling, Marston's Latin dedication reads as follows: BENJAMINO JONSONIO POETAE ELEGANTISSIMO GRAVISSIMO AMICO SUO CANDIDO ET CORDATO JOHANNES MARSTON MUSARUM ALUMNUS ASPERAM HANC SUAM THALIAM. D.[at] D.[edicatque]. Translated, this reads: 'John Marston, disciple of the Muses, presents and dedicates this harsh comedy of his to Benjamin Jonson, the profoundest and yet most polished of poets, his candid and heartfelt friend.'
26. An insightful discussion into these plays as 'tragedies of theodicy' can be found in *The Cambridge Companion to English Renaissance Theatre* (Braunmuller and Hattaway, 1990, pp. 334–47).
27. Poel's Elizabethan-style open-stage revivals of Jonson, Marlowe and Shakespeare in the 1890s and early twentieth century paved the way not only for numerous experimental revivals of Early Modern plays, but also for new published editions of the plays. See Speaight (1954); and O'Connor (1987).
28. In the case of Jan Kott, whose book *Shakespeare: Our Contemporary* (1965) had such an impact on Shakespearean production, the notion of dialogue is more literal, for Kott and Brook had met; and Brook wrote a preface to the English edition of Kott's book.
29. *The Frontiers of Farce* was subsequently published by Heinemann in 1977.
30. Later that year the production transferred to the Royal Court Theatre, London. The text of *Lulu* was published by Heinemann in 1971.
31. Barnes combined the three one-act plays, *Hortense a dit 'Je m'en fous!'*,

Léonie est en avance and *Feu la mère de Madame* into one three-act play, changing the names of the couples in Acts Two and Three. Dukore offers a detailed account of this and other Feydeau adaptations in *Barnestorm* (1995, pp. 265–71).

32. The bedroom farce scene is Act One, Scene 11. See also Chapter 2, pp. 54–6.

33. *Spring Awakening*, Wedekind's first play, for example, was written in 1891, but not staged until 1906 (in a production directed by Max Reinhardt, albeit in a heavily censored version). The play was not performed in England until 1963, and then only for two Sunday-night club performances at the Royal Court Theatre after two years of negotiation with the Lord Chamberlain's office.

34. These are the names used in Tom Osborn's translation, the version used in the first English production at the Royal Court Theatre.

35. Eric Bentley, for example, suggested that 'Wedekind's world is totally devoid of any morality.'

36. Nicholas de Jongh, for example, wrote in the *Evening Standard* (16 June 1999), 'Barnes's black humour . . . resembles a 15-year-old cocking a snook. This self-conscious bad taste trivialises *Dreaming*'s serious aspirations.'

37. A brief account of *Clap Hands Here Comes Charlie* can be found in my introduction, pp. 6–7.

38. See Chapter 5, pp. 111–13.

39. In an unpublished interview given to Brian Woolland on 21 July 1999.

40 In the BBC radio production of the play, broadcast on Radio 3 in 1984, Vanderbilt was played by Peter Ustinov, and Gould by Alec McCowen. The play is published in *Barnes' People II* (1984).

41. Introduction to *Barnes' People III: The Real Long John Silver and Other Plays* (1986).

42. Brecht, *Gesammelte Werke*, xv, p. 301. The translation offered here is by Keith Dickson in *Towards Utopia*, (1978, p. 241).

43. See, for example *Brecht on Theatre* (1964, pp. 281 and 282) where there is an account of his last collection of theoretical writings, 'Dialectics in the Theatre', in which he now begins to refer to his theatre as 'dialectical theatre', and he gives the impression that his earlier 'Short Organum' is 'something of a makeshift, an interim report'.

44. These 'Notes' can be found at the end of *The Real Long John Silver and Other Plays* (1986, p. 113).

45. Although Brecht's work on Shakespeare is well known, he also adapted Marlowe's *Edward II*, first produced in 1924. Between 1943 and 1946 he worked with W. H. Auden (among others) on an adaptation of Webster's *The Duchess of Malfi*. A production of the play opened on Broadway in October 1946, though little of Brecht's adaptation was actually used.

CHAPTER 8

1. *Gay Times*, London, 3 July 1999.
2. This is an extract from Barnes' autobiographical essay in *Contemporary Authors Autobiography Series*, Vol. XII, edited by Nakamura (1990, p. 10).
3. This is not intended as a patriotic puff for British television, but to differentiate between the small-scale projects (discussed in Chapter 6) he has undertaken for the BBC and Channel 4 and the much larger miniseries on which he has worked for some of the American networks.
4. Cited in Dukore (1995, p. 12).
5. Barnes has argued that most of Jonson's plays for the theatre are politically subversive. See, for example, his essays in *Gambit* (1972) and *New Theatre Quarterly* (1987). He is most persuasive in championing *Bartholomew Fair* and *The Devil is an Ass* as radical texts. My essay 'Peter Barnes: His very own Ben Jonson' examines the way that Barnes' writing about Jonson reveals as much about his own writing as it does about Jonson's (Woolland, 2003, pp. 146–59). Barnes' own essay in the same volume discusses *Bartholomew Fair* in just these terms (2003, pp. 40–7).
6. As Julie Sanders observes of *The Magnetic Lady*, for example: 'The backroom spaces of an early modern urban household are vividly conjured up for audience imaginations here, from the sites of food production to the laundry. Elsewhere in the play, of course, we are also made all too aware of that other unseen, "private" space of the birthing room, where Placentia gives birth to her illegitimate son.' She then notes how Jonson had achieved similar effects in his 1618 masque *Pleasure Reconciled to Virtue*, 'where the "downstairs" spaces of production for the feast that would have accompanied the masque are made explicit in the antimasque's opening "hymn"' Sanders (2003, p. 52).
7. Vsevolod Meyerhold worked as an actor in the Moscow Art Theatre under the direction of Constantin Stanislavski, before becoming a director himself. In post-revolutionary Russia his work was rigorously experimental, and he became the most important post-revolutionary director. In 1926 his theatre was renamed the Meyerhold State Theatre. Although Meyerhold never systematically theorised his own work in the way that Stanislavski had done, his work is increasingly recognised as immensely influential. See Braun (1969 and 1970); Gladkov (1997); Hoover (1974); Kiebuzinska (1988); Law and Gordon (1996); and Leach (1989).
8. The example is used by Susan Hayward (2000, p. 96) in her discussion of collision montage. A more detailed account can be found in Eisenstein (1991*)*.

9. Although the term 'the montage of attractions' appears to have been coined by Eisenstein in his essay of that title (first published in *LEF* in 1923), Meyerhold had constructed some of his productions – most notably *The Death of Tarelkin* (1922) – on these structural principles. It has been argued that Mayakovsky conceived of his own play, *Mystery Bouffe* (directed by Meyerhold in 1918 and 1921), as a series of attractions. See Leach (1989, pp. 121 and 164). See also Law and Gordon (1996, note 268); and Hoover (1974, pp. 272–4).

10. Eisenstein's discussion of the importance of the concept of the hieroglyph is reproduced in *An Eisenstein Reader*, ed. Richard Taylor (1998).

11. From a lecture by Meyerhold given on 13 June 1936. Cited in Braun (1969, pp. 318–19).

12. The word 'montage' is based on a Russian word, itself derived from the French verb *monter*, to mount. Montage can be seen as a product of modernism. Although Walter Benjamin developed the literary montage as a form, my concern here is with the effects of theatrical montage and its relationship to cinematic montage.

13. Barnes' enthusiasm for Jonson's *Bartholomew Fair* certainly echoes Eisenstein's: 'The carefully constructed anarchy of the play, its scope and dramatic form – in this case an intimate panorama, as intricately constructed as a Swiss watch, yet ragged as life at the edges – is unique in dramatic literature. There is certainly nothing like it in European drama. You have to go to novels like Rabelais' *Gargantua* and *Pantagruel* and Gogol's *Dead Souls*. Its tough, humorous vulgarity and loose morals makes this the warmest of Jonson's plays' (Barnes in Woolland, 2003, p. 46).

14. At the time of writing, *Arabian Nights* has yet to be screened on British terrestrial television, although it had been extremely successful in America, where it was first broadcast in 2000.

15. The following extracts from reviews of *Dreaming* exemplify such criticism: 'The play's allegorical weight becomes hard to bear, not least because the work contradicts itself in both style and substance' – Jeffrey Wainwright, *Independent*, 31 March 1999; 'The cast are sometimes defeated by the clashes of tone' – Nigel Cliff, *The Times*, 18 June 1999; 'There's no strict dramatic coherence about *Dreaming*, nor a strong narrative line' – Nicholas de Jongh, *Evening Standard*, 16 June 1999.

16. Sebastian Faulks' novel *Birdsong* makes much of the associations in the minds of the combatants between the sounds of birdsong and the temporary lulls that occurred in First World War battles. Far from offering respite and relief, the birdsong creates a terrifying foreboding that the carnage is about to start all over again.

17. See, for example, Eisenstein's analysis of the structure of his production of *The Wiseman* (based on an Alexander Ostrovsky play) (see Taylor,

1998, pp. 31–3); and Meyerhold's rhythmical analysis of his production of *The Lady of the Camelias* (Leach, 1989, pp. 124–5).

18. The quotation originates in Barnes' own introduction to *Barnes Plays: 1* (1989, p. ix).

19. The observation is included in the section 'Meyerhold Speaks' in Gladkov's book, *Meyerhold Speaks Meyerhold Rehearses*. The date of the conversation is not recorded. (Gladkov, 1997, p. 139).

CHAPTER 9

1. 'Peter Barnes' in *Contemporary Authors Autobiography Series*, Vol. XII, edited by Nakamura (1990, p. 13).

2. Gruber (1986, p. 147).

3. Gardner, *Guardian*, 31 March 1999.

4. Barnes' introduction to *Leonardo's Last Supper* can be found in *Barnes Plays: 1* (1989, p. 122).

5. My thanks to Stevie Simkin for coining this term in one of our many stimulating conversations about theatre.

6. Even in Chapter 5 of *Jokes and Their Relation to the Unconscious*, 'Jokes as Social Processes', where Freud turns his attention to the 'Audience', his conclusion configures the response of the audience in terms of the Teller's intentions: 'telling my joke to another person would seem to serve several purposes: first to give me objective certainty that the joke-work has been successful; secondly, to complete my own pleasure by a reaction from the other person upon myself; and thirdly – where it is a question of repeating a joke that one has not produced oneself – to make up for the loss of pleasure owing to the joke's lack of novelty' (1905/1960, p. 156).

7. In a footnote to the introduction to her excellent book *Comedy*, Susan Purdie observes: 'Plato, Sidney, Hobbes and Bergson are prominent examples of superiority theorists; Beattie, Kant, Schopenhauer, R. W. Emerson, Arthur Koestler and Jonathan Miller all offer incongruity approaches. Hobbes's succinct formulation may summarise the first theory's emphasis on the fact that laughter elevates the laughers above other people: "*Sudden Glory*, is the passion which maketh those Grimaces called LAUGHTER; and is caused either by some sudden act of their own, that pleaseth them; or by the apprehension of some deformed thing in another, by comparison whereof they suddenly applaud themselves" (p. 125). Freud's approach to 'the comic' is a form of superiority theory. Schopenhauer, by contrast, exemplifies the alternative emphasis upon the solitary cognitive process of laughter: "the source of the ludicrous is always the . . . unexpected subsumption of an object under a conception

which in some respects is different from it" (quoted in Lauter, 1964, p. 359).'

8. The exchange between Lopakhin and Ranyevskaya can be found in the middle of Act Two. In Michael Frayn's translation (1978), it reads as follows:

    LOPAKHIN   Very good play I saw last night. Very funny.
    RANYEVSKAYA   There's nothing funny in the world. People should-n't watch plays. They should look at their own lives more often.

    (pp. 28–9)

9. Koestler's argument can be found in *The Act of Creation*, Book 1, Part 1, pp. 27–97.
10. Charles Gruner, in *The Game of Humor* (1997), follows this line of argument, expanding on Hobbes' position, insisting that his 'superiority' theory is all-encompassing. In his book he devotes an entire chapter ('Drollery in Death, Destruction and Disaster') to 'sick' humour and joking about death. He argues that 'By telling jokes about death and making fun of those in the life-and-death industries of medicine, grave-digging and undertaking, we enable ourselves to momentarily, at least, feel superior to that final process' (p. 41).
11. This last possibility seems not to have been Barnes' intention; but it is worth noting that Cranach and Gottleb have been on stage until the final moments of the previous scene. There will not have been sufficient time for the actors to have made anything other than the most cursory costume change. In the minds of the audience the association between the different roles that each actor plays is likely to be strong.
12. The English Stage Company, which produces at the Royal Court Theatre, is a subsidised company, but in 1978 its public grant was a small fraction of that received by the National Theatre or the Royal Shakespeare Company.
13. Barnes directed the London revival of *Dreaming* which opened at the Queen's Theatre, Shaftesbury Avenue, in June 1999.
14. A prime example of this was John Peter's review in the *Sunday Times*: 'Here is Peter Barnes's new play, a frisky, jokey number, full of low-grade gallows humour . . . You are treated to such aphoristic gems as "Massacres are rarely 100% proof: there's always someone left." . . . The point about such sarcastic serious bits of bar-room philosophy is that they are (a) trivial, (b) vulgar, (c) crushingly obvious – or indeed all three. The writing is both slick and flabby' (20 June 1999).
15. When the play opened in Manchester, Ian Shuttleworth wrote in the *Financial Times*: 'Either Barnes has given up on laughter or, yet more tragically, it has given up on him' (31 March 1999).

16. Barrett (1978), in Aristophanes, *The Knights, Peace, The Birds, Assembly-women, Wealth.*

17. I readily acknowledge that it is contentious and reductive to refer to Beckett as an absurdist. There is, nevertheless, in the work of both Beckett and Barnes, a vigorous attempt to use theatrical language and theatrical space to express the depravity and desolution of contemporary conditions; and in some of Barnes' later radio plays (and certainly in *Luna Park Eclipses*) there is a minimalism that is reminiscent of Beckett's work.

18. In the absurdist's formulation, the word 'absurd' means much more than its common sense of 'ridiculous'. Barnes frequently points up the ridiculous, but his work avoids the pessimism of absurdism. Ionesco wrote that the 'Absurd is that which is devoid of purpose . . . Cut off from his religious, metaphysical and transcendental roots, man is lost; all his actions senseless, absurd, useless.' This is clearly not Barnes' position.

19. The seemingly oblique title may be intentionally meaningless, but it is interesting to note that the first play by Vladimir Mayakovsky to receive a public performance was performed at the Luna Park Theatre, St Petersburg, in December 1913. Mayakovsky was a Russian poet and playwright whose work Barnes much admires. He wrote political farces, notably *Mystery Bouffe, The Bedbug* and *The Bathhouse* (see also Chapter 7). At the time of writing, the full text of *Luna Park Eclipses* has not been published. *The Head Invents, The Heart Discovers* was, however, published in *New Theatre Quarterly*, 47, August 1996, p. 203 et seq. (1996b).

20. Although I did not attend the National Theatre Studio performances of the play, I have used *The Head Invents, The Heart Discovers* as a workshop exercise with students; and I have witnessed the extraordinary ways in which audiences make meaning from the apparently disconnected fragments. Barnes talks of the same thing happening when the play was performed at the National Theatre Studio.

EPILOGUE

1. Alexander Bakshy. *The Path of the Modern Russian Stage and Other Essays.* London: Cecil Palmer and Hayward, 1916, p. 72

2. Reproduced here by permission of Peter Barnes and Charles Marowitz.

BIBLIOGRAPHY

THE WORK OF PETER BARNES

Awards

John Whiting Award, 1969 (shared with Edward Bond for *Saved*): *The Ruling Class* (Nottingham Playhouse, 1968)

Evening Standard Award for Most Promising Playwright of the Year, 1969.

Giles Cooper Award for Radio Drama: *Barnes' People*, 1981

Laurence Olivier Award for Best Drama, 1985: *Red Noses* (RSC, 1985)

Royal Television Society Award for the Best Drama of 1989: *Nobody Here But Us Chickens* (broadcast by Channel 4, September 1989)

Academy Award best screenplay nomination, 1993: *Enchanted April* (BBC/Miramax, 1991)

Play productions

Time of the Barracudas, 1963, Los Angeles and San Francisco

Sclerosis, 20 June 1965, Traverse Theatre, Edinburgh; 27 June 1965, Aldwych Theatre, London (under the auspices of the Royal Shakespeare Company)

The Ruling Class, 6 November 1968, Nottingham Playhouse.

Leonardo's Last Supper and *Noonday Demons*, 25 November 1969, Open Space Theatre, London

The Bewitched, 7 May 1974, Royal Shakespeare Company, Aldwych Theatre, London

Laughter!, 25 January 1978, Royal Court Theatre, London

Somersaults, 1981, Leicester Haymarket Studio Theatre

Red Noses, 2 July 1985, Royal Shakespeare Company, Barbican Theatre, London

Sunsets and Glories, 28 June 1990, West Yorkshire Playhouse, Leeds
Luna Park Eclipses (in a private performance), 1995, Royal National
  Theatre Studio, London
Corpsing, 1996, Tristan Bates Theatre, London
Dreaming, 17 March 1999, Manchester Royal Exchange; 15 June 1999,
  Queen's Theatre, London
Jubilee, 12 July 2001, Royal Shakespeare Company, Swan Theatre,
  Stratford-upon-Avon.

Television plays
The Man with a Feather in His Hat, 1960, BBC TV
Revolutionary Witness, July 1989, BBC TV
The Spirit of Man, 23 August 1989, BBC TV
Nobody Here But Us Chickens, September 1989, Channel 4
Bye Bye Columbus, 3 February 1992, BBC TV
Hard Times (adapted by Barnes from the novel by Charles Dickens),
  1994, BBC TV
Merlin, 1998, Hallmark/NBC
Alice in Wonderland, 1999, Hallmark/NBC
Noah's Ark, 1999, Hallmark/NBC
Arabian Nights, 2000, Hallmark/ABC

Radio scripts
Eulogy of Baldness, adapted from Synesius of Cyrene, 23 February 1980,
  BBC Radio 3
Barnes' People, 1981, BBC Radio 3
Barnes' 'People II, 1984, BBC Radio 3
Barnes' People III (in *The Real Long John Silver and Other Plays*), August
  1986, BBC Radio 3
More Barne's People, 1989 and 1990, BBC Radio 3

Productions of adaptations and edited versions
The Alchemist (Ben Jonson), 9 February 1970, Nottingham Playhouse
  production, National Theatre at the Old Vic; 23 May 1977, Royal
  Shakespeare Company, The Other Place, Stratford-upon-Avon
Lulu, 7 October 1970, Nottingham Playhouse; 8 December 1970,
  Royal Court Theatre, London
The Devil Is an Ass (Ben Jonson), 14 March 1973, Nottingham
  Playhouse; 2 May 1977, Royal National Theatre

Eastward Ho! (Jonson, Marston, Chapman and Barnes), 1973, BBC
   Radio 3
For All Those Who Get Desperate (cabaret songs, poems and songs from
   plays by Brecht and Wedekind), April 1976, Royal Court Theatre
   Upstairs, London
The Frontiers of Farce (adaptation of *The Purging* by Georges Feydeau
   and *The Singer* by Wedekind), 11 October 1976, Old Vic Theatre,
   London
Antonio (from John Marston's *Antonio and Mellida* and *Antonio's
   Revenge*), 1977, BBC Radio 3; 20 September 1979, Nottingham
   Playhouse
Bartholomew Fair (Ben Jonson), 3 August 1978, Round House Theatre,
   London
Two Hangmen – Brecht and Wedekind, 20 December 1978, BBC
   Radio 3
A Chaste Maid in Cheapside (Thomas Middleton), 1979, BBC Radio 3
The Devil Himself (cabaret review from Wedekind), 23 April 1980, Lyric
   Theatre, Hammersmith
The Soldier's Fortune (Thomas Otway), 1981, BBC Radio 3
The Atheist (Thomas Otway), 1981, BBC Radio 3
The Dutch Courtesan (John Marston), 1982, BBC Radio 3
A Mad World, My Masters (Thomas Middleton), 1982, BBC Radio 3
Actors (from Lope de Vega's *Lo fingido verdadero*), 1983, BBC Radio 3
The Primrose Path, 1983, BBC Radio 3
A Trick to Catch the Old One (Thomas Middleton), 1985, BBC Radio 3
The Old Law (Middleton, Rowley, Massinger and Barnes), 1986, BBC
   Radio 3
Don Juan and Faust (from Christian Dietrich Grabbe), BBC Radio 3
Woman of Paris (from Henry Becque), 1986, BBC Radio 3
Scenes From a Marriage (adapted from three plays by Feydeau: *Feu la
   mère de Madame, Hortense a dit: 'Je m'en fous!'* and *Léonie est en
   avance*), 1986, RSC at the Aldwych Theatre, London
The Magnetic Lady (Jonson), 1987, BBC Radio 3
Tango at the End of Winter (Kunio Shimizu), 1991 (directed by Yukio
   Ninagawa), Edinburgh Festival

Films
This does *not* include any of the numerous film scripts that Barnes has
   written, and to which he refers as 'craft work'.

The Ruling Class, 1972 (directed by Peter Medak), Keep Films, available on DVD from the Criterion Collection (2001)
Leonardo's Last Supper, 1977 (directed by Peter Barnes), British Film Institute
Enchanted April, 1991 (directed by Mike Newell), BBC/Miramax

Books
The Ruling Class (1969), Heinemann, London
Barnes' People II: Seven Duologues (1984), Heinemann, London
The Real Long John Silver and Other Plays (Barnes' People III) (1986), Faber and Faber, London
Barnes Plays: 1 (The Ruling Class, Leonardo's Last Supper, Noonday Demons, The Bewitched, Laughter!, Barnes' People: Eight Monologues) (1989), Methuen, London
Revolutionary Witness and Nobody Here But Us Chickens (1989), Methuen, London
The Spirit of Man and More Barnes' People: Seven Monologues (1990), Methuen, London
Sunsets and Glories (1990), Methuen, London
Barnes Plays: 2 (Red Noses, The Spirit of Man, Nobody Here But Us Chickens, Sunsets and Glories, Bye Bye Columbus) (1993), Methuen, London
Barnes Plays: 3 (Clap Hands Here Comes Charlie, Heaven's Blessings, Revolutionary Witness) (1996a), Methuen, London
Dreaming (1999), Methuen, London
Jubilee (2001), Methuen, London
To Be or Not to Be (2002), BFI Film Classics, British Film Institute, London

Published screenplays
Merlin (1998), Newmarket Press, New York

Essays and periodical publications
'Ben Jonson and the Modern Stage' *Gambit*, 6 (1972), pp. 5–30.
'Hands off the Classics – Asses and Devilry', *Listener*, 5 January 1978, pp. 17–19
'Liberating Laughter', *Plays and Players*, 25 (March 1978), pp. 14–17
'Fresh Fields', in Ann Lloyd (ed.), *Movies of the Thirties*, (1983a), Orbis Publishing, London

'Staging Jonson', in *Shakespeare and Jonson: Papers from the Humanities Research Centre* (Canberra, Australia), Ian Donaldson (ed.) (1983), Macmillan, London

'A Slice of Toast Big Enough to Sit Upon', *Observer*, (19 October 1986), p. 23

'Still Standing Upright: Ben Jonson, 350 Years Alive', *New Theatre Quarterly*, 9 (August 1987), pp. 202–6

'On Class, Christianity, and Questions of Comedy', *New Theatre Quarterly*, 1 (February 1990), pp. 5–24

'Peter Barnes', in Joyce Nakamura (ed.) *Contemporary Authors Autobiography Series*, Vol. XII (1990)c, Gale Research, Detroit, New York, London

'Peter Barnes on American Drama', *Journal of Dramatic Theory and Criticism*, 7 (Fall 1992), pp. 163–73

'Working with Yukio Ninagawa.' *New Theatre Quarterly*, 13 (November 1992), pp. 389–91

'Shaw at Play', in Bernard F. Dukore (ed.) *1992: Shaw and the Last Hundred Years* (1994), Pennsylvania State University Press, University Park

'Democracy and Deconstruction', (1996b), *New Theatre Quarterly*, 47

'On Playing With Her Breasts', *Around the Globe* (1996c)

'"An Uncooked Army Boot": Spike Milligan, 1918–2002', *New Theatre Quarterly*, 71 (August 2002a), pp. 205–10

Peter Bayliss, obituary, *Guardian* (5 August, 2002b)

'*Bartholomew Fair* – All the Fun of the Fair', in Brian Woolland (ed.), *Jonsonians – Living Traditions* (2003), Ashgate, Burlington and London, pp. 40–47

Published adaptations

Lulu (1971), adapted by Barnes from *Earth Spirit* and *Pandora's Box* by Frank Wedekind, Heinemann, London

The Frontiers of Farce (1977), adapted by Barnes from *The Purging* by Feydeau and *The Singer* by Wedekind, Heinemann, London

Tango at the End of Winter (1991), adapted by Barnes from the play by Kunio Shimizu, Amber Lane Press, Oxford

Interviews

'Plays and Playing: Conversations at Leeds'. *Theatre Topics*, 1 (September 1991), pp. 99–116

CRITICAL WORK ON PETER BARNES

Billington, Michael, 'Laughter', *Guardian,* 25 January 1978,
   p. 10

Cave, Richard Allen (1988), *New British Drama in Performance on the London Stage: 1970–1985,* St. Martin's Press, New York

Cohn, Ruby (1991), *Retreats from Realism in Recent English Drama,* Cambridge University Press, Cambridge

Dukore, Bernard F. (September 1987), *'Red Noses* and *Saint Joan',* *Modern Drama,* 30, pp. 340–51

Dukore, Bernard F. (1981), *The Theatre of Peter Barnes,* Heinemann, London and Exeter, USA

Dukore, Bernard F. (1990), 'Peter Barnes and the Problem of Goodness', in Enoch Brater and Ruby Cohn (eds.), *Around the Absurd: Essays on Modern and Postmodern Drama,* University of Michigan Press, Ann Arbor

Dukore, Bernard F., (1995), *Barnestorm: The Plays of Peter Barnes,* Garland Publishing, Inc., New York and London

Hammond, Jonathan (1977), 'Barnes, Peter', in James Vinson (ed.), *Contemporary Dramatists,* St Martin's Press, London, pp. 69–71

Innes, Christopher (1992), *Modern British Drama 1890–1990,* Cambridge University Press, Cambridge, pp. 297–312

Inverso, Marybeth (September 1993), 'Der *Straf-block*: Performance and Execution in Barnes, Griffiths, and Wertenbaker', *Modern Drama,* 36, pp. 420–30

Wardle, Irving, 'Laughter!', *The Times* (25 January 1978), p. 13

Woolland, Brian (2000), 'Peter Barnes', in John Bull (ed.), *Dictionary of Literary Biography – British and Irish Playwrights Since the Second World War,* Vol. III, Bruccoli Clark and Layman, Detroit, San Francisco, London, pp. 22–34

Woolland, Brian (2004), 'Peter Barnes – His Very Own Ben Jonson', in *Jonsonians: Living Traditions,* Ashgate, Burlington and London, pp. 146–59

Worth, Katharine J. (1972), *Revolutions in Modern English Drama,* Bell, London

WORKS REFERRED TO

Archer, William (1923), *Old Drama and The New*, Heinemann, London

Artaud, A. (1964, 1970), *The Theatre and Its Double*, trans. V. Corti, Calder and Boyars, London

Barrett, David (1978), in Aristophanes, *The Knights, Peace, The Birds, Assemblywomen, Wealth*, Penguin, Harmondsworth

Bazin, A. (1982), *The Cinema of Cruelty: From Buñuel to Hitchcock*, ed. F. Truffaut, Seaver, New York

Bergson, Henri (1956), *Le Rire* (1900), trans. F. Rothwell as *Laughter*, in Wylie Sypher (ed.), *Comedy*, Doubleday, New York

Bermel, Albert (1982), *Farce: A History from Aristophanes to Woody Allen*, Simon and Schuster, New York

Billington, Michael (1978), 'Laughter', *Guardian*, 25 January 1978

Billington, Michael (1985), 'Red Noses', *Guardian*, 2 July 1985

Bordwell, D., Staiger, J. and Thompson, K. (eds.) (1985), *Classical Hollywood Comedy*, Routledge, New York and London

Braun, E. (ed.) (1969), *Meyerhold on Theatre*, Eyre Methuen, London

Braun, E. (1970), *The Theatre of Meyerhold*, Eyre Methuen, London

Braunmuller, A. R. and Hattaway, Michael (1990), *The Cambridge Companion to English Renaissance Drama*, Cambridge University Press, Cambridge

Brecht, B. (1938), *Life of Galileo*, trans. John Willett (1980), Methuen, London

Brecht, B. (1940), *Mother Courage*, trans. John Willett (1980), Methuen, London

Brecht, Bertolt (1964), *Brecht on Theatre*, ed. and trans. John Willett, Methuen, London

Brook, Peter (1968), *The Empty Space*, McGibbon & Kee, London

Buñuel, Luis (1984), *My Last Breath*, trans. A. Israel, Jonathan Cape, London

Burton, Richard (1859, reprinted 1978), *Tales From the Arabian Nights*, Avenel Books, New York

Cave, Richard Allen (1991), *Ben Jonson*, Pulgrave Macmillan, Basingstoke and London

Cave, Richard, Schafer, Elizabeth and Woolland, Brian (1999), *Ben Jonson and Theatre: Performance Practice and Theory*, Routledge, London

Chekhov, Anton (1904, trans. Michael Frayn 1978), *The Cherry Orchard*, Methuen, London

Christie, Ian and Taylor, Richard (eds.) (1993), *Eisenstein Rediscovered*, Routledge, London

Christie, Ian (2001), *The Ruling Class*, sleeve notes for DVD, Criterion Collection

Creed, Barbara (1993), *The Monstrous-Feminine: Film, Feminism, Psychoanalysis*, Routledge, London

Dickson , Keith (1978), *Towards Utopia: A Study of Brecht*, Oxford University Press, Oxford

Dollimore, Jonathan (1998), *Death, Desire and Loss in Western Culture*, Allen Lane, The Penguin Press, London

Eisenstein, Sergei M. (1987), *Nonindifferent Nature: Film and the Structure of Things*, ed. and trans. H. Marshall, Cambridge University Press, Cambridge

Eisenstein, Sergei M. (1991), *Towards a Theory of Montage*, ed. Michael Glenny and Richard Taylor, Vol. II, British Film Institute Publishing, London

Freud, Sigmund (1905), *Der Witz und seine Beziehung zum Unbewussten*, trans. J. Strachey as *Jokes and Their Relation to the Unconscious*, SE, Vol. VIII (1960); 1966 paperback edition, Routledge & Kegan Paul, London (from which my citation is taken)

Fromm, Erich (1942, reprinted 1960), *The Fear of Freedom*, Routledge and Kegan Paul, London

Fromm, Erich (1981), *On Disobedience and Other Essays*, The Seabury Press, New York

Gambit (1972), no. 22

Ginzburg, Carlo (1980), trans. J. and A. Tedeschi, *The Cheese and the Worms: The Cosmos of a Sixteenth-Century Miller*, Routledge and Kegan Paul, London

Gladkov, Aleksandr (1997), *Meyerhold Speaks/Meyerhold Rehearses*, Harwood Academic Publishers, Amsterdam

Goffman, Erving (1969), *The Presentation of Self in Everyday Life*, Allen Lane, The Penguin Press, Harmondsworth

Griffiths, Trevor (1976), *Comedians*, Faber and Faber, London

Gruber, William E. (1986), *Comic Theaters: Studies in Performance and Audience Response*, University of Georgia Press, Athens; Georgia, USA; and London

Gruner, Charles R. (1997), *The Game of Humor: A Comprehensive Theory of Why We Laugh*, Transaction Publishers, New Brunswick, USA and London

Hayward, Susan (2000), *Cinema Studies: The Key Concepts*, Routledge, London and New York

Heinemann, M. (1985) 'How Brecht Read Shakespeare', in Jonathan Dollimore and Alan Sinfield (eds.), *Political Shakespeare: Essays in Cultural Materialism*, Manchester University Press, Manchester

Henderson, Brian (ed.) (1985), *Preston Sturges: Five Screenplays*, University of California Press, Berkeley, Los Angeles and London

Hill, Christopher (1972), *The World Turned Upside Down: Radical Ideas During the English Revolution*, Maurice Temple Smith, London; republished 1975, Penguin, Harmondsworth

Hirst, David L. (1993), *Giorgio Strehler* (Directors in Perspective), Cambridge University Press, Cambridge

Hobbes, Thomas (1968), *Leviathan*, ed. C. B. Macpherson, Penguin, Harmondsworth

Hoover, Marjorie L. (1974), *Meyerhold: The Art of Conscious Theater*, University of Massachusetts Press, Amherst, USA

Innes, Christopher (1992), *Modern British Drama: 1890–1990*, Cambridge University Press, Cambridge

Jacobson, Howard (1997), *Seriously Funny: From the Ridiculous to the Sublime*, Viking/Penguin Books, London

Jonson, Ben, *The Alchemist*, ed. F. H. Mares (1966), Revels Plays, Manchester University Press, Manchester

Jonson, Ben, *Bartholomew Fair*, ed. E. A. Horseman (1960), Revels Plays, Manchester University Press, Manchester

Jonson, Ben, *Sejanus His Fall*, ed. Philip J. Ayers (1990), Revels Plays, Manchester University Press, Manchester

Jonson, Ben, *Volpone or, The Fox*, ed. R. B. Parker (1983), Revels Plays, Manchester University Press, Manchester

Kiebuzinska, Christine (1988), *Revolutionaries in the Theater: Meyerhold, Brecht and Witkiewicz*, UMI Research Press, Ann Arbor and London

King Lear (1970), directed by Grigori Kozintsev, USSR

Kleiman, N. (1993), 'Arguments and Ancestors' in Ian Christie and Richard Taylor (eds.), *Eisenstein Rediscovered*, Routledge, London

Koestler, Arthur (1964), *The Act of Creation*, Hutchinson, London

Koestler, Arthur (1967), *The Ghost in the Machine*, Hutchinson, London

Kott, Jan (1965), *Shakespeare: Our Contemporary*, Methuen, London

Kristeva, Julia (1982), *Powers of Horror: An Essay on Abjection*, trans. Leon S. Roudiez, Columbia University Press, New York

Lauter, Paul (ed.) (1964), *Theories of Comedy*, Doubleday/Anchor, Garden City, New York

Law, Alma and Gordon, Mel (1996), *Meyerhold, Eisenstein and Biomechanics: Actor Training in Revolutionary Russia*, McFarland & Company, Jefferson, North Carolina and London

Leach, Robert (1989), *Vsevolod Meyerhold* (Directors in Perspective), Cambridge University Press, Cambridge

Levin, Bernard (1977), The Ungentle Art of Doctoring Jonson', *Sunday Times* (8 May 1977), p. 37

Levin, Bernard (1978), 'Possession is Nine Points of the Law', *Sunday Times*, (5 February 1978), p. 35.

Malory, Sir Thomas, *Le Morte D'Arthur*, ed. Janet Cowen (1981), Penguin Books, London

Mamet, David (2003), 'The short and the fat of it', *Guardian*, (6 June, 2003), p. 5

Marowitz, Charles (1966), 'Notes on the Theatre of Cruelty', *Tulane Drama Review*, 34 (Winter 1966)

Nada, John (1962), *Carlos the Bewitched: The Last Spanish Hapsburg, 1661–1700*, Jonathan Cape, London

O'Connor, Marion (1987), *William Poel and the Elizabethan Stage Society*, Chadwyck-Healey, Cambridge

Orgel, Stephen (1981), 'What is a Text?', in *Research Opportunities in Renaissance Drama*, 26, pp. 3–6

Pepys, Samuel, *The Diary of Samuel Pepys*, ed. Robert Latham and William Matthews (1970–1983), 11 vols., Vol. II (1970), Bell, London

Peter, John (1999), *Sunday Times*, 20 June 1999

Purdie, Susan (1993), *Comedy: The Mastery of Discourse*, Harvester Wheatsheaf, Hemel Hempstead

Rosenbaum, Ron (1998), *Explaining Hitler: The Search for the Origins of His Evil*, Macmillan, London.

Sanders, Julie (2003), '*The New Inn* and *The Magnetic Lady*: Jonson's Dramaturgy in the Caroline Context' in Brian Woolland (ed.), *Jonsonians: Living Traditions*, Ashgate Burlington and London, pp. 48–61

Schaeffer, Neil (1981), *The Art of Laughter*, Columbia University Press, New York

Selbourne, David (1982), *The Making of A Midsummer Night's Dream*, Methuen, London

Shuttleworth, Ian (1999), *Financial Times*, 31 March 1999

Speaight, Robert (1954), *William Poel and the Elizabethan Revival*, Heinemann, London

Sturges, Sandy (ed.) (1991), *Preston Sturges by Preston Sturges*, Faber and Faber, London and Boston

Taylor, Richard (ed.) (1998), *The Eisenstein Reader*, British Film Institute Publishing, London

Thomson, David (1998), *Beneath Mulholland: Thoughts on Hollywood and Its Ghosts*, Little, Brown and Company, London

Thomson, Peter and Sacks, Glendyr (eds.) (1994), *The Cambridge Companion to Brecht*, Cambridge University Press, Cambridge

Trussler, Simon (1994), *The Cambridge Illustrated History of British Theatre*, Cambridge University Press, Cambridge

Turner, Elaine, *Contemporary Playwrights and Production – Unit Four, Red Noses*, Rose Bruford College, London

Wedekind, Frank (1969), *Spring Awakening*, trans. Tom Osborn, Calder and Boyars, London

Williams, Raymond (1976), *Keywords: A Vocabulary of Culture and Society*, Fontana, London

Woolland, Brian (ed.) (2003), *Jonsonians: Living Traditions*, Ashgate, Burlington and London.

Yutkevitch, Sergei (1971), 'The Conscience of the King', *Sight and Sound*, pp. 192–6, London (translated from an article in *Isskustvo Kino*)

FILMS

King Lear (1970), directed by Grigori Kozintsev, USSR

INDEX

Notes

All works indexed by title are by Peter Barnes, and are for the stage unless otherwise indicated.

Literary/stage works by other authors appear as subheadings under the author's name.

Films are indexed by title, with director, year and (where appropriate) Peter Barnes' contribution.

n = endnote

295

Peter, John 281*n14*
physical illness/disability, treatments of
  46, 49–50, 52–4, 60, 90–1, 160–1,
  163–8
Pinter, Harold 272*n9*
  The Birthday Party xi, 27
Pleasance, Donald 272*n10*
Plowright, Joan 127, 272*n13*
Poel, William 193, 276*n27*
political satire 134–5, 168, 173,
  199–200
politics *see* community; historical
  subjects, contemporary relevance;
  humour, social function
popular culture, role in PB's/others'
  work xiii, 94–6, 198–9, 202, 251,
  267*n13*
  see also song
postmodernism xiii, 171
Potter, Dennis 40, 267*n13*
Priestley, J. B., *An Inspector Calls*
  266*n11*
Pudovkin, Vsevolod xiii
Purdie, Susan 246, 280–1*n7*

Rabelais, François 279*n13*
radio *see Barnes' People*
Rea, Stephen 274*n34*
Red Noses **85–103**, 220
  awards/nominations xi
  characterisation 8, 93–4, 252
  comic/dramatic tone 86, 243
  critical commentary 87, 269–70*n8*
  historical setting 10, 12, 87
  optimism of outlook 86–7, 89, 91–3,
    102, 103
  performance (within play) 90–1,
    98–101
  political/philosophical content 86,
    89, 90–3, 96–7, 103, 252
  production history xii, 14–15, 86, 87,
    105, 263*n4*, 269*n2*, 271*n2*
  relevance to time of writing 102–3,
    269–70*n8*
  thematic links with other works 15,
    106–7, 243
  treatment of disease/physical
    disability 90–1
Reinhardt, Max 277*n33*
religion

appearance/intervention of sacred
  figures 17, 56–7, 116–17, 158–9,
  246–7
and ignorance/superstition 13–14,
  61–2, 85, 151–3, 154
inadequacies of participants 17, 85
insensitivity to suffering 110–11,
  135–7, 158–60
as instrument of repression 57,
  59–60, 90, 92–3, 95, 97, 102,
  226–7, 252
and laughter 59–60, 87, 90–3, 245–7
medieval/early modern sects 87–8,
  155, 273*nn27–8*
positive attributes 86
prayer 51, 153–4, 158–9
rejection of 56–7, 145–6, 159, 160
as tool of Establishment 29, 37, 38,
  85
Renoir, Jean xiv
Revolutionary Witness (TV) 140,
  141–50, 182, 200–1, 273*n20*
  characterisation 141–2, 143–6, 147,
    150
  contemporary relevance 142–3, 150
  historical setting 10, 12
  influences 273*n23*
  links with other works 157
  structure 150, 219
Rickman, Alan 273*n26*
Ring of Spies (Tronson, 1963, PB
  screenplay) 5
Rodway, Norman 274*n34*
Rosenbaum, Ron, *Explaining Hitler*
  268–9*n10*
The Ruling Class 7–9, **27–42**, 44
  awards/nominations xi, 28
  casting 8, 264*n8*
  characterisation 8–9, 32–5, 41–2, 58,
    180, 265*n20*
  critical comment xi–xii, 27, 28, 105,
    266*n2*, 266*n10*
  film (Medak, 1972) 8, 264*n8*, 266*n8*,
    266*n12*
  levels of meaning 19–20, 122, 266*n5*
  political content 10, 28, 213, 266*n5*
  production history 27–8, 263*n4*
  structure 37–41
  thematic links with other works 13,
    17, 57, 58, 76, 85, 89